HERE LIES
VIRGINIA

HERE LIES VIRGINIA

AN ARCHAEOLOGIST'S VIEW OF
Colonial Life and History

with a New Afterword

B Y

IVOR NOËL HUME

UNIVERSITY PRESS OF VIRGINIA

Charlottesville and London

THE UNIVERSITY PRESS OF VIRGINIA
Copyright © 1963 by Ivor Noël Hume

Preface to the New Edition and Afterword
Copyright © 1994 by Ivor Noël Hume

First University Press of Virginia printing 1994

Chapter III, slightly shortened, appeared originally in
American Heritage. A portion of Chapter VIII, in somewhat different form, appeared originally in *Antiques*.

Library of Congress Cataloging-in-Publication Data
Noël Hume, Ivor.
    Here lies Virginia : an archaeologist's view of colonial life
and history / by Ivor Noël Hume.
    p. cm.
    Originally published: New York : Knopf, 1963. With new
preface and afterword.
    Includes bibliographical references (p.) and index.
    ISBN 0-8139-1528-7 (paper)
    1. Virginia—History—Colonial period, ca. 1600–1775.
2. Virginia—Antiquities.   I. Title.
F229.N83   1994
975.5'02—dc20
                                        93-43413
                                        CIP

Printed in the United States of America

TO
Jean C. *and* Virginia Harrington
Pioneers of Historical Archaeology

Preface to the Virginia Edition

Save at gunpoint, only the most narcissistic or masochistic of authors ever reads his own books. For my part, on receiving my advance copy, I open it at what I hope is the only typographical error, shut it, consign it to a shelf—and never look at it again. I do not recall whether I found a spelling error in *Here Lies Virginia* because it reached its shelf almost exactly thirty years ago; but I do know that when I was asked to reread it and provide a new introduction, I approached the task with all the confidence of a tender-footed fire walker. It was, I recalled, a precocious, even a presumptuous book written only five years after I came to America and while most of the people who had done the work were still very much alive. And not only that—I wasn't an anthropologist!

The intent of the new introduction is (or rather *was*) to comment on the sites, events, needs, and archaeological practices discussed in these chapters in 1963, describing how they have advanced, changed, or whatever, in the subsequent decades. I quickly found, however, that doing so was akin to criticizing a picture before it was painted, and that the place for a "what happened afterwards?" essay is afterwards. So that is where you will find it.

Whether or not *Here Lies Virginia* was the spark that put fire under what was then called "historic sites archeology" is neither for me to say or to know. Nevertheless, the 1960s did see a rising awareness of its potential as a handmaiden to history—a now clichéd term that I find I claimed to have coined in a speech delivered in December 1963. Hitherto, certainly in Williamsburg, archaeology had served a different mistress—architecture. Consequently, architects resisted beating their hands to pulp in wild applause when I argued that old buildings are but frames around pictures of past life, and that it is the life rather than the inanimate monuments and artifacts that interests the public.

In the days of theatrical censorship in England, the Lord Chamberlain, responding to complaints about nudity at the Windmill Theatre, decreed that if it's still it's art, but if they move it's rude. That might have been said of historic sites interpretation in the 1930s and 1940s when tourists walked awestruck through silent rooms frozen in what curators determined was the appropriate time. Eventually, however, the social revolution of the late 1960s and 1970s spilled over into historical interpretation. Graciously guiding hostesses began to be augmented and sometimes even replaced by "reenactors" who would squabble in the street over a stolen chicken and slaves who would not only rail against their lot but throw in modern analogies the better to make their point. In once pristinely tidy exhibition rooms a drawer would be left coyly open with a dirty sock hanging out. Indeed, this advance became known as the dirty sock syndrome. Inevitably, these innovations sometimes got out of hand, and in time a surfeit of socks became self-defeating; nevertheless, the trend provided a milieu in which people-seeking archaeology could flourish.

Just as the first life-on-the-scene reenactors were amateurs who honed their skills on the streets, so the early historical archaeologists were novices in the sense that they lacked prior experience and had to learn to adapt skills and knowledge acquired in other fields. Some did so with great success; others believed that it was not they but the archaeology that should adapt. Before the dust settled on that debate, we had entered the computer age and the balance began to tip away from down-in-the-dirt fieldwork toward an abstract and printout-precise approach wherein percentages rode roughshod over people.

The 1963 edition of *Here Lies Virginia* closed with the hope that in future years the Commonwealth's buried past would be better served; this 1994 edition ends with the hope that it will fare no worse.

I.N.H.

July 10, 1993

Preface

"How to save the old that's worth saving, whether in landscape, houses, manners, institutions or human types, is one of our greatest problems, and the one that we bother least about." So wrote John Galsworthy nearly thirty years ago. Today the problem is no closer to being solved, although it has certainly become more urgent. Historians, archaeologists, conservationists, and people the world over who believe that the past should not be sacrificed on the altar of tomorrow, are fighting their small battles on many fronts. This book is devoted to one of them.

The story of colonial Virginia is a comparatively recent chapter in the annals of recorded history. So one might assume that we should have little difficulty in assembling sufficient facts to create a complete picture of life as it was lived in the colony in the seventeenth or eighteenth century. It often comes as a surprise, therefore, when we discover that we know no more about certain aspects of it than we do about comparable facets relating to the Romans or Egyptians.

In these chapters I have tried to demonstrate that archaeology and recorded history can and must combine together to fill in the missing details. Although the result is a somewhat ragged patchwork of successes and failures, I hope it will show that America's colonial past is worth saving, and that if we are to do so we must make use of the same disciplines, sciences, and skills that are so freely lavished on the remains of the more remote past.

Somewhere along the line it is usual for an author to slip in a few apologies disguised as explanatory notes in an attempt to disarm his critics. Not wishing to break with tradition, I must therefore explain that this is not a textbook for would-be archaeologists, nor is it a history of colonial archaeology in Virginia. The sad fact that you can count the published complete reports on excavated colonial Virginia sites on the fingers of one hand means that much key data is no longer available for study. My constant reference, therefore, to the work of the National Park Service and of Colonial Williamsburg does not mean that all the important discoveries have been made by those organizations. On the contrary, some of the most valuable contributions both to archaeology and the conservation of historic sites in the State have come from the Association for the Preservation of Virginia Antiquities. The fact that many of those contributions were made in the early years of this century before modern archaeological techniques were understood or detailed recording thought necessary, makes it difficult for us now to review them. Nevertheless, every visitor to Jamestown Island or to Williamsburg, for that matter, owes a debt of gratitude to the A.P.V.A. for having preserved for us many buildings and sites which otherwise would have been mutilated or lost. However, there is no denying that in recent years the principal archaeological contributions have been made by the staffs of Colonial Williamsburg and of the National Park Service, both of whom have kept fairly detailed records of their excavations. In using this material which has been generously made available to me by both Colonial Williamsburg and the Park Service's Colonial National Park, I have occasionally been prompted to draw conclusions other than, or in addition to, those put forward by the original writers. As many of them are no longer here to discuss their work, I have been forced either to extend my neck or to omit certain seemingly relevant matters; more often than not I have chosen the former course.

It may be that my approach to Virginia's history and archaeology lacks the usually expected note of dusty reverence: but for that I make no apology. Instead, I recall the comment of the late Rear Admiral E. W. Sylvester when I asked him how, after a distinguished career in the navy, he liked being director of the Mariners' Museum at Newport News. Without hesitation he replied that slightly to his surprise he found it "more darned fun than a barrel of monkeys." I feel precisely the same way about the archaeology of colonial Virginia.

I do not agree that it is necessary for those of us who devote our lives to history or archaeology to hide behind a mask of erudite solemnity to prove that we treat our work seriously; nor do I believe that by "popularizing" it we are automatically guilty of lowering our standards. On the contrary, it can be argued that the only good reason for studying the people of the past is to introduce them to the public of today. If we make that introduction so dry and forbidding that nobody enjoys the experience, we have surely been wasting our time. If this heresy causes some of my colleagues to turn yellow at the edges, I can only urge them to read no further.

I have used innumerable quotations from contemporary sources, and I know that from the scholar's point of view it is unpardonable to provide no bibliographic footnotes. But as this is not a scholar's book I have somewhat reluctantly omitted them. There is, however, a full list of my source material at the back, tabled in the order in which it has been used in each chapter.

No doubt I have many other causes for apology, but as yet I am blissfully unaware of them. There is, perhaps, merit in such ignorance in that it avoids an otherwise interminable preface.

I. NOËL HUME

March 1963

Acknowledgments

IN A BOOK that relies as heavily as this does on the work of others it is well nigh impossible to give adequate credit to all those who have contributed knowingly, or more often unknowingly, to these pages. I must confine myself, therefore, to those persons and organizations that have helped me personally by the provision of information, illustrations, and encouragement.

I am particularly indebted to personnel of the United States National Park Service and of Colonial Williamsburg. But lest they should be blamed for my own shortcomings, I wish to make it clear that the named persons have assisted me with specific problems and are not responsible for my general conclusions and opinions. I am most grateful to Paul Buchanan, John Dunton, George B. Eager, William D. Geiger, Mrs. Mary Goodwin, A. Edwin Kendrew, James M. Knight, Dr. E. M. Riley and Miss Mary Stephenson of Colonial Williamsburg, and to Dr. John L. Cotter, J. C. Harrington, Charles E. Hatch, Jr., J. Paul Hudson and Mrs. Louise M. Meekins of the National Park Service. In addition I owe much to the help and guidance of the late Col. J. P. Barney, Elwood L. Boyce, Mrs. Lloyd Overton Bullock, Mrs. Joseph Childs, Mrs. H. G. Dashiell, Mr. and Mrs. William Jenkins, James P. Maloney, Joseph A. Miller, C. Malcolm Watkins of the Smithsonian Institution, and James Wharton.

I am also grateful to the following for permission to quote from the named books: to Cassell & Company, publishers of *The Tomb of Tut·Ankh·Amen* by Howard Carter and A. C. Mace; and to the

Acknowledgments

Houghton Mifflin Company, publishers of *People of the Serpent* by Edward Herbert Thompson.

Finally, I wish to express my gratitude to my wife who brewed coffee of varying quality throughout the painful period of gestation and to Dr. Thad W. Tate who reviewed the infant opusculum and ministered to its imperfections.

Contents

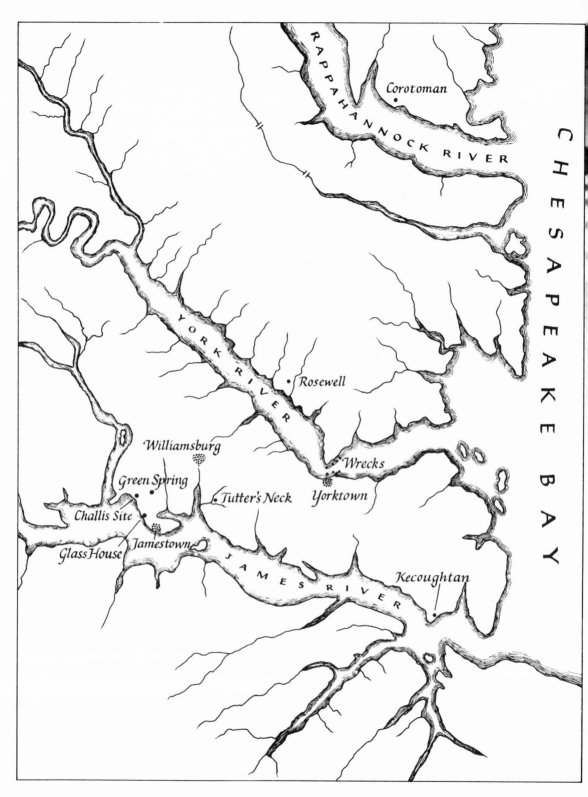

Map of Tidewater Virginia. The principal archaeological sites and locations.

Illustrations

Illustrations

CHAPTER VIII

CHAPTER IX

CHAPTER X

xxiii

Illustrations

FOR the provision of illustrations and permission to use them, and for permission to make photographs from original paintings and drawings and to use them in this book, grateful acknowledgment is made to the following organizations and individuals:

The United States National Park Service and its Colonial National Historical Park for Figures 4-8, 11, 13, 16, 18, 45, 47, 54, 63-67, 74, and 78.

Colonial Williamsburg, Inc., for Figures 1-3, 15, 21, 23-27, 29-33; 35, 40, 49, 51-53, 55, 57-62, 71-73, 77, 82, 86, 87, 89-104, 110, 111, 115-117, and 123-128.

The Smithsonian Institution for Figure 12.

The Massachusetts Historical Society for Figure 28.

The late Mr. T. T. Waterman for Figure 36.

The Colchester Museum, Essex, England, for Figure 43.

Mr. Clyde Holmes for Figure 50.

Mr. J. Paul Hudson for Figure 68.

The Mariners' Museum, Newport News, for Figures 69 and 70.

Mr. John V. N. Dunton for Figure 84.

Mr. Joseph T. McClenny for Figure 88.

The Historical Society of Pennsylvania for Figure 107.

Guildhall Museum, London, for Figure 116.

The Worshipful Company of Fishmongers of London and the *American Heritage Book of the Revolution* for Figure 129.

Mr. Sidney King who painted the originals of Figures 11 and 54.

Mr. Richard Stinely whose work is depicted in Figures 51, 82, 93, and 97.

HERE LIES
VIRGINIA

In Defense
of Yesterday

A FEW YEARS AGO, while plowing in the thinly populated Guinea section of Gloucester County, Virginia, a farmer unearthed a Roman bronze coin. In England or on the continent of Europe this would not be either exciting or important, but in America it is positively sensational. The only snag is that I have been completely unable to substantiate this story, either by examining the coin or even finding the farmer who unearthed it. Consequently, we have no alternative but to file the story away with the little men from flying saucers and the frogs that rained down in Alabama.

My reason for perpetuating the story even to this extent, is simply that I want to use it as an introductory exercise. Suppose for a moment that a Roman coin *was* found. What conclusions could we draw from it?

Our first cynical explanation for its presence might be that it came from the collection of someone who lived in the district. But

3

this is a poor area, and always has been—hardly a likely place for the home of a collector of Roman coins. In the days and centuries before the arrival of the first Virginia colonists, however, the whole section was inhabited by the Indians, and Indians would appreciate such baubles as coins with pictures on them, although they would almost certainly have been strung around someone's neck.

If Leif Ericsson could reach North America by direct route from Norway in A.D. 1000, it is not beyond the realms of possibility that a Roman merchantman could have been blown across the Atlantic seven or eight hundred years earlier. It is true that the Norse ships were built to ride the treacherous northern waters, but Roman vessels constantly made their way out beyond the Pillars of Hercules and up through the Bay of Biscay to Britain, some of them carrying marbles and stone columns of prodigious weight and size. Suppose, then, that a Roman merchantman was wrecked on the Outer Banks of North Carolina. It is possible and even likely that the Indians would have salvaged anything they could, and from there it is only a small feat of imagination to see Roman coins finding their way north to Virginia's York River and the Indians whose settlements flanked its shores.

Unfortunately, there is another explanation that is a good deal easier to swallow. English monarchs from Charles II to George III, all of whose coins circulated in Virginia, were generally portrayed in classical guise with laurel wreaths around their heads, and Roman armor or togas draping their shoulders. Furthermore, the legend around the edge was always in Latin. It is quite reasonable to suggest, therefore, that the person who found the coin mistook an English coin of the seventeenth or eighteenth cenury for one that was much older.

The point that I am making is not that the Romans came to Virginia, but simply that the discovery of an artifact—in this case a coin—makes us want to know how it came to be where it was found. The object itself is of secondary importance. The same is true of all archaeological research. The objects that we dig up are merely clues to the story of past events, pieces of a jigsaw puzzle which, when correctly fitted together, recreate a picture of life as it was lived in colonial Virginia.

Many people find it faintly amusing that the techniques of archaeology should be employed on colonial sites. They even consider it

1. Part of the Fry-Jefferson map of Virginia, the first edition of 1751, marking the principal towns and plantations.

slightly pretentious—an attempt to impart an importance to these quite recent centuries that should be rightly reserved for the more venerable and scabrous antiquities of prehistory. The truth of the matter is that the techniques of archaeology can be usefully practiced on any site, no matter how recent it may be, if by digging something up we can hope to learn more than is to be discovered from written sources. After all, nobody questions the use of archaeology in Egypt or on Roman sites, and we have documentary records surviving from both those civilizations. When I was working as an archaeologist in London in 1954, I was once called in by the police to help determine how long a suspected murder victim had been in the ground. The answer—on archaeological evidence—was about three hundred years, and the police quickly lost interest.

It follows as an obvious corollary that if some people think that archaeology is useless when applied to colonial sites, they must also consider the sites, themselves, not worth studying or preserving. That outlook is all too prevalent and every year dozens of important sites are lost amid the whirling, grinding, Wellsian contraptions that churn up the ground for modern construction jobs, highway improvements, and reforestation projects. Most of us appreciate the dangers to prehistoric Indian sites, and all over the country trained archaeologists are working against time to salvage what they can before the key sites are ruined or drowned beneath the waters of vast new reservoirs. Colonial remains, on the other hand, have only about a dozen adequately trained professional archaeologists to champion their cause. This is odd, when you consider the immense popular interest in American history that is so graphically expressed each year in Virginia by the hundreds of thousands of visitors who stream through restored Williamsburg and visit Jamestown, Yorktown, and the great James River plantations. Yet even some of these visitors question the purpose of digging up a past that is so recent. Why not leave it in the ground a few hundred more years so that it can acquire the venerable patina of antiquity?

The sad truth is that if we do not preserve America's past now there will be nothing left for the future to enjoy. The constant spread of urban development, although only one of many dangers, is certainly the most devastating. Whereas few prehistoric settlements were deliberately chosen as sites for colonial towns and villages, the latter pro-

6

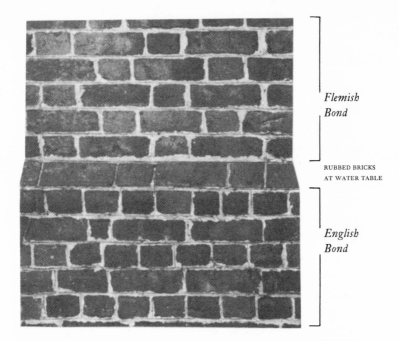

Flemish Bond

RUBBED BRICKS
AT WATER TABLE

English Bond

2. A typical example of 18th century brickwork: foundations laid in English bond (alternating rows of headers and stretchers), a single course of ground-bricks providing the water-table offset, and Flemish bond above (headers and stretchers alternating in each course). In the 17th century, English bond was generally used throughout. Note the scored lines in the oystershell mortar around the bricks, a feature not usually encountered after the end of the 18th century.

vided the roots from which the great towns of the Eastern states have sprung. As a result, the remains of the colonial communities are disturbed whenever new utilities are laid and gardens dug. In the nineteenth century, building regulations were not as specific as they are today, and builders would not think twice about putting up a building on top of the foundations of an earlier structure. But today it is mandatory to seat one's building on ground that is known to be of adequate stability, and that means rooting out all the rubble, fill, and old foundations of earlier structures. To the construction engineer these are just sources of irritation, and to the fellow who is paying for the new building their presence represents increased costs for the concrete that will be needed to fill the holes. To the archaeologist, on the other hand, the old cellars, wells, and trash pits are the stuff of history. Their unrecorded destruction is to him as appalling to consider as is the unthinking destruction of family documents to a historian.

7

The relationship between the historian and the archaeologist is often rather curious, each eying the other with slightly irritable distrust. This brings us back to the popular delusion that archaeology stops where history begins. That this fallacy should be accepted by some laymen is saddening, yet hardly surprising; but when historians voice the same opinion we have cause for general and noisy lamentation.

It is perfectly true that when a historian can produce a document to show that a house burned down at 3 a.m. on January 14, 1762, he is way ahead of the archaeologist who scrapes through the burned remains and deduces that the fire occurred at some date between 1750 and 1770. But there are a great many occasions when the historian has no documentary evidence and it is then that the archaeologist can make his contributions. At other times the historian may be able to tell only part of the story. This often happens when an old building is being restored and refurnished on the basis of contemporary inventories. An invoice of 1770 may list "1 Dozn. white Chamber Pots" and "2 Blue & white China Bowls." While it is nice to know that these items were in the house, a number of tiresome questions remain unanswered. Were the white basins and chamber pots made of white delftware or were they of white salt-glazed stoneware? What form of ornament adorned the blue and white china bowls? No value is given in the invoice and we are left wondering whether they were of good, bad, or indifferent quality. The historian is certainly not going to provide the answers. If the information is not in the documents, he has usually shot his bolt. However, if an archaeologist excavating in the vicinity of the building finds a refuse pit of the appropriate period and in it discovers fragments of white wash basins and chamber pots as well as pieces of blue and white china bowls, these questions can be answered. If it appears that by such a stroke the archaeologist has scored off the historian, that is hardly the intention. One is merely complementing the other. Archaeological evidence has provided the appearance of the items, but it has required historical data to determine whence they came, when, and for whom they were purchased.

Bringing back the past has become a popular, though often expensive project for many Americans from wealthy philanthropists to the working members of local garden clubs, and their efforts run the

8

3. The laboratory treatment and study of the artifacts plays a major part in modern archaeology.

gamut from the preservation and restoration of Williamsburg to the patching up of an old tobacco barn. Between these poles is a multitude of projects both large and small, all of them needing precedent from the past to aid them in their pursuit of that most elusive attribute —authenticity. Most of the guiding spirits behind these enterprises realize the importance of historical documentation; but all too few appreciate the potential contribution of archaeology.

At the root of the trouble lies an imperfect understanding of the basic principles of archaeological practice. Of course I fully realize that the words "principles of archaeological practice" are likely to send the ladies of well-meaning restoration committees running from the room in coveys. This is a pity, because they only need to absorb two very simple facts, neither of them demanding any more mental versatility than a little common sense.

The first arises from the fact that the ground is made up from a

9

series of layers; most of them have been created by natural agencies through the centuries, but others have been deposited or disturbed by the hand of man. He digs drainage ditches, excavates cellars for houses, cuts terraces in his gardens, all of which change the appearance of the ground. Nature's contributions are largely governed by wind and water that causes the ground to erode from one place and build up in another. In wooded areas the annual shedding of leaves causes a slow and steady increase in the topsoil at the feet of the trees. People who know a little about archaeology often assume that the soil increases in thickness throughout the world at an even and predictable rate. I have heard such figures quoted as an inch a year, one foot in a decade, and a foot per century. None is correct, for the increase in soil at one point is frequently occasioned by its erosion from a point close by, a process which may or may not be repeated annually. But even without a simple formula to gauge the speed at which soil is laid down, the fact remains that it does accumulate at different times and speeds and often with dirt of different colors and textures.

In 1956 I was excavating on the site of the *Virginia Gazette* printing office on Duke of Gloucester Street in Williamsburg. The building had stood in a valley and when the street was raised in the eighteenth century, clay was dumped into that valley, setting the street grade at the printing office's second floor. Today we would call it a split-level building. The foundations, at the valley floor level, were uncovered in the summer and as a result, the face of the clay fill under the street was exposed to a depth of about nine feet. In the autumn the leaves fell from the neighboring trees and blanketed the old foundations. Then in the late fall and winter, rain and frost started to erode the clay bank, which was washed in the form of mud, out across the site until much of the old brickwork was completely buried again. The following spring we returned to the site to find that the mud had dried out and appeared to be of identical color and consistency as the now much mutilated clay bank. A test hole cut down through the newly deposited clay to the brick floor below revealed that four inches of pale yellow clay had been deposited in less than five months. At the bottom, where it rested on the bricks, this clay was blackened to a thickness of half an inch. The change of color had resulted from the presence of the dead leaves which had quickly decayed when covered

10

by the wet mud, all that remained of them being a dirty stain in the clay. If that site were not touched for a number of years, and providing that the same natural conditions prevailed, a new black and a new yellow layer would be created every year. If, by some lucky chance, a passing tourist should have tossed a Lincoln penny of, say, 1956, down onto the bottom washed-clay layer, a future archaeologist would be able to deduce that the top of that clay layer was exposed in or after 1956 and, consequently, the black and yellow strata above it would each date one year later.

In the foregoing example the two basic principles of archaeology are employed, the first being that if layer "A" sits on top of layer "B," "A" was deposited after "B." The second is that each layer of soil, regardless of whether it represents wash from a bank or excrement in a trash pit, is dated by the most recent artifact that it contains. This dating is called a *terminus post quem*, the date after which the bank was washed or the pit filled. Just because our Lincoln penny was minted in 1956, it does not follow that it was thrown away in that year. In the same way, we may find all sorts of glass and ceramics in the remains of a burned house. But as these things may have been collected by their owner over a long period of time, they must be studied together to determine the most recent of them, for it is the newest items that give us the *terminus post quem*.

These basic archaeological principles are both newly realized and long forgotten. Throughout the entire nineteenth century there were hundreds of antiquaries both in Europe and in America who knew nothing of the stratification of soil layers and cared less. They were digging for objects and the relation of one to another was quite unimportant—except when it was a question of whether the treasures should wind up in their own collections or in the cabinet of a rival scholar.

The discovery of the importance of stratigraphy has often been attributed to an Englishman, General Pitt Rivers, who, in the 1880's, inherited his great-uncle's estates at Cranborne Chase in England. The area was rich in prehistoric and Romano-British remains, and the retired Indian Army general embarked upon their excavation with military precision and a somewhat unmilitary amount of perception. Between 1887 and 1898 he published four monumental volumes in which

11

he recorded every detail of his work, reports which would do credit to the most skilled modern archaeologist. Pitt Rivers's careful recording of every artifact in relationship to the layers in which they were found leaves no doubt that he was fully aware of the importance of stratification. On the basis of these reports, the general has been hailed as the father of scientific archaeology. But in actual fact the honor belongs to a Virginian who published his report a century earlier.

In 1784—a generally busy period for most American patriots—Thomas Jefferson found time to publish his *Notes on the State of Virginia* in which he gave an account of his excavation of an Indian cemetery. The following extract from the *Notes* clearly establishes Jefferson as the first scientific archaeologist, illustrating a quite remarkable ability to assimilate archaeological evidence and to read the soil's subtle clues as easily as we read his words today.

> I proceeded then to make a perpendicular cut through the body of the barrow, that I might examine its internal structure. . . . At the bottom, that is, on the level of the circumjacent plain, I found bones; above these a few stones, brought from a cliff a quarter of a mile off, and from the river one eighth of a mile off; then a large interval of earth, then a stratum of bones, and so on. At one end of the section were four strata of bones plainly distinguishable; at the other, three; the strata in one part not ranging with those in another. . . . Appearances certainly indicate that [the burial mound] has derived both origin and growth from the accustomary collection of bones, and deposition of them together; that the first collection had been deposited on the common surface of the earth, a few stones put over it, and then a covering of earth, then the second had been laid on this . . . and so on. The following are the particular circumstances which give it this aspect. 1. The number of bones [approximately 1,000 skeletons]. 2. Their confused position. 3. Their being in different strata. 4. The strata in one part having no correspondence with those in another 5. The different states of decay in these strata, which seem to indicate a difference in the time of inhumation. 6. The existence of infant bones among them.

Here, written more than 170 years ago, we have as lucid a tabulating of archaeological evidence as you could wish to see today. The stratigraphy of the mound is recorded and deductions are made on the evidence of the relationship of one layer or stratum to another. In addition, the components of the layers are clearly noted and their sources indicated. The bones, too, are carefully studied to determine the number of burials present as well as the ages of the people interred. Most important of all, both the evidence of the bones and the stratigraphy are used to infer that the burials occurred at different times.

Had Jefferson found man-made objects such as weapons or pottery, we may be sure that he would have had something enlightening to say of them. He would surely have known, just as General Pitt Rivers did later, that the ability to determine when an artifact was manufactured would be an immensely important step toward knowing when it got into the ground, and thence to being able to date the events that served to change the face of the earth around it.

The ability to identify and date the relics of the past is the first requirement for an archaeologist, no matter in what period of history or prehistory he specializes. In colonial archaeology, when exact dating is of the essence, it is imperative that the excavator's knowledge be as broad as that of a museumfull of curators. He must be an expert in ceramics, a student of glass, have a working knowledge of colonial crafts and trades, be able to identify and date a musket when only a rusted fragment of its lock survives, or know that a pin with a twisted wire head is of colonial date, but that one with a stamped flat head is not. Clues like these are the bones of archaeology. If we fail to make correct use of them, we are heading straight for disaster and the destruction of irretrievable archaeological evidence.

When Howard Carter was excavating the tomb of Tut-Ankh-Amen in 1923, he eloquently described the duties of an archaeologist to his discoveries. "The things he finds," wrote Carter, "are not his own property, to treat as he pleases, or neglect as he chooses. They are a direct legacy from the past to the present age . . . and if, by carelessness, slackness, or ignorance, he lessens the sum of knowledge that might have been obtained from them, he knows himself to be guilty of an archaeological crime of the first magnitude. Destruction of evidence is so painfully easy, and yet so hopelessly irreparable."

I believe that those words would make an excellent creed to hang over the bed of every aspiring archaeologist. They apply to those of us who are working on colonial Virginia sites just as much as they did to Carter in Egypt. When we dig our trowels into the ground, the future of the past is in our hands, and that is not a responsibility that we can take lightly.

From time to time archaeologists working on Indian sites come upon artifacts of European date and, not being trained to identify such things, they generally send them away to a specialist in the colonial field. This is a perfectly legitimate thing to do. But when someone who is deliberately excavating a colonial site has to do this, all is definitely not well—and it happens much too often. The reason is simply that colonial archaeology is still in its infancy, and consequently there is a desperate shortage of archaeologists, either professional or amateur, with the necessary knowledge of the artifacts.

I can but hope that if you have the intestinal fortitude to delve with me through the pages that follow, you will be encouraged to take up a trowel in defense of America's colonial past.

The Roanoke
Adventure

Virginia's archaeological history falls into three conveniently tidy segments: the eighteenth century or Williamsburg period, the seventeenth century Jamestown era, and the sixteenth century adventure on Roanoke Island. The last of these is short, dramatic, and inconclusive, and as it has little or no connection with the evolution of the colony in the subsequent centuries, we may reasonably consider it here and now in its brief entirety, examining first the history and then the scraps of evidence provided by archaeology.

The mystery of the "Lost Colony" and the romantic yet pathetic birth of Virginia Dare have excited school children and scholars alike. Yet after a great deal of careful historical research and archaeological excavating, we are no closer to knowing the fate of the colonists than we were fifty years ago.

English interest in establishing a colony in the New World was stimulated by the successes of the Spanish and Portuguese, who were busily milking the wealth of South and Central America. In 1578, Sir Humphrey Gilbert obtained a charter to establish a settlement on any site not already claimed by a Christian kingdom. He thereupon personally financed an expedition and finally set sail in 1583, landing first in Newfoundland and then voyaging south down the coast. Unfortunately, after a surfeit of storms and other tribulations, Gilbert decided to turn for home only to be drowned on the way. Sir Humphrey Gilbert's half brother, Sir Walter Raleigh, had been interested in the first voyage, and when Gilbert's charter expired in 1584, Raleigh applied to Queen Elizabeth for similar privileges. These were granted, and in April of that year two ships under the command of Captains Arthur Barlowe and Philip Amadas set out to explore the North American coast. They duly arrived off the Outer Banks of what is now North Carolina and in July 1584 found the area much to their liking. Fortunately for posterity, one of the captains prepared a written account of their impressions, initially for the benefit of Sir Walter Raleigh. He told of grapes so plentiful that they spilled from the land into the sea, of cedars finer than any elsewhere in the world, and of woods filled with "Deere, Conies, Hares, and Fowle, even in the middest of Summer in incredible abundance."

It seems that the Indians were remarkably hospitable and entertained their curiously pink visitors, washing their clothes, providing food, and generally making them welcome. Wingina, the chief of the Indians on Roanoke Island, did not have the pleasure of meeting his English visitors as he had been "shot in two places through the body, and once clean through the thigh" while warring with a neighbor. Instead, the chief's brother, Granganimeo, acted as host and made somewhat limited conversation with the aid of smiles and slaps on the head and chest "making shewe the best he could of all love and familiaritie." It is somewhat doubtful whether Messrs. Amadas and Barlowe tried to get across the rather provocative idea that the Indians' land no longer belonged to them, and that henceforth it was the property of Queen Elizabeth of England, the "rightful Queene." It is almost certain that in the manner of most colonial enterprises, the tiresome details needed only to be understood by the new management. As it was, the Englishmen parted from their hosts on the best of terms.

16

As their sails disappeared over the horizon, we may assume that the Indians settled down to enjoy the clothes, tin dishes, copper kettles, and goods that they had acquired in barter, blissfully unaware that they were now living on English property.

Archaeology has nothing to tell us of this first exploratory effort, and it is extremely unlikely that it ever will. The English built nothing and so left no lasting mark on the ground. It is possible that some of their trade goods may one day be found in Indian graves on the island, but it is doubtful whether they would be sufficiently distinctive for anyone to be able to distinguish between relics of the first expedition and those from subsequent trading. Indeed, we know from the account of the first voyage that some European objects had reached those shores twenty years earlier, having been retrieved by the Indians from a wreck. Just how much the Indians were able to salvage is not clear, but mention is made, without comment, of the presence among them of "children that had very fine aburne and chestnut coloured haire."

The Captain's report to Raleigh contained enough references to objects of gold and boxes of pearls to encourage investors to contribute to a larger and more purposeful expedition. This duly set sail in the following spring under the command of Raleigh's cousin, Sir Richard Grenville, who was later to carve his niche in the annals of gallantry aboard the *Revenge* at Flores in the Azores. Now he sailed with a fleet of seven ships with instructions to set up an English community in the colony that Queen Elizabeth had officially named Virginia. The company consisted of 108 men (but no women), among whom were Captain Amadas and Simon Ferdinando who had been on the previous voyage, Grenville's brother-in-law John Stukeley (and father of the guardian of Pocahontas's son, Thomas Rolfe), Thomas Cavendish who was later to follow Drake in circumnavigating the world, Ralph Lane who was to govern the colony and who subsequently wrote a detailed account of his stay there, as well as John White, the now famed illustrator, and scientist Thomas Harriot. Together they represented as formidable a group of Englishmen as had ever put to sea on a punitive expedition. They were not, however, necessarily the best suited to found a colony, to live in virtual exile, tilling fields and being friendly with the natives.

The fleet reached Puerto Rico in May and after repairing damage

17

suffered in crossing the Atlantic, it made its presence felt by seizing a couple of Spanish frigates and raiding the Spanish settlement at "Roxo bay." Grenville then moved on to Hispaniola where he entertained the Spanish Governor at a banquet that was clearly designed to impress. The meal was served "all in plate," i.e. silver-gilt, a fact that throws an interesting light on the inventories of ships of gentlemen adventurers in the sixteenth and early seventeenth centuries. While it could be argued that some of Grenville's plate had only recently been stolen from the Spaniards, it is reasonable to expect that his ship would have carried most of the amenities of home, everything from pomanders to Venetian glass.

Objects being the lifeblood of the archaeologist, we are constantly searching, not only in the ground where they lie buried, but also in the records that give clues to the sorts of things that we may hope to find. The reference to Grenville's use of "plate" makes us wonder whether he took it all home with him or whether any pieces remained behind in Virginia. Although none has been unearthed, the records suggest that not all of it remained aboard his ship.

In July 1585, before reaching their destination at Roanoke Island, the fleet dropped anchor in what is now Ocracoke Inlet, south of Cape Hatteras, and from there made several sorties to the mainland. One of these forages included the burning of Aquascogok, an Indian village, as a reprisal for the theft of a silver cup. It is possible, therefore, that someone will eventually find an Indian grave containing an English silver cup. If it should bear the engraved arms or crest of Sir Richard Grenville, it will rank among the greatest "documentary" treasures of American history.

Ralph Lane's narrative mentions that the colonists' equipment included such items as "mattocks, spades and axes," tools that would have been essential to any agricultural endeavors. These, however, were primarily carried for the purpose of constructing "sconces," which a seventeenth century dictionary describes as "a term in Fortification, a Block-house, or chief Fortresse." Lane had planned to build a series of these forts which he proposed to construct "upon some Corne fielde, that my company might have lived upon it"—hardly a plan calculated to win friends and influence Indians. We do know, however, from the writing of Thomas Harriot, the expedition's scien-

18

4. The Roanoke fort, seen from the east, as reconstructed by the National Park Service.

tist, that the Indians were much impressed by the colonists' gadgets and mechanical devices, which led them to believe that the white men had close connections with gods, but whether they were good or bad gods no one has bothered to record.

"Most things they sawe with us," wrote Harriot, "as Mathematicall instruments, sea Compasses, the vertue of the load-stone in drawing yron, a perspective glasse whereby was shewed many strange sights, burning glasses, wilde firewoorkes, gunnes, hookes, writing and reading, spring-clockes that seeme to goe of themselves and many other things that wee had were so strange unto them, and so farre exceeded their capacities to comprehend the reason and meanes how they should be made and done, that they thought they were rather the workes of gods then of men, or at the leastwise they had bene given and taught us of the gods."

On arrival at the northern end of Roanoke Island the colonists, under the direction of Ralph Lane, set about building a fort that would afford protection against both Spaniards and Indians. The plan of the fort was simply a square with V-shaped bastions protruding from the sides which gave the structure a star-like appearance. Although John White's famous series of drawings do not include a view of the Roan-

19

oke fort, they do show "The forme of a fort w^h was made by Mr.^r Ralfe Lane in a parte of St Johns Ilande neere Capross where we toke in salt the xxvj^th of May. 1585." This was one that had been built by Lane during Grenville's highly provocative trip through the West Indies on the way to Roanoke, and there is little reason to suppose that there would have been much difference between the two forts. Both were purely military structures containing, one supposes, the arsenal, a well, and accommodation for the storage of food and other provisions. The Roanoke fort was not a fortified township, but rather a refuge to which the colonists living outside could retire should the need arise.

Our knowledge of the houses built by Lane and his fellow colonists is confined to scraps of information written by Lane himself plus statements from less authoritative sources. They would seem to have been similar to the small, yeomen's cottages of England, a story and a half in height and with thatched roofs. The windows would have been unglazed and the walls constructed of wattle and daub, perhaps with brick foundations. This last refinement might not have been expected were it not for the statement of one of the settlers who noted that "as soon as they had disembarked they began to make brick and fabric for a fort and houses." Like the low-lying peninsulas of Tidewater Virginia, Roanoke Island consists of clays that can serve for brick making, but has no natural stone.

We do not have a list of the trades to which the first colonists had been trained, but we do have Richard Hakluyt's *Discourse of Western Planting* that he had prepared for Sir Walter Raleigh in 1584, in which he lists those trades that he thought essential. Among these were brickmakers, tilemakers, limemakers (for mortar), bricklayers, tilers, lathmakers, carpenters, and thatchers, these last being able to work with "reedes, rushes, broome or strawe." It is interesting to note that Hakluyt's carefully prepared and persuasive document giving "Certain Reasons to induce her Majesty and the state to take in hand the western voyage and the planting therein," was presented by him, at Raleigh's instigation, to the queen, who was apparently singularly unimpressed. As a result the state put up none of the money for any of the early efforts at colonization. Elizabeth was well known for her cautious, if not parsimonious, attitude toward investing money in projects that involved any element of risk. Had the Virginia adventures enjoyed the advantage of state support, their fate might well have been different. But as it was, they were ineptly staffed, improperly supplied, and like all private enterprises, their needs were ignored when their best brains were conscripted at a time of national emergency.

Grenville remained with the colonists for one month to help them get settled, and then lay off the Outer Banks for another, possibly to see if any Spaniards intended to dislodge the new settlement. When nothing happened, he set sail for home—to the relief of Ralph Lane who cordially and sincerely loathed him. Getting down to hard work was not the strong suit of Englishmen in the golden age of Elizabeth; they had yet to develop the traits of sobriety and industry that colored (a rich drab) the Puritan philosophy of the next century. Consequently, the first settlers were made up of the same ill-balanced components that nearly wrecked the Jamestown venture twenty years later—a hierarchy of lesser nobility and gentlemen to whom work was socially unacceptable, and beneath them a mixed bag of the "common sort" who believed that they would find life less hard and more profitable than it had been at home. At either social level, simple hard work was far less attractive than exploring, hunting, searching for gold, or just plain lazing in the sun. It was probably for this reason that Lane contrived to make an agreement with the Roanoke Indians that they should increase their corn planting to take care of the settlers' requirements as well as their own. As for the rest of their needs, the colonists had to rely on supplies from home.

To keep afloat in so fragile a bark, it was essential that the colonists retain the friendship of the Indians. But although they clearly enjoyed it at the outset, relations steadily deteriorated as the months went by, until, by the beginning of June 1586, the English were openly at war with their providers. So bad had the situation become that Lane had been forced to split his settlers up into small groups and to send them away to neighboring islands to live off oysters. The cause of the trouble can be traced to the cartoonist's well-known delight—the character of the Englishman (or for that matter, the American) abroad, who likes to shout and throw his weight about in an attempt to convince his unfortunate hosts that he is a great deal better than they are. The results are invariably the reverse, as, indeed, they were

21

in Virginia in 1585-86. Lane had made a number of exploratory trips onto the mainland and had ventured as far north as what is now Norfolk, leaving a trail of dead Indians and burned villages along the way. He had even carried along as hostages members of the families of chiefs who were initially friendly to him. It was altogether a remarkably foolhardy approach. Although Lane's own account gives every indication that his actions were necessitated by the untrustworthiness of the Indians, a hint of regret, if not of reproach, is to be found in the report of Thomas Harriot.

"And although some of our company towards the end of the yeere," wrote Harriot, "shewed themselves too fierce in slaying some of the people in some Townes, upon causes that on our part might easily ynough have bene borne withall: yet notwithstanding, because it was on their part justly deserved, the alteration of their opinions generally and for the most part concerning us is the lesse to be doubted."

To add to the settlers' troubles, Roanoke Island had been hit by a tornado that had wrought considerable damage to the houses. So it was that when Sir Francis Drake and a fleet of privateers hove in sight at the beginning of June, the colonists' morale was in their boots. Sir Richard Grenville had failed to return with supplies promised from England, the Indians were taking pot shots at them whenever a target presented itself, they had failed to find either the fabled short cut to India or the treasures of gold and pearls that the Indian possessed, and, furthermore, they were sick to death of oysters. Small wonder, then, that when Drake offered to take the whole lot home with him, there were those who would have been glad to go. It was to Lane's credit, therefore, that he settled for Drake's alternative proposal, the provision of a ship to take the settlers back to England and enough supplies to last them for another month while they waited to see whether Grenville would turn up.

Fate, the will of heaven, or whatever we may care to call it, devises extraordinarily callous tricks from time to time, and it played one of them on England's colonial aspirations by whipping up a storm that cost Lane his ship and most of his possessions, including the few specimen pearls that he had acquired from the Indians. This was the last straw, and when the weather cleared the colonists went aboard

Drake's fleet and on June 18, 1586, began the long voyage home.

Hardly had Drake's fleet departed than a supply ship sent out by Raleigh appeared on the horizon. Its master made a brief search for Lane and his settlers and then went on his way. Soon afterward Grenville turned up with three vessels and he, too, sought in vain for the colonists. He found various abandoned English settlements, probably those constructed by the groups who were sent off on their own by Lane. Not knowing that the entire company was sailing happily home, Grenville was left wondering whether all had been wiped out by the Indians (who had been reasonably friendly when he left in 1585) or whether, perhaps, they had moved inland to set up a town and that some misfortune had befallen the rear guard left behind to await his coming. He rightly decided that the English were no longer in Virginia and he consequently resolved to leave fifteen men and supplies for them for two years so that the colony should be held for Elizabeth. This done, he set course for home.

Grenville has been criticized by some historians for not having used his three ships and their company to found a second colony. But it is hard to judge him when we do not know the details of his orders. It may be that his instructions were to enlarge the settlement; on the other hand, he may have been told only to furnish supplies. In either case, it is highly improbable that those instructions included a "rain plan" to be put into effect if the initial colonists were no longer there. Furthermore, Grenville's ships and their cargo represented a considerable financial investment by Raleigh and his associates, one that was not to be lightly squandered on what must have seemed to be throwing good money after bad.

In 1587 Raleigh tried again, sending out another colonizing expedition carrying a hundred and fifty settlers, or "planters" as they were called, under the Governorship of John White. This—as every school child knows—was destined to become history's romantic and ill-fated "Lost Colony." Less well known is the fact pointed out by the distinguished historian, A. L. Rowse, that John White's instructions were not to return to the well-worn site on Roanoke Island, but to set up another to be called the "Citie of Ralegh in Virginia" in the Chesapeake Bay area. This new settlement was to be governed by White with twelve assistants and he carried a charter to this effect with him. But for reasons that are not clear, the crew refused to go any further than Roanoke. A party duly went ashore to make contact with Grenville's fifteen men, and, as was par for the course for new arrivals at Roanoke, they found the settlement deserted—except for the bones of one of the fifteen.

The fort, earthworks, and palisade were in a deplorable state, but, as White wrote later, they found "all the houses standing unhurt, saving that the neather rooms of them, and also of the forte, were overgrown with Melons of divers sortes."

It is not my purpose to hash over the well-known stories of the birth of Virginia Dare and the baptism of the Indian, Manteo, or even to explore John White's repeat performance of Ralph Lane's experiences with the Indians at large. We are here concerned only with these factors that have a bearing on the tangible remains that the "planters" did leave, or could have left, behind them.

The premier difference between White's colonists and those of Lane and the Amadas-Barlowe expeditions was that White's included no fewer than seventeen women and nine children among their company. Consequently, to an archaeologist, the presence of these folk might be perceived through the discovery of toys and, perhaps, by such things as pins, needles, or fan handles. Unfortunately, the Indians were as eager collectors of such trivia as are modern archaeologists, and there is every reason to suppose that they picked the Roanoke site clean just as often as an opportunity presented itself. This was certainly the case when John White, who had been sent home for supplies only a month after they had arrived, finally returned to his "Citie of Ralegh" on August 16, 1590.

Presumably because of the previous state of the old fort, White found that since his departure in August 1587, a new and strong palisade had been built, but all the houses had been torn down and such heavy objects as bars of iron, pigs of lead, small iron cannon, and saker-shot were littered about and almost obscured by the tangle of weeds that had grown up around them. On the strength of the latter evidence he deduced that the township had been abandoned for some time. However, anyone who has lived in Virginia for one summer knows very well that weeds grow as high as a small elephant's eye almost before you can say "lawn mower." Thus, if the settlement had

24

been abandoned as recently as the beginning of June, it would have been healthily overgrown by mid-August. In truth, using only that evidence, the disaster or decision that caused its abandonment could equally well have occurred a few months or even as much as two years earlier.

A group of sailors scouting the area of the fort encountered the remains of five chests that had been buried by the colonists and subsequently broken open by the Indians. Governor White was appalled to find that three of the chests were his own and had contained personal possessions that he had left in the safekeeping of the "planters" on his return to England in the summer of 1587. There were, he said, ". . . about the place many of my things spoyled and broken, and my bookes torne from the couers, the frames of some of my pictures and Mappes rotten and spoyled with rayne, and my armour almost eaten through with rust . . ."

As Professor David Quinn has pointed out in his standard work, *The Roanoke Voyages 1584-1590*, the fact that White's possessions included framed pictures and maps suggests that the governor may have been the artist John White whose magnificent sketches are our only pictorial record of the earlier ventures. If this is true, one cannot help wondering what precious drawings of the "Citie of Ralegh" were lost to posterity when the Indians broke open the three chests.

Had Sherlock Holmes been a member of Governor White's party, he would doubtless have been able to deduce from the positions of the papers and the condition of the armor, just how long they had been exposed to the weather. Assuming that the Indians had watched the chests being buried, it follows that they would have set about digging them up again just as soon as the colonists had departed or were removed. Thus, Holmes would have known how long before White's arrival the site had been abandoned. Using the same evidence, but relying only on White's description, it seems reasonable to suppose that if the chests had been opened a year or so before he found them, the maps and drawings (frames or no frames) would have been almost totally destroyed by summer sun and winter frost and rains. The armor, which under normal conditions would take a considerable time to be "eaten through with rust," could reach this sorry state in a few months of contact with the salt-laden air of the Outer Banks. In short,

25

it is possible that White's return may not have been as long after the colonists' departure as he supposed.

The mystery of the "Lost Colony" is as intriguing as any modern detective story, and many attempts have been made to reconstruct the events that surrounded it. The testimony of the grass, the papers, and the armor given above are but three of the clues that can be used in evidence by the historian-detective. The archaeological detective employs the same powers of reasoning—which in plain terms amounts to no more than using a little common sense—although he bases his deductions on things that are more tangible than the written statements of long-dead witnesses. The historian may know that a murder was committed, but it is left to the archaeologist to find the bullet. It was to be hoped, therefore, that the excavator might be able to solve the mystery of Fort Raleigh where the historians had failed.

The eroded remains of Ralph Lane's fort, which he had named "The New Fort in Virginia," managed to survive the centuries and were still discernible on the ground when the United States National Park Service began excavations there in 1947. Unlike its inhabitants, the site had never really been lost. In 1653, English traders were taken there by friendly Indians and came back with the inevitable souvenirs. In 1709, John Lawson wrote that a gun of brass, another made of iron staves and hoops, a powder horn, and English coins had been found in the fort area. This statement is slightly surprising in that one would have expected that the Indians would have searched most diligently for anything that was worth carrying off. Had they not, after all, discovered the hiding place of White's chests?

The romantic and mysterious aspects of the "Lost Colony" gave the site a piquancy denied most historic locations. It was for this reason that it continued to come to mind whenever Roanoke Island was mentioned. When the island was mapped in 1770, it was not surprising that the word "Fort" should have been written close to the shore line at the northeast side. Dr. Charles Porter, III, who has written the National Park Service's handbook describing the history of the site, notes that in 1850 the historian, Benson J. Lossing, stated that slight traces were still visible; ten years later Edward C. Bruce, writing in *Harper's New Monthly Magazine*, reported that the fort ditch could be seen forming a square some forty feet in each direction. He added

26

that pieces of brick and stone were found. The brick could conceivably have been pieces from the footings or chimneys of Lane's houses; the stone is less easy to explain. Remembering that no natural stone outcrops occur on Roanoke Island, it follows that it must have been brought from elsewhere. The usual source would have been ballast dumped by ships on arrival in Virginia before taking on cargoes for the return voyage to England. So common did this practice become in the James and York rivers in the eighteenth century that strict regulations were issued demanding that ballast be brought ashore and not thrown into the river where it would foul the channels and become a danger to shipping. The snag about applying this convenient explanation to the Roanoke stone is that, as far as we know, the only substantial cargo ever taken from the sixteenth century settlement was the settlers themselves when carried home by Drake. On that occasion it is hardly likely that anyone would have bothered to cart ballast ashore before leaving.

In 1894, a group of public-spirited North Carolinians formed the Roanoke Colony Memorial Association and purchased the fort site along with ten surrounding acres to ensure its continued preservation. In the following year limited archaeological excavations were undertaken that resulted in the confirmation of the extent of the fort. Two years later, in 1896, a rugged stone marker was set up commemorating the building of the first fort and the birth of Virginia Dare. It was not until 1935 that the area became a state park and until 1941 that it became the Fort Raleigh National Historic Site and was transferred to the National Park Service. Like most such projects, it lay fallow during the war years. Then, in 1947, intensive excavations were conducted in the immediate vicinity of the fort, under the direction of J. C. Harrington, one of the Park Service's most able archaeologists.

If it had been hoped that these excavations would have solved the mystery of the "Lost Colony" or have provided quantities of relics that would have helped to reconstruct the settlers' daily life on the island, those hopes were groundless. They did, however, establish the definite outline of the fort area as well as the depth and width of the defensive ditch. A careful study of the latter's fill showed that it had started to silt up almost as soon as the earthwork was constructed. This you would expect. The dirt removed from the ditch was piled behind it to form the breastwork, and at first this dirt would have been extremely loose, lacking the bonding effect of roots and the protective covering of grass that subsequently grew over it. In its initial raw state, the first rain would start to wash the piled clay back into the ditch. But once the bank was protected, the erosion would have come largely from the sides of the ditch itself, until eventually the cut would have become sufficiently rounded and shallow for it, too, to be effectively blanketed with grasses. This softening of the ditch contours might take two or three years and would, of course, have been delayed if the colonists kept it cleaned out. It would seem that after John White left the final group of settlers there in 1587, they did not bother with the old fort, but constructed the wooden palisade that afforded protection for a much larger area, and presumably encompassed the whole settlement.

Harrington's excavations of the interior of the fort unfortunately provided very little information, a disappointment that was explained by the fact that "the interior had been dug into so many times and in so many places by Indians, later settlers, soldiers of the Civil War period, and by Talcott Williams that the National Park Service archaeologist was unable to say for sure what structures had been inside the fort." This statement in the official handbook goes on to conjecture that there would have been a well and a powder magazine. This is certainly sound reasoning, but one wonders why no well was found. Such a feature would undoubtedly have been six, ten, or even more feet in depth, and it is hard to believe that the disturbing agents listed above could have destroyed every trace of it. As for the powder magazine, if its foundations had been shallow and it had had no cellar, all traces could very easily have disappeared, particularly if someone had later carried off the bricks for re-use elsewhere.

No evidence to establish the location of the houses outside the fort was forthcoming, and, of course, we know from White's own statement that they had gone when he returned to the site in 1590. It is understood that the National Park Service plans new excavations on land recently acquired and we can still hope that the area of habitation will be located. Just what can the archaeologists expect to find?

If the buildings had no brick foundations, a careful scraping of the clay beneath the topsoil would be likely to reveal the now dirt-

5. A large brass finial, probably from an andiron, found amid the roots of a tree blown down outside the Roanoke fort.

6. One side of a Nuremberg counter found on the Roanoke fort site.

filled holes where posts had been inserted into the ground. In the same way, if the chimneys were also of timber and clay, the bases of these would have been imbedded in the clay. If, on the other hand, the chimneys were of brick, it is possible that the holes for scaffold poles erected while building them would also be seen in the ground. As we are told that the colonists did make brick, it seems reasonable to suppose that some buildings would have had brick foundations. It is extremely unlikely that such bricks would have been laid directly on the existing land surface; they would have been set in a prepared trench that served to prevent them from shifting in bad weather and also to ensure that the first course was properly horizontal. Even if, years later, someone came along and dug out the bricks for use in some other project, he could still not obliterate the outline of the houses that had been marked out by the digging of the builders' trenches. The salvaging of bricks from abandoned structures has been common in all periods of history and the familiar trenches left behind have come to be called "robber" trenches by archaeologists.

29

Fallen brick chimneys can often be confused with brickbat-paved paths when seen by a layman, and traces of a supposed brick path were recently encountered while landscaping in the vicinity of the museum to the west of the fort. Scattered fragments of brick still turn up from time to time, but none so far has displayed any characteristic that definitely dates it to the sixteenth century. It is true that brick sizes were controlled by statute in the colonial period, but as nobody stuck very rigidly to it, it is possible to find bricks of various sizes in a single wall. This is hardly surprising when you realize that although the wooden forms in which the bricks were molded may have been of standard dimensions, the quality and the consistency of the clay varied from place to place and maker to maker. The amount of shrinkage in firing the bricks varied accordingly; indeed, the proximity of the bricks to the source of heat in the clamp would have had a bearing on their ultimate measurements. All in all, bricks do not make the best archaeological clues.

Much more easily attributable to the period was the discovery, a few years ago, of a magnificent brass finial from an andiron that turned up clutched in the roots of a tree blown over in a storm. This object (Fig. 5), like all the other artifacts from the "Citie of Ralegh" and its predecessors, is in the National Park Service museum on the site. Also in the collection is half a silver sixpence bearing on one side the profile portrait of Queen Elizabeth and on the other, the arms of Tudor England. Although the source of this coin is uncertain, if it was recovered (as has been suggested) in the vicinity of the fort, it would serve to confirm John Lawson's statement of 1709 that old English coins were then still to be found.

From the National Park Service's excavations came three coin-like objects of latten (an alloy of copper, zinc, and lead) which were mathematical aids, casting-counters or "jettons" as they are usually termed (Fig. 6). Nuremberg was the principal center for the manufacture of jettons in the second half of the sixteenth century and Hans Schultz, who made these examples, was one of the most prolific minters, operating there from 1550 until 1574. The jettons themselves are not notably fine examples, nor is it particularly surprising to find them on this site; the feature that gives them a special interest is that each has a small hole punched through it close to the edge. There

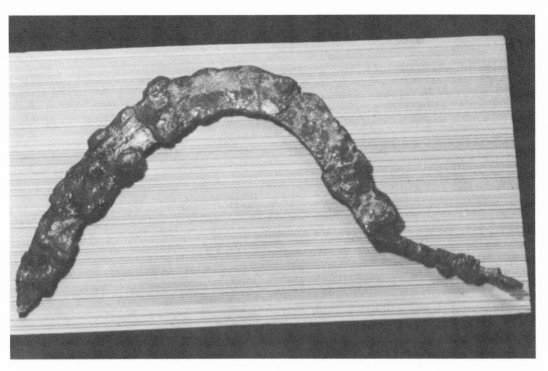

7. An iron sickle found at the bottom of the Roanoke fort ditch.

1 inch
3 cms.

8. Neck of a Spanish oil or wine jar, perhaps brought to Roanoke by Sir Francis Drake.

is every reason to suppose that they had served as part of a necklace and had hung from the neck of an Indian—one, perhaps, who knew what became of the "Lost Colony."

Another jetton from the same die as two of the Fort Raleigh examples had previously been found on an Indian site near Cape Hatteras, not far from the village of Croatoan as marked on John White's map. Remembering that the only clue to the fate of the "Lost Colony" was the word CROATOAN carved on the palisade, we may wonder whether the counter was among the settlers' possessions that went with them when (and if) they left Roanoke Island. But a more probable explanation must be that the jetton was acquired by an Indian through trade during the life of the colony or was afterward picked up on the site of the settlement.

Archaeological evidence of Indian occupation of the fort site, in the form of broken, bag-shaped Indian cooking pots found in various levels of the ditch silt, clearly showed that the Indians were camped in or near the fort soon after its English defenders had gone. It is quite probable that the same Indians and their families returned many times to seek the treasures of clocks, burning glasses, lodestones, and whatnot, that the colonists had shown them but had refused to part with in their more arrogant days. The discovery of John White's buried chests may well have sent the Indians into a prolonged (and archaeologically disastrous) digging spree that may have continued on and off for years.

At the bottom of the fort ditch were found three objects of considerable interest: an iron sickle that had probably helped to hack away the underbrush when Lane's men first set to work (Fig. 7), an Indian clay tobacco pipe through which a colonist may have first savored the weed that made Virginia, and thirdly, part of the neck of a Spanish pottery wine jar (Fig. 8). The last is historically the most interesting, for it gives us an opportunity to test our powers of deduction.

The shape of the fragment itself is not very helpful in that it is of a type that was common from the sixteenth to the late eighteenth century. However, its position "at the bottom of the fort ditch" leaves no doubt that it belongs in the general period of the "Lost Colony," though probably not to it. We do not know how fast the fort ditch silted up or how often it was cleaned out. In addition, there is the possibility that, being heavy, the jar fragment was thrown into the ditch after prolonged rain and that it sank into the saturated silt. Thus its position in the ditch does not, alone, preclude it from having been brought to the colony by John White's settlers. Much more conclusive evidence is provided by the origins of the jar. Spanish goods would not at that time have been among the provisions of a ship setting out from England, but they could have been—and frequently were—acquired by trade or force of arms as the English vessels made their belligerent way through the Spanish West Indies. The only snag is that we know that in 1587 White did not trade in the Indies, but made his way with all speed toward Virginia. On the other hand, as we have already seen, when Sir Richard Grenville carried Ralph Lane and his colonists to the same destination in 1585, numerous stops were made along the route providing ample opportunity for the acquisition of Spanish oil or wine.

More intriguing, though not necessarily more logical, is the possibility that the jar was brought to Virginia by Sir Francis Drake when he stopped to aid Lane's beleaguered colonists in the summer of 1586. We know that in fulfillment of his initial offer, Drake provided provisions to last the settlers another month, provisions which he had doubtless obtained in his enormously successful attacks on Spanish shipping and settlements in the Caribbean. Having supplied Lane with those stores, it is hardly likely that Drake would have sucked them back when, after the storm, the colonists decided to accept the second proposal and return home with the fleet. The empties, at least, would have been abandoned along with anything else that was not wanted on the voyage or worth carrying back to England. After all, the colonists themselves must have taken up a good deal of space aboard the already richly and heavily laden ships.

The most persuasive argument for Drake's having been responsible for the jar's presence, comes from a documentary account of Drake's exploits in the Caribbean which actually states that his ships did carry wine jars obtained from the Spaniards. The reference was found by Robert Charleston of the Victoria and Albert Museum in London in a *Narration du Voyage de François Draeck*, printed in Amsterdam in 1638. Describing Drake's journey through the West Indies, the author stated that "they had landed at the harbour named

Azycke where they found two ships, one carrying Spanish merchandise out of which they siezed only two hundred 'Botigas' or
Spanish jars of wine." Two pages later he mentioned that ". . . they
hung behind some Spanish oil jars full of water." No one will ever
know whether the Roanoke jar had held wine, oil, or water, but we
can be reasonably certain that it was of the type seized by Drake at
Azycke.

Two other pottery items from the National Park Service excavations provide useful, if tantalizing clues. The first comprises two
pieces of a tin-glazed earthenware or maiolica ointment jar of the
sort used by apothecaries. The sherds have tentatively been identified
as of Spanish origin; but very similar wares were being made in the
Netherlands, and in 1570 emigrant potters from Antwerp had set
up the first London factory for the making of paving tiles and "vessels
for apothecaries." So alike were the utilitarian maiolica products of
London, the Netherlands, and Spain that a chemical analysis of the
clay and glaze can provide the only sound basis for identification,
and even this may not be conclusive. All one can say of the Roanoke
fragments is that they come from a jar that had probably held some
form of medical supply.

The final pottery clue is provided by a group of small fragments of
crucible, probably all from the same small vessel. Intact it would have
stood about three inches in height and have had a circular base and
triangular mouth, a shape that dated back to medieval times and was
common all over Europe in the sixteenth century. The interesting
thing about this pot is the fact that examples of its size were generally
used by workers in fine metals: gold and silver. As we shall see in a
later chapter, after use crucibles generally wind up with their insides
incrusted with the residue of the borax that had served as a flux, in
which one can often find minute traces of the metals. In the present
instance, however, there were no such traces. The crucible had not
been used.

A return to the documentary history of the Roanoke settlements
helps us to guess at the explanation for the presence there of so
specialized a vessel—always supposing that you have not already
figured it out. Sir Walter Raleigh and his associates were something
short of generous, open-hearted nationalists whose only interest in

34

colonization was to engrave the name of England on the heart of the New World. On the contrary, their efforts had been triggered by the sight of the plunder that the galleons of Spain had been hauling merrily homeward. In their planning of a colony in Virginia they imagined that the Indians there would be as well supplied with gold as were the Incas and Aztecs. Doubtless, the colonists themselves expected to find the source of the supposed wealth and they would have carried with them the necessary equipment for preparing it—and this would have included crucibles of the type and size found at the fort site. That the crucible was unused, provides us with a silent yet eloquent commentary on the whole endeavor.

The physical remains of Sir Walter Raleigh's dreams are still few and far between. It may be that more will be found in future Park Service excavations, and that traces of the small encampments made by the groups of settlers who were sent away to fend for themselves by Ralph Lane will turn up on the mainland or will emerge from amid the shifting sands of the Outer Banks. There is always the chance that the one word message CROATOAN, which gave hope to John White that his daughter and granddaughter Virgina Dare might still be alive on Croatoan Island, may yet lead us to them four hundred years or so later.

If capricious nature had not whipped up a storm almost at the moment that White read CROATOAN cut onto the palisade post, one of history's most intriguing mysteries might have withered ere it was born. As it was, White was forced to hurry back to his ships and head for deep water, planning to return as soon as circumstances permitted. But fate, being no more generous than mother nature, ensured that circumstances never did permit.

In 1589 Raleigh had disposed of his interests in the Virginia project (but he retained a fifth of any gold and silver that might come out of it), and in 1592 his affair with Elizabeth Throckmorton resulted in a forced marriage and a lengthy sojourn in the Tower of London. It was not until 1602, after White was dead, that Raleigh was able to mount another expedition. But although this reached land at a point some forty leagues southwest of Hatteras, it obtained no news of the "Lost Colony." In 1607, George Percy, one of the first Jamestown colonists, noted that in exploring up the James River he had come upon "a Savage Boy about the age of ten yeeres, which had a head of haire of a perfect yellow and a reasonable white skinne, which is a Miracle amongst all Savages." Perhaps the child's mother had been one of John White's settlers.

Although one talks of the first Englishmen to build a settlement in Virginia as colonists and settlers, it is unlikely that many of them expected to end their days there. It was for this reason that there were so many "gentlemen" among them and it explains the fact that few took readily to the drudgery of farming. Instead, they preferred to go out on exploratory sorties that might bring them to a Virginia Eldorado and ultimately enable them to return home with their pockets heavy with gold. But even if none of them did so, those who were lucky enough to return to England took back memories of adventures stirring enough to make them the envy of their friends for as long as they lived. In the little church of Burghill in Herefordshire is the tomb of a man whose name does not figure in Virginia history; but he was there, on the ship captained by Thomas Cavendish, one of the seven in Grenville's fleet that landed the first Roanoke colonists in 1585. The engraved brass on the tomb reads:

> HERE LYETH THE BODYE OF ROBERT MASTERS
> GENT: LATE LORD OF THIS MANNOVR, WHO TRAVEL
> LED WTH THOMAS CANDISH ESQ^{R}: TO VIRGINIA AND
> AFTERWARD ABOVTE THE GLOBE OF Y^{E} WHOLE
> WORLDE & AFTER HIS RETVRNE MARRYED WINEFRI^{D}
> Y^{E} DAVGHT^{R} OF THOM^{S}: CORNWALL OF BVCKLAND GE^{NT}.
> BY WHOM HE HATH 2 SONES & 7 DAVGHTERS. HE
> DEPARTED THIS LIFE THE .3. OF IVNE A^{O}. 1619.

It was thirty-four eventful years since Robert Masters had seen the dunes at Nags Head and watched the spray lifting over the Diamond Shoals, yet Virginia remained with him even in death.

Upon a Goodly and Fertile Island

EVEN THOUGH many visitors arrive at Jamestown and ask to be shown Plymouth Rock and the relics of the Pilgrims, I do not propose to wade too far into the murky waters of early Jamestown history. They contain strong currents of controversy in which one can very easily be swept away and drowned. Some authors have used the abundant contemporary narratives to show that the 1607 colonists were a dedicated group of intensely religious idealists bringing civilization into a savage land; others have used different passages from the same sources to prove that the colonists were little better than a pack of rabid dogs. But dogs or demigods, there is no denying that they had immense courage and a fortitude that is rarely matched in this twentieth century.

We are not here concerned with the squabbling of the Wingfields, Newports, Percys, Gosnolds, and the like, nor should we try to pontificate on the validity of the story of Pocahontas and that celebrated exaggerator, John Smith. That carcass has been picked many times before. We are concerned, however, with those pages of the history that relate to the marks that the settlers left behind in the ground. From these come the archaeologists' deductions and ultimately the reconstructions and interpretations that are enjoyed by modern visitors to the island.

Unfortunately, no seventeenth century ships have been found nestled in the muddy bed of the James River, and consequently the most impressive and evocative of all the sights to be seen at Jamestown have no archaeological background. Yet to ignore them would make no more sense than to ignore Sir Walter Raleigh when writing about Roanoke. I am, of course, referring to the three ships, the *Susan Constant*, the *Godspeed*, and the little *Discovery* that brought the first Jamestown colonists to Virginia in May 1607. As part of the 350th anniversary celebrations of 1957, all three ships were reconstructed and they now lie moored in the James close by the reconstructed fort as lasting reminders of the courage, not only of the 1607 colonists, but of all who braved the oceans in the days of sail. The largest of the three, the *Susan Constant* of one hundred tons, carried seventy-one persons, the *Godspeed* of forty tons, fifty-two people, and the *Discovery* of twenty tons, twenty-one people. This last was only forty-nine feet in length, little more than a fishing boat and was of a type known as a "pinnace" from the Latin *pinus*, "i.e. a pine tree, of which it was commonly made." Pinnace was not, as a leading encyclopaedia has stated, the name of the ship. The sight of this little vessel bobbing at its moorings in the James brings home to us, as nothing else can, the courage and faith of those first passengers. Many of us would have doubts about the safety of crossing the James in it on a rough day, let alone attempting a five-month journey across the Atlantic. Quite apart from the impact of their small size, the sight of their masts and spars in the distance as one leaves the island, gives one a vision of the past that is unforgettable. I have seen these ships a thousand times, silhouetted against a setting sun, rising ghost-like from a shroud of early morning mist, and frozen fast into a sea of winter ice. But I doubt if I shall ever cease to be thrilled by the awareness that I am surveying a scene almost exactly as

9. The replica of the *Susan Constant* at her moorings at Jamestown Festival Park.

it was viewed through the eyes of colonists and Indians alike, three hundred and fifty odd years ago.

I am certain that some archaeologists will claim that such romantic notions have no place in the serious study of the past. If, in admitting them, I am thought to be letting the team down, I can only counter that if we are unable to use the surviving words and relics of history to enable the past to live again in our own minds, how can we ever hope to make it of interest to others? A great deal of time and money has been spent (some of it hideously wasted) up and down the country in enabling tourists to enjoy looking at the past—from a safe distance. Rarely has a project been as successful as the reconstruction of the fort at Jamestown. It is true that it is not on the original site, and that it is rather more sturdy and certainly much cleaner than was the original. But as you walk among its wattle and daub houses on a cold winter day, you begin to feel what it must have been like to be far from home, cabined, cribbed, confined behind mud walls, longing for spring and the sight of a sail bringing food and succor from England.

The site of the fort has never been found, but it is generally believed to have been built toward the western end of the island and so, being close to the river, it has since been washed away. Some authorities have suggested that part of it may lie beneath the Confederate earthworks immediately to the west of Jamestown's brick church. Careful excavations were conducted there by the National Park Service in 1955, but no traces of it were forthcoming. In the same year off-shore attempts were made to haul up artifact clues in a clam bucket lowered from a barge. Sixty-five "drops" were made, as a result of which the Park Service is now the proud possessor of as fine a collection of old beer bottles, brickbats, and nineteenth and twentieth century crockery as ever graced a city dump. No doubt it was hoped that informative seventeenth century artifacts would be found—and a few were. But short of finding an inscribed tablet giving the position of the fort, it is hard to see that any amount of artifacts could have done more than confirm that a good deal of heavily inhabited land surface had been washed away in the ensuing years.

The colonists landed on Jamestown Island on May 14 and

10. The interior of the fort at the Jamestown Festival Park in course of reconstruction, looking much as it would have when first built.

immediately set about building themselves some sort of fortification which probably amounted to little more than a breastwork of brushwood. On May 21 Captain Newport, John Smith, and twenty others set out to explore the upper reaches of the James. When they returned on May 27, the fort had been surprised and many of the colonists had been wounded before the Indians had been driven off. Immediate efforts were made to improve the defenses and by June 15, according to George Percy, ". . . we had built and finished our Fort, which was triangle wise, having three Bulwarkes, at every corner, like a halfe Moone, and foure or five pieces of Artillerie mounted in them." It is noticeable that the Jamestown fort was not in the least like that built by the earlier settlers at Roanoke. Quite apart from its difference in shape, "James Fort" enclosed the entire settlement (Fig. 10) and was not merely a keep to which the colonists could withdraw in an emergency. This was just as well as they spent most of their time in a state of emergency, the Indians delighting to shoot at them whenever an opportunity arose.

The appearance and substance of the colonists' dwellings within the fort in the summer of 1607 is not clear. There are references to both tents and cabins, and on the basis of the latter, it has sometimes been assumed that the settlers had log cabins. But in the seventeenth century the word cabin could describe the meanest hut—and that was almost certainly the James Fort connotation. It had been a month after they landed before the colonists got around to digging a well in the fort. Until then they had drunk the dirty river water. To make matters worse, they were forced to deal with problems of sanitation within the confines of the palisades, as those who had ventured out to attend to these needs had been sitting ducks for Indian marksmen. What with one thing and another, it was not surprising that the "men were destroyed with cruell diseases" and that as famine, heat, and the Indians crept upon them, they were in no mood or condition to indulge in architectural extravagances.

As George Percy pointed out, "If it had not pleased God to put a terrour in the Savages hearts, we had all perished by those vile and cruell Pagans, being in that weake estate as we were; our men night and day groaning in every corner of the Fort most pittifull to heare." After supplies arrived and the weather became more temperate, the situation somewhat improved. But in the winter of 1607-08, an accidental fire destroyed the entire fort, a catastrophe that occurred soon after Captain Newport had returned from England, and one that may have resulted from the carelessness of his companions. Dr. William Simmonds in his *Proceedings of the English Colonies in Virginia* (1612) tells us that "... where this New Supply being lodged with the rest, accidentally fired the quarters, and so the Towne, which being but thatched with reeds, the fire was so fierce as it burnt their pallizadoes (though 10. to 12 yeardes distant), with their armes, bedding, apparell, and much private provision. Good Mr. Hunt our preacher, lost all his library, and all that he had but the cloathes on his backe . . ."

With the help of Captain Newport and his sailors the palisades were rebuilt along with the church and storehouses; but when he returned again to England in April 1608, the repairs were still not complete. Nevertheless, we may assume that it was in the spring and summer of 1608 that the colonists managed for the first time to build themselves a reasonably solid settlement. This was virtually the same assemblage of buildings that William Strachey saw when he arrived as first secretary of the colony in 1610 and whose fortifications he described as having "... the side next the River extending one hundred and forty yeards; the West and East sides a hundred onely. At every Angle or corner, where the lines meete, a Bulwarke or Watch-tower is raised, and in each Bulwarke a peece of Ordnance or two is well mounted. To every side, a proportioned distance from the Pallisado, is a setled streete of houses, that runs along, so as each line of the Angle hath his streets; in the midst is a market place, a Storehouse, and a Corps du Guard, as likewise a pretty chapel . . ."

Strachey goes on to describe the chapel itself, and from it we can gain an idea of its character and stability. It was, he wrote, "... in length threescore foote, in breadth twenty foure, and a Chancell in it of Cedar, and a Communion Table of the Blake [black] Walnut, and all the Pewes of Cedar, with faire broad windowes, to shut and open, as the weather shall occasion, of the same wood, a Pulpet of the same, with a Font hewen hollow, like a Canoa, with two Bels at the West end." Those bells, which could ring out so merrily when the occasion demanded, were destined more often to toll out the notes of doom as the colonists' death rate continued to mount as the months and years

43

11. An artist's impression of Jamestown about 1625 after the town had spread beyond the confines of the fort.

slipped by. The horrifying figures have been succinctly stated by National Park Service archaeologist John L. Cotter in his report on the archaeology of Jamestown. "Between December 1606,'" he wrote, "(when the first vessels of the Virginia Company left England) and February 1625, 7,289 immigrants came to Virginia. During this period 6,040 died. . . . Allowing for a proportion of these settlers to have been buried on plantations and settlements on the mainland, it is evident that more persons were buried on Jamestown Island during the first few years than lived there at any one time thereafter."

Although the infant settlement had endured many privations, the winter of 1609-10 exceeded all the horrors that had gone before. An accumulation of increased Indian hostility, disease, and almost nonexistent food supplies whittled the colonists' numbers down from about five hundred to as few as sixty. This terrible winter, now remembered by historians as the "starving time," probably left its mark in the ground in the form of a large concentration of graves beneath the east end of an extensive foundation complex which included the site of the third State House later destroyed in Bacon's Rebellion of 1676. It is estimated that the graveyard contained as many as three hundred burials, most of them clustered together, but with a few stragglers extending almost to the present river's edge. As all of them predate the earliest of the overlying foundations, we know that they stem from the first years of the colony. Furthermore, the facts that the bodies were interred without coffins and that they lay with heads and feet in all directions, strongly suggest that they were laid to rest in haste without the niceties of formal Christian burial. The "starving time" could well have provided both the large number of dead and the frame of mind in which disposing of the remains was more important than the paying of final respects.

Scattered burials have been found in various parts of Jamestown and its environs, most of them the bones of colonists, but a few being skeletons of Indians. One of these, a male aged about thirty, was found to have died in an advanced stage of syphilis, a reminder that along with potatoes and tobacco, this disease is often claimed to have been one of America's first exports. Some indication of the date at which the Indian died was provided by the presence of a small fragment of window glass beneath the skeleton. As the first settlers did not possess such glass, we can reasonably assume that the interment did not occur before the second quarter of the seventeenth century.

A second early graveyard was situated in the vicinity of the brick church and a third, which visitors can still see today, surrounds the building itself. About a mile and a half to the northeast of the church stands yet another cemetery containing the restored tombs belonging to the Travis family that owned a large tract on the island from the seventeenth century onward. The cemetery comprised more than sixty graves, but the stones of only a few can now be seen.

The disposal of human remains is always a problem when the deaths come too quickly one upon another. Just how and where the early settlers dealt with this problem is still unknown, for apart from

45

the three hundred or so under the third State House complex and the small early cemetery by the church, no traces have been found of the six thousand who perished in the first quarter of the seventeenth century. The positions of the two cemeteries, however, provide us with clues to the position of the fort site, supporting the theory that it stood in the vicinity of the surviving confederate earthwork.

The hazards of venturing outside the fort were constantly brought home to the settlers, and consequently they would undoubtedly have dug their graves in the best protected area that they could find. The island being roughly pear-shaped and the settlement being situated toward the narrow end, the greatest natural protection would have been found up-river in the lee of the fort toward, as it were, the stalk of the pear. On the basis of this reasoning it would follow that the fort must have been east of the "starving time" graveyard. The second cemetery, on the other hand, was almost certainly of later date and was in use when the settlement was outgrowing the fort and when the danger from the Indians seemed to be waning. Thus, with the town growing in a down-river or easterly direction, the second cemetery would have been below the fort; so together the two graveyards provide brackets between which the fort site probably existed.

In May 1610, along with the approach of spring, came Sir Thomas Gates, the colonists' new governor, who had been delayed for almost a year in Bermuda. The sight that greeted him on arrival was enough to make him decide to pack up and take the surviving settlers home. In the words of his report ". . . the pallisadoes he found tourne downe, the portes open, the gates from the hinges, the church ruined and unfrequented, empty howses (whose owners untimely death had taken newly from them) rent up and burnt, the living not able, as they pretended, to step into the woodes to gather other fire-wood; and, it is true, the Indian as fast killing without as the famine and pestilence within." After careful deliberation Gates took the colonists on board and set off down the James toward the sea and England. Had he started two days earlier the story of Jamestown would have been a duplicate of Ralph Lane's first Roanoke colony, the settlers giving up just before relief arrived. As it was, Gates was already under sail when news arrived that Lord Delaware, well supplied and with a hundred and fifty fresh colonists, had reached Port Comfort at the mouth of the river.

This was the turning point, not only for Gates, who hurried back to the fort to dust it down before his Lordship arrived, but also for the entire history of the colony. The fort was rebuilt, and peace was made with the Indians: Jamestown would survive. But people do not change their character as readily as fate may change their fortunes, and when Lord Delaware returned to England in March 1611, the colonists immediately relaxed. John Smith, in a moment of exasperation, dubbed the early settlers as being as unfit to found a colony as to sustain it, and if proof were needed, it was to be found in the spring of that year when, knowing that the grain store could not last three months, the settlers still could not be bothered to plant the corn on which their existence would depend. When, in May, Sir Thomas Dale, the new deputy governor, arrived in Jamestown, he found "most of the companie were at their daily and usuall works, bowling in the streets . . ."

It took a firm hand, martial law, and a variety of necessary though unpopular measures, before the young colony was ready to present a bold face to Spaniards, Indians, or even the weather. But a year later Jamestown could boast "two rowes of houses of framed timber, and some of them two stories, and a garret higher, three large Store-houses Joined together, [a hundred and twenty feet in length], and hee [Sir Thomas Dale] hath newly strongly impaled the towne." Before long the settlement began to burst out of its wooden womb and to grow up into a community of streets, stores, taverns, and frame residences not unlike an English village in, say, Kent or Essex.

Once the fear of Indian attack was removed, the settlers began to move further afield, building themselves farms away from the island. In addition, three other comparable settlements were established; the first was set up at Kecoughtan, originally an Indian village below Old Point Comfort on Hampton Roads, while the others were up-river from Jamestown a distance of some fifty miles and were named Charles City and Henricus (also Henrico or Henricopolis) respectively.

If all had gone according to plan, Henricus would ultimately have become more important than Jamestown. It was founded in 1611 by Sir Thomas Dale on land now known as Farrar's Island in a bend of the James River called Dutch Gap. "This towne," wrote John Smith, "is situated upon a necke of a plaine rising land, three parts environed with the maine River; the necke of land well impaled, makes it like an Ile; it

47

hath three streets of well framed houses, a handsome Church, and the foundations of a better laid (to be built of Bricke), besides Store-houses, Watch-houses, and such like. Upon the verge of the River there are five houses, wherein live the honester sort of people, as Farmers in England. and they keepe continuall centinell for the townes securitie." Here, incidentally, was the first reference to a building being constructed of brick. Robert Johnson, writing of Henricus in 1612, refers to the houses (as well as the new church) having "the first story all of bricks."

As Henricus gained in stature, plans were developed to build a hospital there, and the Virginia Company granted ten thousand acres for a university and one thousand for an Indian school. During this same era of increasing optimism both in England and Virginia, an iron-works was constructed further upstream at Falling Creek; Charles City was well established as also were seven "Hundreds" or plantations, tracts deeded to groups of Virginia Company stockholders for the founding of individual settlements. But on Good Friday, 1622, the In-dians made it clear that they had no wish to go to school or to be wooed away from their native gods. Working by a carefully pre-arranged plan, they fell upon the isolated farms and settlements, burn-ing the houses and slaughtering every man, woman, and child they could lay their hands on. Fortunately for Jamestown, a friendly Indian servant chose to tell his master of the plan just in time for the town to be warned. But the outlying areas received no warning; the ironworks at Falling Creek was destroyed, and so were the towns of Henricus and Charles City, as well as most of the isolated farms. At Martin's Hundred, only seven miles from Jamestown, seventy-three people were killed, and the total for the entire massacre has been set between three hundred and three hundred and forty-seven persons.

Although the Virginia Company ordered that Henricus should be rebuilt and that brickmakers already there to build the university and school should get on with the job, the project was never revived. Today the site on Farrar's Island is extremely difficult to reach. The palisaded neck referred to by John Smith has been cut through by a canal ironing out a bend in the river, while most of the island has dis-appeared into a vast gravel-mining project engineered by a local ce-ment company. Overlooking the canal at Dutch Gap is a marker recalling that here was the site of Henricus and of the first intended university in America. But it is my personal belief that the marker is too close to the end of the island and that Henricus, one of the "Four Ancient Boroughs" of Virginia, has been sacrificed on the gravel-tempered concrete altar of progress. As far as I can discover, no archaeological work was ever done there and my own small attempts to find traces of it, either on the bluff or on the shores of the river, yielded nothing.

There has been talk in recent years of undertaking extensive archaeological work on the ironworks site, but as yet nothing has come of it. The same is true of Charles City. On the south shore, opposite Charles City, is the site of Bermuda Hundred, which also suffered in the massacre, but which went on to achieve lasting importance in the later seventeenth and eighteenth centuries. Traces of foundations of uncertain date have been found in this area, but my one day spent there resulted in the recovery of nothing more spectacular than a couple of fragments of eighteenth century pottery. Nevertheless, Bermuda Hundred remains an area of considerable archaeological promise for anyone with the time and money to spend on it.

Of the four "Cities" of early seventeenth century Virginia, only Kecoughtan (renamed Elizabeth City in 1621) was sufficiently far away to have heard nothing of the 1622 massacre. It was at the Indian village there that Captain Newport had stopped when bringing the first settlers into the James in 1607, and it was there that John Smith went in the fall of the same year in an attempt to trade trinkets for food, and finding that there was nothing to be had, "he was by necessitie inforced, though contrary to his commission to let fly his muskets." Here, later he spent more than a week as a guest enjoying the Indians' good food and remarking that he had never had "better fires in England than in the dry, smoky houses of Kecoughtan." In July 1610, Lord Delaware had begun to build two small forts, one on either side of what is now Hampton Creek. No traces of these structures have been found and as the area is now built over, it is unlikely they ever will.

In 1940, about a mile to the west of the creek, facing Hampton Roads, a site of both Indian and colonial occupation was encountered and subsequently partially excavated. A large brick chimney founda-

49

tion was encountered, along with the remains of a Dutch oven, a lime kiln, and numerous refuse pits. From the pits came a fine collection of colonial artifacts, including brass spurs, a brass andiron finial, a glass linen smoother, scissors, fish hooks, the guard from a basket-hilted sword, agricultural tools, and various items of European pottery. The whole area was liberally sprinkled with Indian pottery, some of which was present in the same pits as the colonial material. This led the excavator, Mr. Joseph B. Brittingham, to the conclusion that the site was that of a trading post established before Lord Delaware built his forts and that it "unquestionably" proved "that the Whites and Indians lived together before the Colonists' occupation in 1610." If this is so, we have evidence for the existence of brick chimneys in Virginia earlier than was provided by the previously cited Henricus references. Unfortunately, a note of caution is sounded by the presence on the site of a Rhenish stoneware bottle of a type that cannot date much earlier than 1630–40 (Fig. 12). Evidence to the contrary lacking, it seems safer to attribute the colonial occupancy to the second quarter of the seventeenth century, when the site formed part of a tract patented by one Elizabeth Dunthorne, and to its continuance throughout the colonial period. The nature and duration of the Indian occupancy of the site was not clear from Joseph Brittingham's published report and it seems that he had been forced to abandon the project before it was completed, largely because the Mariner's Museum of Newport News which was sponsoring the project, considered "that sufficient artifacts had been found to make an impressive display and, since a larger collection of artifacts would tend to overbalance the Museum's nautical character, further work would not be warranted." Warranted or not, the unhappy fact remains that the area has now been built over and the site of Kecoughtan, if such it was, has gone the way of Henricus.

The aftermath of the massacre of 1622 resulted, not too surprisingly, in a hardening of the colonists' attitude toward the Indians. John Smith made no bones about it, urging that they should be destroyed by all means possible and beaten out of the country. He pointed out that the Spaniards had had the right idea in the West Indies, having reduced the rebellious infidels to slavery—the Indians being civilized by conquest rather than kindness. From a purely practical viewpoint, Smith also noted that hitherto, in a self-sacrificing attempt at peaceful co-

12. Rhenish stoneware "Bellarmines" of about 1630-40 with similar medallions. Left, from Kecoughtan. Right, from Jamestown.

existence, the Indians had been left to live in "the pleasantest places in the Countrey," while the colonists had been forced to hack their fields out of the jungle. Now, after the massacre, the colonists needed no fiery oratory to send them out after their enemies. Although the Indians as individuals were hard to pin down, there was little difficulty in destroying their villages, crops, and canoes. Just as the modern Virginia hunters go out in the fall of the year to slaughter more or less anything that moves, so the colonists went out in the summer after the Indians, catching them in their attempts to grow the corn that they had to garner before the winter came. Year after year the open season on Indians and the resulting famine thinned the ranks of the colonists' foes. Nevertheless, twenty-two years after the first massacre the same Indian leader, Opechancanough, staged a repeat performance. Once again the colonists were taken by surprise, once again the outlying farms and settlements were destroyed, and once again the settlers' death roll numbered more than three hundred. But this time there was a difference: instead of killing some three hundred and forty-seven out of an estimated thirteen hundred, in 1644 the Indians took a similar

51

number out of eight thousand. But if the Indians' successes were pro-
portionately less, the retribution was even more severe than before.
Opechancanough was caught and killed and the great Powhatan Con-
federacy, which had controlled Tidewater Virginia when the colonists
arrived, was now destroyed. Although fierce fighting was to break out
again in the 1670's, the center of the trouble would then be seated inland above Richmond. Never again would the farms around Jamestown suffer a major Indian attack. Indeed, by the end of the century
the Indian population of Virginia had been reduced to two thousand
from the estimated eighteen thousand that had lived there in 1600.

Regardless of the fact that neither Indian uprising changed the
course of history, at least as far as the colonists were concerned, one
fact is irrefutable: considerable damage was done and a great deal of
blood was shed. There is every reason to suppose that here and there
the soil of Tidewater Virginia is still stained, still scattered with broken
artifacts, and the clay still reddened by the fires. It may seem curious,
therefore, that no site has yet been found that can be definitely associated with either massacre. A possible candidate was the site found by
Mr. Floyd Painter of Norfolk, which is now situated on federal property five miles below Jamestown. After the land immediately above
the river had been cleared by bulldozing, Painter found, in the side of
an open ditch, two refuse pits, both containing artifacts dating no later
than about 1640 and both containing ashes and quantities of clenched
nails that could have been the residue of anything from a few old
crates to a burned homestead. From these pits the amateur archaeologist recovered a quantity of pottery, Indian copper beads, a lead bale
seal for cloth, issued in the reign of James I, iron tools, and an iron
siege helmet. This last was an item of head armor of excessive weight
and strength generally worn by military engineers who were likely to
be working while exposed to enemy fire.

Mr. Painter's helmet is one of the very few pieces of armor found
in Virginia and the only English siege helmet found in America. Its
great weight would have made it a most tiresome item of headgear for
a hot Virginia summer and one may wonder, therefore, how it ever
came to be there. A possible explanation comes out of the knowledge
that a quantity of armor was sent over in the Third Supply from London in 1608, most of it apparently being unwanted pieces from the

52

Tower of London. As far as the London agent was concerned, a helmet was a helmet and if the colonists did not like it there was little they could do about it. Mr. Painter noted that his helmet had a dent in it which he attributed to a musket ball, an observation that sired various conjectural explanations ranging from the helmet's having been used for target practice to its having seen service against the Spaniards. Unhappily the noted military historian, Harold L. Peterson, spoiled these romantic excesses by explaining that the impression was merely that of a testing dent administered when the helmet was manufactured.

Another helmet of rather similar shape but of normal weight, was found in a refuse pit on the Naval Mine Depot property near Yorktown. This helmet, known as a cabasset, was associated with numerous weapon fragments, all of the first half of the seventeenth century. From Jamestown itself have come a small number of items of body armor, the most interesting pieces being a breastplate and backplate of light pikeman's armor, found in a single refuse pit filled prior to 1650. In the same pit were a cutlass, the guard from a basket-hilted sword, a musket barrel, and a fine swept-hilt sword from the workshop of Johannes Wundes of Solingen, Germany (Fig. 13). The only other substantial piece of armor from Jamestown was found by Confederate soldiers while digging their breastworks near the church during the

13. Swept-hilt rapier of about 1610 made by Johannes Wundes of Solingen, Germany. Found at Jamestown, washed, and then returned to the ground more or less in its original position.

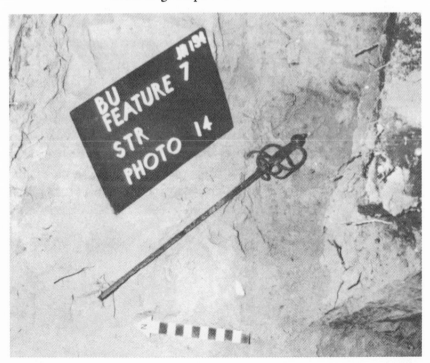

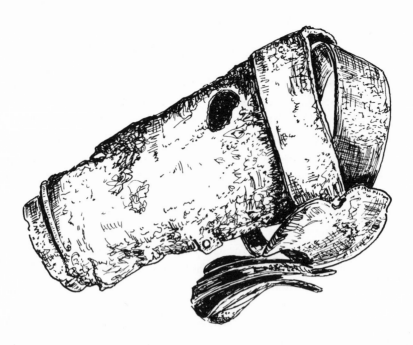

14. Arm section from a three-quarter suit of armor. Found during the Civil War at Jamestown while the Confederate fort was being built.

Civil War (Fig. 14). This took the form of a hinged arm section that could have come either from a light suit or from a three-quarter suit of a type worn by officers in the seventeenth century.

No doubt as time went by, a great deal of Jamestown's armor was turned over to the blacksmith for scrap. Nevertheless, the records list so much that it is surprising that so little has been found. Harold Peterson, in his book *Arms and Armor in Colonial America*, has noted that after the 1622 massacre the colony was supplied with no fewer than two thousand helmets, forty plate cuirasses, four hundred shirts and coats of mail, and a hundred jackets armored with small metal scales. This store was in addition to the armor already in Virginia before the massacre, some of which had probably been looted by the Indians.

It has often been said that armor was found to be too heavy to be worn in Virginia and that the colonists quickly abandoned it. This may be true of the heavier three-quarter length suits, but it would seem that the protective merits of breastplates, helmets, and mail continued to be appreciated as late as the 1620's. Earlier, in 1611, William Strachey, whose description of the fort was so valuable, described the order of dress for those who had to venture on punitive missions beyond its palisades. Every musketeer, he said, ". . . shall either be furnished with a quilted coate of Canuas, a headpeece, and a sword, or else with a light Armor, and Bases quilted, with which hee shall be furnished; and every Targiteer [one who carries a shield] with his Bases to the small of his legge, and his headpeece, sword and pistoll or Scuppet provided for that end." Strachey concluded by stating that the Governor should ensure that he "vse his Garrison to the dayly wearing of these Armors, least in the field, the souldier do finde them the more uncouth strange and troublesome."

No identifiable fragments of shields or "targets," as they were called, have yet been found in Virginia excavations. Although it was a form of defense that was on its way out in Europe by the end of the sixteenth century, in Virginia it had much to commend it. When the Indians loosed their arrows in a high arc, the colonists could see them coming and use their shields to push them aside. Equally helpful was the fact that with the protection of a shield it would not be essential to wear plate armor, but only a padded or leather coat. The shields, themselves, were generally circular, about three feet in diameter, and made of steel or more commonly of wood covered with leather. It was the latter variety on which, in the first days of the 1607 landing, a naïvely confident Englishman invited a visiting Indian to try his luck. George Percy recalled that the savage "tooke from his backe an Arrow of an elle long, drew it strongly in his Bowe, shoots the Target a foote thorow, or better: which was strange, being that a Pistoll could not pierce it. Wee seeing the force of his Bowe, afterwards set him up a steele Target; he shot again, and burst his arrow all to pieces."

Indian quartzite projectile points and blades have been found all through the Tidewater area, scattered over the fields, along the shores of the rivers, and in colonial rubbish pits of the seventeenth and eighteenth centuries. It is hard to tell how many of these Indian lithic objects were in use in the colonial period, as they could have found their way into the pits in dirt dug from elsewhere. In 1960 an excellent red quartzite point of large size turned up in a Williamsburg trash pit that had been in use about 1820.

No Indian bows have been found in Virginia excavations; being of wood they would not normally survive. But if they were deposited in permanently wet soil they could, and there is every reason to suppose that the marshes of Jamestown Island may hold many such treasures. In such conditions, as we shall see in a later chapter, metals and organic material can be preserved in virtually the same condition they were in on the day they were lost. An Indian canoe, burned and scraped out of a single tree trunk, was found some years ago in fine shape in the mud of the York River near West Point and is now exhibited in the Valentine Museum in Richmond. Another, twelve feet long and shaped with iron tools, was found in the silt at the bottom of a pond in Caroline County when a dam broke in the spring of 1962. This one was acquired by the Jamestown Foundation and is to be seen at the Festival Park. However, the obvious marks of iron tools suggest that it was made well into the colonial period. Although such objects survive intact as long as they remain incased in mud, once they begin to be washed out of it they quickly go to pieces. This is particularly true of fabrics and slender pieces of wood such as arrows or bows. Pottery or stone implements are easily spotted by archaeologists and collectors, but a very sharp eye is needed to recognize the curve of a bow amid the mass of roots and twigs that habitually protrude from the river banks.

Although the English were all too aware of the effectiveness of the bow and arrow in the hands of the extremely mobile Indians, there is no indication that the colonists made use of the same weapons. Firearms were considered much more useful in that the report of the gun would often disperse the enemy even when the ball missed by a country mile. As every student of European history knows, the English longbow with steel-tipped arrows had been a combination to be feared since the Middle Ages. Although this weapon was still in use in the early seventeenth century, there is evidence to show that the colonists deliberately refrained from importing it for fear that one might fall into Indian hands and serve as a prototype for them to improve their already deadly armament. As recently as 1792 an English army officer was championing the advantages of the bow over a flintlock musket, and his points in favor of the former well summarize the Indians' advantages over the colonists. First, he claimed that the bow was as accurate as the musket; second, an infantryman could discharge four arrows in the time it took to load and fire one bullet; third, the enemy was not obscured by smoke from his own gun; fourth, a flight of ar-

56

rows "terrifies and disturbs the enemy's attention to his business"; fifth, "an arrow sticking in any part of a man puts him *hors de combat* till it is extricated"; and lastly, bows and arrows could be more easily made and supplied than muskets and ammunition. All these considerations would have been painfully obvious to the early Jamestown settlers.

The heavy crossbow, with its equally cumbersome quarrels or bolts, had been a standard European weapon in the early days of Spanish incursion into America. But it was troublesome to carry and slow to load. On the credit side, it could pierce plate armor at sixty yards; but against Indians, who frequently wore little more than a frown, such power was hardly necessary. Light crossbows were used as sporting weapons and part of one of them was found in excavations at Green Spring, the great seventeenth century plantation of Governor Berkeley. The piece found was the cocking lever used to draw the string back and engage it to the tricker-lock or trigger, the latter incidentally being the crossbow's contribution to the evolution of the musket.

Many musket fragments have been found in excavations at Jamestown, the most informative being locks or firing mechanisms, which well illustrate the various stages in the development of the firearm. The musket was simply a device used to ignite a small quantity of gunpowder that burned through a touchhole into the barrel of the gun, setting off the compressed charge that it contained. In the course of the seventeenth century various mechanisms were developed to achieve this simple result. The first, and least complicated, was the matchlock, which comprised nothing more than a covered pan for priming powder and a length of potassium nitrate-soaked cotton cord that provided a constantly burning match. The end of the match was attached to a lever on the side of the gun and when the trigger was pulled the glowing end was thrust down into the powder—always providing that you remembered to open the lid of the pan first. The matchlock was the principal weapon of the 1607 colonists, but by 1624, as Harold Peterson has pointed out, a military census showed that there were only 47 matchlocks out of a grand total of 1,098 firearms in the colony. In England, however, the matchlock continued to be used by the army until its use was officially abolished in 1690.

A much more complicated and expensive weapon was the wheel lock, of which there were a few in Virginia in the early days of the

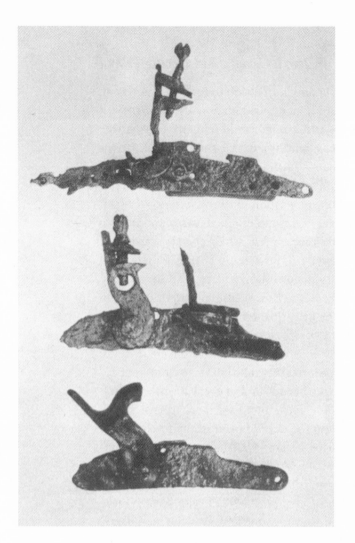

15. Gun locks from Williamsburg. Top, a 17th century snaphance (minus its battery). Center, a flintlock of the Revolutionary period. Below, a percussion lock of the Civil War period from the Harper's Ferry Arsenal.

colony. This device ignited the priming powder by means of a serrated steel wheel beside the pan which was wound up on a spring by a key. When the spring was freed, the wheel ground against a lump of iron pyrites that sent a spark into the powder. Fragments of at least one of these have been found at Jamestown. A third mechanism used by the first colonists was known as the snaphance. This device was much simpler than the wheel lock and was really the ancestor of the flintlock of the eighteenth century (Fig. 15). The snaphance comprised a hammer holding a piece of flint which, when the trigger was pulled, sprang forward and scraped against a vertical block of steel called a battery that sent a spark downward into the priming powder. An obvious refinement was soon developed; a reversed L-shaped cover for the pan

58

also served as a striking surface for the flint. When the trigger was pulled, the flint slammed forward striking the vertical face of the cover or frizzen, pushing it up and away from the pan. Thus in one movement the priming powder was uncovered and a spark struck down into it. There were various evolutionary refinements of this type of lock and many examples have been found in Virginia. I do not propose to dwell on their subtle differences here. But before leaving the subject, it is worth noting that although there are many contemporary references to the use of snaphances in Virginia, very few fragments of them have been found. The total to date amounts to two locks and three batteries from Jamestown and two locks from Williamsburg. These last pose a curious problem in that they were found on the site of the eighteenth century printing office on Duke of Gloucester Street, an area that yielded no other objects of the previous century. Nevertheless, we do know that in the 1670's there were more than 230 snaphances in the magazine at Williamsburg, then called Middle Plantation.

Other weapons represented among the fragments from Jamestown are the three basic polearms, the halberd, bill, and pike (Fig. 16). The first had become little more than a badge of rank carried by sergeants while inspecting the guard or being inspected themselves. Only

16. Examples of bill and halberd shapes from Jamestown.

one example has been found. On the other hand, six bills have been re-covered, coming, perhaps, from the 950 shipped into the colony after the 1622 massacre. This weapon was a simple development of the common agricultural implement; it had a broad chopper-like cutting edge slightly hooked at the end, a long spike extending from behind the hook, and generally another smaller spike protruding from the back of the blade. On a short handle, it was an excellent tool for slashing underbrush, but on its long military pole, its principle use was against cavalry. This was also true of the pike, which was generally a stout double-edged blade on the end of a pole some fourteen or even sixteen feet in length. Pikemen would kneel with these polearms at a forty-five degree angle to prevent horsemen from charging the musketeers while they were going through the lengthy process of reloading their weapons. However, as the Indians did not possess horses, and there seems to have been only one at Jamestown as late as 1624-25, the usefulness of polearms was somewhat limited. They would, of course, have been invaluable if the Indians had dashed into the field with clubs and hatchets swinging. But they had more sense than to engage in such excesses, and so preferred to remain discreetly in the woods.

Undoubtedly the most unusual weapon or military device surviving from seventeenth century Virginia is known as a caltrop, a single example of which has been found at Jamestown (Fig. 17). It is a widely spread iron tripod about three inches long with another leg sticking vertically upward, so that however you throw it down, one spike always sticks up. A contemporary dictionary describes it as "an instrument used in War; being great pricks of Iron, four square, to cast in an Enemies way, when they would break in on the contrary side." This unpleasant little device has an extremely long history going back to Roman times and was generally used to deter the horse of advancing cavalry. In 1622 Francis Markham, in his *Five Decades of Epistles of Warre*, noted with concern that in warfare "Foards are soon choakt up with Calthorpes" making them impassable long after the conflict was over. Soldiers were urged to wear steel soles on their boots, and horses' hoofs were often similarly shod. There is no doubt that the most inscrutable Indian treading on a caltrop would be shocked into noisy comment. The snag with these things would have been that you needed so many of them. A thick concentration neatly arrayed outside

60

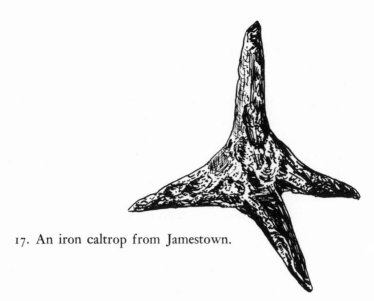

17. An iron caltrop from Jamestown.

the fort gates might have been effective, providing the colonists themselves did not plan to venture out. In the same way, discreet little clusters on woodland trails might have had nuisance value. But in the sort of guerrilla warfare favored by the Indians, it seems improbable that they would have been of much use. The fact that only one caltrop has been found would seem to suggest that they were used little, if at all. As with all military equipment designed for European wars, the caltrop's presence in Virginia must be considered in the light of possible attacks by the Spaniards as well as assaults from the Indians.

By the middle of the seventeenth century, fear of both enemies had dwindled and Jamestown was settling down to a reasonably comfortable and predictable existence. The Virginia Company's charter had long since been revoked, and Virginia, now a royal colony, was answerable to the king and his ministers. In one of many letters sent home to the authorities in London, Governor Harvey wrote proudly of the blossoming of Jamestown in 1639. ". . . there are twelve houses and stores built in the Towne," he stated, "one of brick by the Secretayre, the fairest that ever was knowen in this countrye for substance and uniformitye, by whose example others have undertaken to build framed houses to beautifye the place, consonant to his majesties Instruction that wee should not suffer men to build slight cottages as heretofore . . . A Levye likewyse by his majesties commands is raised for the building of a State howse at James Cittie, and shall with all diligence be performed."

In the early days of the colony the council had met either in the

61

church or in the house of the governor. The acquisition of a specific structure for these deliberations was an important step forward in the history of American government. The property acquired for this purpose was the home of the late Governor Sir John Harvey and was purchased by the colony in 1641. A deed of 1671 described the structure as then comprising three houses, one, at least, of them built of brick and measuring forty feet by twenty feet. The same document adds that the center unit of the three attached "tenements" had been the old State House.

The State House complex provided the residence of three royal governors, the most famous of whom was Sir William Berkeley, whose great plantation site on the mainland north of Jamestown was to become one of the most important colonial archaeological sites yet excavated in Virginia. The State House was the political and judiciary center of the colony, a meeting place for the Assembly, a place where taxes were levied, complaints heard, punishment administered and where on one dramatic day in 1652 the colony surrendered to the enemies of the king. Parliamentary commissioners sent over by Oliver Cromwell there received the reluctant allegiance of the royalist Governor Berkeley and through him that of the colony as a whole.

By the time that Charles II was restored to the long vacant throne of his father, the first State House of Virginia had ceased to serve as

18. The foundations of the first State House at Jamestown. View toward the ruined Ambler House.

19. A large Rhenish stoneware "Bellar-mine" dated 1661, found in the ruins of the first State House.

the seat of government. Indeed, it was no longer so used in 1656, though it remained as a residence for some years to come. By 1696 we know from documentary sources that only one of the three joining buildings was still standing, the rest being in a state of ruin. The nature of the disaster that befell the building will probably never be known—unless its site still remains to be excavated.

The general consensus of modern opinion is that the site has already been found, and that it lies toward the east end of what was known as "New Towne." Visitors to Jamestown can see part of the open brick-lined cellars of a large building complex comprising three basement sections (Fig. 18), each entered by its own bulkhead steps leading down into it from the outside, suggesting that the whole consisted of three individuals units. This complex was discovered as long ago as 1901 by Colonel Edward Barney who then owned a large part of the island. He and his wife dug down through the debris-filled

63

20. A magnificent Westerwald blue and gray stoneware jug of about 1610. Its ornamental frieze is from the same mold as sherds found at Jamestown. Height 13 inches.

east basement and found a brick fireplace in which, resting on the ashes of a fire, was a tripod-legged cooking pot still containing bones that had been stewing there when the building was destroyed. Colonel Barney also found, along with a large quantity of not too impressive domestic debris, a fine pewter basin more than a foot in diameter.

The Colonel did not go on to explore the whole building complex and the site was virtually forgotten until 1932 when a Richmond antiquary, George C. Gregory, was looking for the site of the first State House and came upon these foundations. He duly uncovered the outline of the triple structure and concluded that this was the State House. Two years later the site, along with all that part of the town not owned by the Association for the Preservation of Virginia Antiquities, was acquired by the National Park Service. Almost immediately work began on the total clearance of the foundations laid bare by Gregory. Large quantities of artifacts including fragments of wine bottles, clay tobacco pipes, and ceramics were recovered. In the latter category was a large proportion of a massive Rhenish stoneware bot-

64

tle known as a "Bellarmine" (see p. 286) bearing on its sides molded medallions carrying the date 1661 (Fig. 19). It had been badly burned and one might be tempted to argue that it was in the building when it was destroyed. However, the fact that the whole of the base and part of the neck are missing must either be explained as careless excavating or, more probably, by the fact that the vessel was broken elsewhere and the body thrown into the already ruined building. In any case, the bottle's presence there shows that it could not have found its way into the cellar before 1661, five years after the structure had ceased to serve as the State House. The large quantity of other relics, particularly the pipes and bottles, suggested that the cellars were still open to receive refuse into the early eighteenth century. The presence of so many bottles has been interpreted to suggest that part of the building may have been used as a tavern in its later days. But evidence of this kind can be very misleading, particularly in the eighteenth century when wine, beer, cider, even paint and oil were stored in precisely the same sort of bottles, and when inventories of private homes list as many as three or four hundred bottles in their cellars.

There is little doubt that the building complex found first by Col. Barney and later by Mr. Gregory fits most of the requirements for the first State House as culled from the scrappy documentary information. The measurements are right, so are the three divisions, and so is the style of building. On the other hand, no evidence was found to suggest that any of it dated prior to 1640—which it should have done if part of it had been the home of Governor Harvey before it became the State House. But such negative evidence must always be treated with extreme caution. Less easy to overlook is the fact that two houses shown on original surveys to be in certain locations in relationship to the State House, could not be found when their supposed positions were plotted in relation to the triple foundation. Attempts were made to find them by Park Service archaeologist H. Summerfield Day in 1935 and again by Dr. John L. Cotter in 1956. Both drew a blank. But as Cotter has pointed out in his report on the site, had these missing buildings been of light construction, it is possible that all traces of them might have been obliterated by subsequent plowing.

Even if this structure was not the first State House, there is no doubt that it was in existence in the second half of the seventeenth century and that it possessed most of the construction details that one would expect of such a structure or, for that matter, of any well-built residence or commercial building of that period. The walls were made of red brick laid in English bond (Fig. 2) and anchored with mortar mixed with lime from burned oyster shells. The floors of two of the cellar units were of ordinary red brick, but that at the east had originally been laid with small yellow Dutch bricks set on edge, only a few of which remained in position at the time of the 1934 excavation.

The use of small bricks about an inch in thickness and laid on edge goes back to Roman times. These were used for floors that were going to take a good deal of heavy wear and the bricks were set in herring-bone patterns. The Dutch made great use of such brickettes in the seventeenth century and, rather surprisingly, there is no doubt that they were shipped to America and not made here in the Dutch style. Examples have been found on sites as far apart as Van Cortlandt Manor on the Hudson and in the Dutch colony of Surinam. I say that it is surprising that they should be exported only because bricks were not nearly as frequently shipped to America as is popularly believed. Scores of old houses up and down the country are claimed by their owners to be made from English brick, but while their measurements may conform to English statutes regulating sizes, most of them were made in the colonies. This is particularly true of Tidewater Virginia where much of the clay is excellently suited for brickmaking. The basis for the belief that the bricks are English is that bricks were used as ballast in ships, and there is no doubt this was done from time to time. However, quite apart from the fact that few ships could have carried enough to be really useful, bricks made somewhat treacherous ballast. Unlike most Dutch brickettes, English bricks were not very tightly grained and so tended to be porous. Consequently, if the vessel shipped water, much of it would be absorbed by the bricks and so increase the weight of the ballast. An example of this was provided on the James River some years ago when a barge towing bricks down river from Richmond sank from the increased weight of its water-logged cargo.

The red bricks of the supposed State House were of English sizes, but were almost certainly made in the colony. In 1630 Governor

Harvey had written to England complaining of the lack of artisans, among whom he named brickmakers and bricklayers. This is slightly curious in that we know that both brickmakers and bricklayers had been sent over to work on the college and school at Henricus and that after the massacre of 1622 the Virginia Company specifically urged these people to get back to work. Even if those buildings were never completed, one might have expected that the brickmakers would have been around to provide their important services elsewhere. Be this as it may, we do know that in 1639 the Secretary of the colony had a brick house and that in the same year work was in progress on the new brick church. It was at this time that a brickmaker by the rather incongruous name of William Stoner was listed among new arrivals at Jamestown.

Further evidence of the appearance of the State House complex was provided by a quantity of builders' hardware discovered scattered through the cellar filling. Among the relics were fragments of iron casements and leaded diamond-shaped glass panes or "quarrels" from windows. The presence of the casements showed that at least some of the windows were entirely glazed. This was not always the case, particularly in areas where glass was hard to obtain; there wooden shutters took the place of casement windows, glazing being confined to small non-opening frames above. The pintle-hung casement was the common window form of the seventeenth century and one that probably continued well through the first quarter of the eighteenth. Many fragments of leaded panes have been found in contexts of the latter date, while an iron casement frame was discovered in the burned debris of Corotoman, the great Carter plantation in Lancaster County that was destroyed in 1729.

Other iron items from the so-called State House included numerous strap hinges, pintles, H hinges, hooks, staples, locks, and keys. Also present were fragments of tiles, both of flat and pan forms. The flat, rectangular red clay tile was the most common roofing device used on substantial buildings in the Jamestown period. Two holes were driven through one end of each tile before it was fired so that it could be attached to the rafters of the steeply pitched roof. These were laid from the eaves working upward to the apex of the roof, a thick dab of mortar often being slapped onto the middle of each tile so that

67

the end of the next row up would adhere to it. Such a technique must have been a particularly wise precaution in Virginia where hurricane-force winds could easily rip lightly anchored tiles from their moorings and turn them into damaging, if not lethal, projectiles. In addition, a few fragments of slate were found in the State House debris and it has been suggested that this was also used in roofing.

Flat roofing tiles similar to those from the "State House" were found sun-dried and ready for baking when the site of a large brick kiln was discovered north of the church in 1941. The kiln was excavated by J. C. Harrington, the same Park Service archaeologist who had directed the work at Fort Raleigh on Roanoke Island. Harrington estimated that the kiln would have held as many as fifty thousand bricks and that a large pit beyond it to the north had provided clay for about half a million bricks in all. He also noted that the bricks made in this kiln were of the same size as those used in the building of the presumed first State House.

Brick houses were naturally much less prone to fire than were those of wood and it was with that in mind that the Assembly passed the Town Act of 1662. This stated that the town should consist "of thirty two houses, each house to be built with brick, forty foot long, twenty foot wide, within the walls, to be eighteen foote high above the ground, the walls to be two brick thick to the water table, and a brick and a halfe thick above the water table to the roofe, the roofe to be fifteen foot pitch and to be covered with slate or tile." The Act goes on to state that those who build houses to these specifications shall be allowed land on which to build a store, but that those who do not do so shall not be allowed to construct storehouses. In a later passage the Act admits that "it might seem hard to demolish any wooden houses already built in the towne, yett it is hereby *provided and enacted* that noe wooden houses shall hereafter be built within the limitts of the towne, nor those now standing be hereafter repaired, but brick ones be erected in theire steads."

With the Indian menace long since gone, Jamestown had remained the administrative center and a port for all merchandise reaching and leaving the colony, but it had not blossomed as the thriving residential community that the Assembly naïvely envisaged. Embraced to the north and east by swamp and on the south and west by the muddy waters of the James River, the town was both damp and un-healthy. Nothing but a mosquito could really want to call it home. Consequently most of the colonists had moved away and only went to Jamestown to conduct their business. Some indication of this is pro-vided by a well-known description of 1676 which tells us that the town then consisted of some "16 or 18 houses, most as is the church built of brick, faire and large; and in them about a dozen families (for all the howses are not inhabited) getting their liveings by keeping ordnaries, at extreordinary rates." The tourist industry would seem already to have emerged in Virginia.

Regardless of whether the houses of Jamestown were of brick or wood, they were not immune to the hazards of fire—at least not when they were deliberately put to the torch. In 1676, the planter Nathaniel Bacon led an insurrection against the governorship of Sir William Berkeley (resulting in part from his handling of Indian affairs), and having forced the Governor to flee he proceeded to set fire to James-town. It is noteworthy that the wealthy plantation owner William Drummond was one of Bacon's supporters and that he deliberately fired his own house, a residence that was second in substance to only one other in the town—presumably the Governor's residence or State House. But as a result of this dramatic act, Drummond was not roofless, for he possessed another large house in the mainland—on land which he rented from the Governor. Such a person having two houses would help to account for the previously quoted statement that some of the houses of Jamestown were not occupied. One cannot help thinking that Drummond must have been very sure that he was on the winning side when he burned the Jamestown house and left himself and his family with only the property rented from the same governor that he had just chased out of town. Unhappily, he was in error, Bacon took sick and died, and the rebellion promptly fell apart. Drummond was caught, and hung within half an hour of being brought before the irate Berkeley. The latter duly evicted Drummond's widow and family—which though unkind, was hardly surprising.

A contemporary account of the uprising stated that "The towne consisted of 12 new brick Houses besides a considerable number of Frame houses with brick chimneys, all of which will not be rebuilt (as is computed) for Fifteen hundred pounds of Tobacco." Here, then, we

69

have evidence that regardless of the Town Act of 1662, all Jamestown's houses were not of brick. The same authority listed both church and State House as being among the buildings destroyed. The State House was the third—the second having been a rented property—and was built to the west of the church and overlying the early cemetery discussed at the beginning of this chapter.

Whereas the first State House was part of a three-structure complex, the third was the most northerly of five, all linked together with common walls. This group of buildings was largely excavated in 1903 and a second survey (never a very promising operation) was undertaken in 1954-55. The same foundations served as the site of the fourth State House, built after the rebellion of 1676, and archaeological evidence suggested that the third State House was roofed with tiles and the fourth with slate. Beyond that, little useful information was forthcoming. John Cotter, in his report on the excavations at Jamestown, noted that the foundations of the third State House revealed no traces of chimneys, which he suggests might represent an early attempt at fire prevention in line with the absence of chimneys in the early eighteenth century capitol at Williamsburg. Such measures were certainly admirable though the results were less so. The third State House was burned by Bacon as already described, the fourth burned in 1698, the first Williamsburg Capitol in 1744 and the second in 1832, all of them brick buildings and all, save the last, without chimneys.

The destruction of the fourth State House marked the end of Jamestown as the administrative capital of Virginia; the legislators voted to move inland to Middle Plantation where the College of William and Mary had been erected in 1695. The legend has long been fostered that at the end of the seventeeth century immediately prior to the burning of the State House, Jamestown "was a crowded, cluttered town." It has been inferred that when the legislators moved their meeting place, the inhabitants of the "crowded" town also packed their bags and moved to the new site. Had this been true it would be reasonable to expect that they would have carried their seventeenth century glass, pottery, kitchen utensils, and what-not along with them, and that in the course of time a reasonable percentage of those things would have found their way into the ground of Middle Plantation or Williamsburg as it had been renamed. However, in thirty years of excavation, Williamsburg archaeologists have come up with no more than a handful of fragments of seventeenth century pottery—and most of that dating so close to the end of the century that there is no reason to associate it with Jamestown. On the basis of archaeology's negative evidence, it could be supposed that there was no domestic exodus from Jamestown to Williamsburg. The documentary evidence suggests quite convincingly that in 1676 Jamestown possessed fewer than twenty good houses and a community of some twelve families, most of whom were probably engaged in the tavern trade. Although the town's importance sharply declined when the Assembly moved away, ships continued to lie at anchor in the James and sailors still needed to be entertained and suitably primed for the long voyage back to England.

According to the Reverend Hugh Jones, whose *Present State of Virginia* is a principal source of information on the domestic life of the colony in the first quarter of the eighteenth century, in 1724 Jamestown comprised ". . . nothing but abundance of brick rubbish, and three or four good inhabited houses . . ." This statement does not rest at all comfortably alongside the comments of a Frenchman who traveled through Virginia in 1765 and who "hired a Chair and took a ride to Jameses City formerly the Capital of the Province . . . it consists of about 70 Houses, the Seat of Government was here formerly but was caryed to Williamsburg on Account of the unhealthyness of this Place, some Ships anchor of the Town." If both writers were to be believed, we would be presented with a resurrected Jamestown blossoming in the mid-eighteenth century into a community larger than it had been in its heyday. Such an interpretation is no more palatable than the idea that the town site was completely deserted after the move to Middle Plantation.

Archaeological work at Jamestown has shown that the percentage of artifacts found there of the first quarter of the eighteenth century is just about as great as those of the last quarter of the seventeenth, indicating that there was no immediate decline in the intensity of occupation. Probably more lethal to the life of Jamestown than the departure of the Assembly was the rapid increase in the importance of the port of Yorktown and the slower development of Archer's Hope and later College Landing as the port for Williamsburg, both of which kept shipping down-river from Jamestown. Later still, Burwell's Landing on Kingsmill Plantation yet further down the James River became the customs office and a settlement with jetty, store, and tavern facilities.

In the course of the eighteenth century most of Jamestown Island became the property of two families, Ambler and Travis. The former owned a large brick residence with two flanking outbuildings that stood right in the middle of Jamestown's "New Towne"; its landscaped gardens, extending down to the river, overlaid the buried remains of the first State House complex. The ruined shell of the Ambler House still stands as a memorial to eighteenth century Jamestown, though how long it will continue to do so is anybody's guess, a further section of wall having collapsed even while this chapter was being written. The house was built in the mid-eighteenth century and it appears, along with its two outbuildings, on the map of 1781 made by Colonel Desandrouin of the French army. This map also shows at least nine other buildings on the site of the old town, and in letters bold and clear, the cartographer calls it Jamestown. The island saw a good deal of coming and going during the Revolution, most notably the going of Lord Cornwallis and his British army after the Battle of Green Spring. This had been his last, somewhat valueless victory and the beginning of the hard, ignominious road to Yorktown.

Just as the memory of the adventures of the "Lost Colony" on Roanoke Island had remained alive through the seventeenth and eighteenth centuries, so the memory of the ordeals of Jamestown's motley band of Founding Fathers glowed brightly through the nineteenth century. Their fortitude was praised at the Bicentennial of 1807, their sacrifice was lauded at the Virginiad of 1822 and again at the 250th Anniversary in 1857. At the Tercentenary of 1907 they shared the spotlight with Mark Twain, Buffalo Bill, a German beer garden, a re-enactment of the battle of the *Monitor* and *Merrimac*, and as many other exposition attractions as its organizers could dream up. For five glorious months the suffering, courage, and perseverance of the Jamestown colonists was feted in a bombardment of fireworks and candy, highlighted by the presence of President Theodore Roosevelt, who arrived in Hampton Roads to review the fleet, rather thoughtlessly one might think, aboard the presidential yacht *Mayflower*. Happily the

1907 circus was held outside Norfolk and not on the historic site itself. Had it been on it, there is no doubt that the archaeological remains of Virginia's first capital would have been destroyed. As it was, the destruction was left to nature, whose winds and waters whittled away at the historic shoreline until an extensive riprap protection project was undertaken in 1935, continuing the old protective wall of 1901 which had extended no further east than the church.

With the approach of the 350th Anniversary celebrations, the National Park Service undertook a liberal program of excavation under the direction of Dr. Cotter, lasting from 1954 until 1956. But even when this work was completed, more than half of Jamestown's soil remained unexplored. At the present time, 1963, the Park Service has no immediate plans for further excavations, although work on the huge collection of artifacts goes on, and will do so for many years.

No attempt has been made to reconstruct the houses of Jamestown as has been done at nearby Williamsburg. Instead, most of the old foundations have been reburied and the outlines of the buildings marked out on the surface by modern low brick walls whose uneven height creates an impression of weathered antiquity. About a mile to the west on the mainland stands the 1957 Festival Park and it is there that the fort has been reconstructed, the reproduction ships moored, and various exhibit buildings erected. Unlike the Exposition of 1907, the Festival Park was not abandoned when the year was out. It continues as a permanent museum and memorial to the Jamestown story.

Healthful and Thriving City

THE DECISION to build the fifth State House at Middle Plantation was not nearly so hard to reach as had been agreement on the site for the new college. In 1691 the Burgesses had believed that Gloucester County on the north side of the York River would be the best place. But this proposal was never acted on, and in the two years that followed numerous alternatives were put forward. Then, in October 1693, the Burgesses finally decided on Middle Plantation, thus, unwittingly, preparing the stage for some of the great scenes of American history.

There was nothing very impressive about Middle Plantation beyond the fact that it was situated on a pleasantly high ridge (by Jamestown standards) between the James and York rivers. It had been established in 1632 as part of a project to stretch a defensive palisade across the peninsula between the two rivers, the settlement being a

74

base from which the colonists could police it. Governor Harvey enacted that each man who moved to Middle Plantation and built a house there, should be given fifty acres of land. At that time the colony's physician, the not very worthy Dr. John Pott, already had his home there. George Sandys, Secretary of the colony, wrote of him in 1623 that "he kept Companie too much with his Inferiours who hung upon him while his good Liquor lasted." Regardless of this little weakness the good doctor went on to greater fame, becoming Governor in 1629 and being indicted for stealing cattle in 1630. Nevertheless, in spite of his shortcomings, John Pott has the honor of being the first inhabitant of Middle Plantation and, by extension, the first citizen of Williamsburg.

Very little is known of the appearance of Middle Plantation, always supposing that it had any collective appearance at all. There is no evidence of town planning, but merely a scattering of houses and worked fields extending along the line of the palisade. We do not know how the settlement fared in the Indian uprising of 1644, but the few records of the subsequent years show no slackening of the intensity of occupation. In 1676 Nathaniel Bacon made Middle Plantation a temporary headquarters and there rallied many of the most influential planters to his cause. The seed of rebellion sprouted there as it would again almost exactly a century later. However, the ground was destined always to tremble at the roar of oratory rather than at the clash of arms; Bacon fought neither Indians nor the Governor at Middle Plantation, and neither General Washington nor Lord Cornwallis fought through Williamsburg during the Revolution, although both occupied it at different times. Even the Battle of Williamsburg in the Civil War was fought at a discreet distance from the town.

Bacon's Rebellion left no mark on Middle Plantation—other than the melancholy spectacle of William Drummond, his second in command, swinging gently in the wind from a gallows where he had been hanged (either whole or in part), on the sentence of Governor Berkeley. (See Chapter VII, p. 174.) With Jamestown burned, the Assembly met at Middle Plantation in 1677 and there a royal proclamation was read pardoning all who had taken part in the rebellion, save for the deceased Bacon himself. No doubt the ghosts of Drummond and the other ringleaders who had been so quickly dispatched, were suitably appreciative. The same year, the Governor summoned the chief men of the surviving local Indian tribes, representing ten nations, to meet at Middle Plantation, where they signed a treaty of allegiance to the English crown, thus surrendering their freedom in exchange for the colony's recognition of their rights to specific tribal lands. The distinguished Virginia archaeologist, Dr. Ben C. McCary, has noted that many students consider the Middle Plantation treaty to have marked the end of the Indian as a force in the colony's history.

With the rebuilding of Jamestown, Middle Plantation settled down once more to the quiet life. But it was not to last; the Assembly had noticed that it was possible to sleep through its meetings there without being constantly assaulted by mosquitoes, and that the humidity was lower than on the flat marshy island. Even before Jamestown was rebuilt, proposals had been made to move to Middle Plantation, but the Governor decided otherwise.

A brick church had been erected at Middle Plantation in 1683 and when the site of the college was to be chosen, it was resolved that

21. The restored "Wren Building" of the College of William and Mary at Williamsburg.

it should stand "as near the Church as Convenience will permit." The foundations were laid in 1695 with the intention of completing the building as a large square block surrounding a quadrangle, but only the eastern section was ever finished. In 1724 the Reverend Hugh Jones stated in his *Present State of Virginia* that the college building had been "first modelled by Sir Christopher Wren," and "adapted to the nature of the country by the gentlemen there." No substantiating evidence has ever come to light to support Jones's claim. He, himself, went on to say that the building was not unlike Chelsea Hospital near London—which we know was designed by Wren. Unfortunately, only one picture of the first college building has been found and this was drawn extremely badly by a Swiss traveler, Franz Ludwig Michel, in 1702. It does not look in the least like Chelsea Hospital.

In 1698 when the fourth Jamestown State House went up in smoke, the College was still not completed. But when the Assembly met in Middle Plantation in May 1699, the College already possessed a student body from whose ranks came a number of young orators with speeches urging that the Burgesses move their seat to Middle Plantation. One described the site as being a "good Neighbourhood of as many Housekeepers that could give great Help towards the Supplying and Maintaining of a constant Market, as is to be found again in the whole Country. Here," he added, "are great Helps and Advances made already towards the Beginning of a Town, a Church, and Ordinary, several Stores, two Mills, a Smiths Shop, a Grammar School, and above all the Colledge: . . ."

It is doubtful whether the students' praise of Middle Plantation had any bearing on the decision of either the Assembly or the Governor. Nevertheless, the move was proposed by Governor Francis Nicholson on May 18, approved by the Burgesses, and on June 7 an act was passed directing the building of "the Capitoll and the City of Williamsburgh." Thus ended the seventeenth century and with it the history of Middle Plantation. Although extensive archaeological excavations have been conducted throughout most of the heart of colonial Williamsburg, few traces of Middle Plantation have yet been found. Most informative so far was the discovery of the basement of one early building beneath what is now Nassau Street, its position on a skew to the formal right-angled layout of the eighteenth century

22. Leaded windows found on the floor of a late 17th-century cellar in Williamsburg.

town, clearly associating it with the earlier settlement. The remains of two leaded windows were found on the floor (Fig. 22), the best preserved examples yet unearthed in Virginia; but we do not know when the building was constructed or when destroyed. The only clue to the latter date is a large collection of artifacts, said to have been found in the basement's filling, that ranges from broken wine bottles of about 1700 to crockery of the nineteenth century. Regardless of the later objects, which probably came from the topsoil, it is reasonable to suppose that the house was torn down when Williamsburg was laid out in the early eighteenth century. The *Journals of the House of Burgesses of Virginia* show that buildings that did not fit into the new scheme of things were removed in much the same manner that condemned property is handled today. On April 27, 1704, Governor Nicholson suggested that the Burgesses "give Directions that the old House belonging to Mr. *John Page* standing in the Middle of *Gloucester* Street be pulled downe that the Prospect of the Street between the Capitol and Colledge may be cleer and that you take Care to pay what you shall judge those Houses to be worth." Eight days later the

78

Governor's suggestion was implemented and it was "*Ordered* that Mr. *Henry Cary* forthwith sett the Labourers imployed about the Building of the Capitol to pull down the four old Houses and Oven belonging to Mr. *John Page* which stands in *Gloucester* Street and have been appraised and that they lay the Bricks out of the Street on the Lott of the said *John Page*."

It seems that Governor Francis Nicholson fancied himself as a town planner, having a gentleman's eye for design and a taste for "significance." As Governor of Maryland before coming to Virginia, Nicholson had been instrumental in the baroque plan of the new city of Annapolis. In Williamsburg he had another opportunity to exhibit his talents and there, according to Hugh Jones, ". . . he laid out the city of Williamsburgh (in the form of a cypher, made of W. and M.) on a ridge at the head springs of two great creeks . . ." The cipher, of course, was that of William III, for whom the city was named, and Mary, his queen. Happily for posterity, this design was more significant than practical, and it was never completed. Instead, a simple gridiron plan was adopted, dividing the ground into square or rectangular blocks, the *insulae* of classical Roman planning. It was the simplest and tidiest form, and one that had been successfully adopted at such places as Kingston and Port Royal in Jamaica, and at Charleston and Philadelphia. A classical trend is also to be found in the use of the word Capitol instead of State House, as the meeting place for the Assembly had always been termed in the days of Jamestown.

Governor Nicholson loved nothing and nobody better than Francis Nicholson and he was doubtless vastly pleased to see two of the three principal east-west streets named Francis and Nicholson respectively. The third was named after the heir presumptive to the English throne, the Duke of Gloucester. At one end of it stood the College of William and Mary and at the other the Capitol. The latter was designed as an H with a third shorter member turning the horizontal bar into a cross. This is how the building's plan appeared on Theodorick Bland's town platt of 1699, a map, incidentally, that shows only the main street, Duke of Gloucester Street, and three buildings, the College, church, and Capitol; although, when Bland made his map, the Capitol was still little more than a good idea. By the time that the foundations began to be laid on August 8, 1701, a number of changes

79

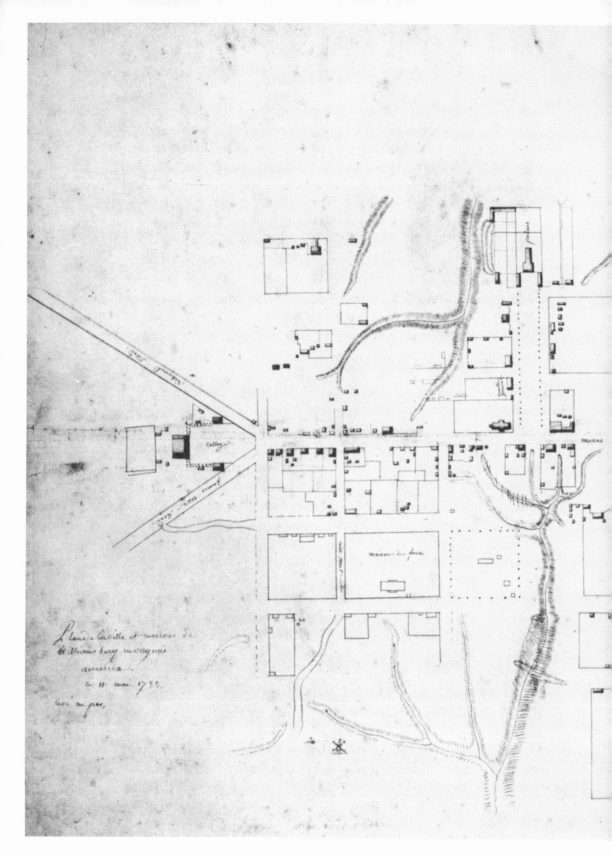

23. A French army cartographer's map of Williamsburg, probably made in 1782. This map, owned by the College of William and Mary, was one of the principal guides for the restoration of the city.

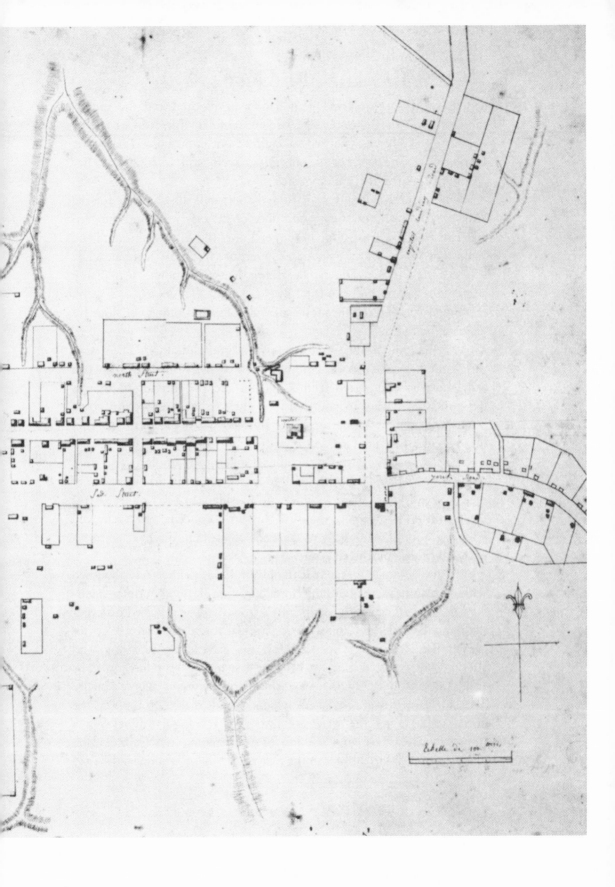

had occurred; a regular H plan had been adopted and the top or southern ends of the letter had become apsidal. But even as late as August 21, as Marcus Whiffen has pointed out in his book *The Public Buildings of Williamsburg*, committees were still looking at other possible plans for the building.

The Capitol as finally constructed contained the chamber for the House of Burgesses on the ground floor of the east wing and the general court on the west. On the upper floor, the east wing contained committee rooms and the west the Governor's Council Chamber, while between the wings, over a piazza linking the two members, was a large conference room. To keep the Lords from the Commons, as it were, each wing was entered through separate doors and the upper floor by separate staircases.

The building of the Capitol was no mean undertaking. The design was without parallel in the colony, much of the stone and ironwork was laboriously imported from England, and the interior finish was sufficiently elaborate to add considerably to the construction costs. Indeed, not only was the finish not finished when the Burgesses met there for the first time in May 1705, but by the time the last touches had been applied, its autocratic genius, Governor Nicholson, had been recalled to England—thanks, in large measure, to the machinations of the Reverend James Blair, founder and President of the College. After the Governor's departure many of his little conceits were removed from the Capitol, among them the arms of his family which were replaced by those of Queen Anne.

Regardless of the fact that the Capitol was deliberately designed without chimneys, the building burned in 1747, leaving nothing standing but "the naked Brick Walls." In 1749 an Act was passed ordering the rebuilding of the Capitol on its original foundations at a cost not greater than £3,000. The act refers to "rebuilding, repairing, and altering," the most distinctive of these last being the removal of the apsidal ends from the southern extremities of the wings. These visually pleasing features were replaced by square ends matching those at the north and turning the structure into two rectangular blocks in a straightforward H plan. The job of resurrecting the Capitol took longer than it did to build it in the first place, and it was not until 1756 that it was finally completed.

It was this, the second Capitol, that witnessed the tempestuous events that preceded the Revolution: Patrick Henry's famous speech against the Stamp Act in 1765, the adoption of the Virginia Resolution for American Independence in May 1776, and the adoption of George Mason's Declaration of Rights in the following month. Outside in the courtyard, drums rolled and banners waved as the men of Virginia mustered to embark on a rebellion that would stamp them traitors or heroes, depending on the outcome. But when victory came, the Capitol's fortunes had faded along with those of the British. The seat of government had been moved to Richmond in 1780, and the building's glory had departed. It continued to stand in a state of increasing dilapidation until, in 1832, it followed in the tradition of all the preceding state houses and was destroyed by fire. Much later the site was acquired by the Association for the Preservation of Virginia Antiquities, which set up a commemorative marker and exposed the top of the foundations to enable visitors to see the plan of the old building. Subsequently, the A.P.V.A. deeded the site to Colonial Williamsburg, Incorporated, so that the Capitol could be reconstructed (Fig. 24).

The history of practically every building in Williamsburg ends with the words—and was restored (or reconstructed) by Colonial Williamsburg. I suppose, therefore, that this is as good a time as any to leap from the eighteenth century into the twentieth long enough to summarize events there in the last forty years.

The Williamsburg that thousands upon thousands of visitors see each year, is the realization of one man's dream. Without his vision, Williamsburg would today be just another down-at-heel small Virginia town, brightened here and there by disarticulated neon lights over the doors of diners and the tawdry streamers and whirligigs that rustle over brightly painted gas pumps—those phallic emblems of our machine age. As early as 1924, Dr. W. A. R. Goodwin, who was then on the faculty of the college, bemoaned the fact that new concrete roads linking Richmond and Newport News were "fast spoiling the whole appearance of the old streets and the old city." One of the most attractive of the surviving eighteenth century buildings, the Archibald Blair Storehouse on Duke of Gloucester Street, was in use as a garage and its handsome colonial brick walls were hidden behind advertisements announcing "Vulcanizing," "Sinclair Oils," and "Water, Air,

83

24. An aerial view of Williamsburg's reconstructed Capitol from the south, with the 18th-century brick records office to the left, the Coke-Garrett House to the right, and the public gaol to the rear.

25. Duke of Gloucester Street as it appeared at the end of the 19th century. View to the west toward the brick Paradise House and Bruton Parish Church.

Quick Tire Changing Service." In all, some eighty-three colonial buildings were still standing in 1924, but many of them were so patched and hidden behind later additions that only a bird dog could flush them out.

Among the more obvious of the surviving eighteenth century structures were Bruton Parish Church, parts of the College, the Wythe House, Paradise House, Court House, Magazine, and Blair House, the last of which was saved by Dr. Goodwin in the nick of time when he learned that it was to be torn down to provide the site for a garage. For two years between 1924 and 1926, Dr. Goodwin spent every available moment trying to interest philanthropists in restoring the historic city. "It would," he wrote, "be the most unique and spectacular gift to American history and to the preservation of American traditions that could be made by any American." But the philanthropists did not see it—even if they saw his letters, which in some cases seems doubtful. The cold replies would have chilled the hearts of lesser men, while snide editorial comments in the newspapers might well have caused him to abandon the project in the heat of righteous anger. When the *Baltimore Sun* discovered that attempts were being made to obtain financial interest in restoring the city, its editorial writer peered into a cracked crystal ball and saw "the spectacle of the Old Dominion huckstering off her ancient capital to an outsider, in order to get a flivver imitation of departed glory," a sight "to bring a flush of shame to the pale cheeks of her mighty shades." But Dr. Goodwin had quite a different vision, and he was not to be deterred. In 1926, the late Mr. John D. Rockefeller, Jr., visited Williamsburg and met Dr. Goodwin there for the first time, thus beginning an association with the city that was to last until he died, one that he, himself, claimed to be among the most rewarding of his life.

In November 1926, Mr. Rockefeller agreed to finance a preliminary survey of the town—providing that his name was not linked with it. About a week later he purchased the Paradise House on Duke of Gloucester Street and so made the first decisive step toward the restoration of the city. During the next twelve months further properties were purchased in different parts of the town, although Mr. Rockefeller's part in the transactions remained carefully concealed. It was not until June 1928 that Dr. Goodwin revealed at a town meeting

85

that John D. Rockefeller, Jr., was behind the recent purchases and that the city was about to enjoy a somewhat surprising metamorphosis.

"Buildings in that part of the city which is to be restored," explained Dr. Goodwin, "and which do not harmonize with the plan of the colonial restoration will probably be taken away or rebuilt. Some of the notable old buildings destroyed by fire will be rebuilt according to details and descriptions gathered from many sources. These will include the Palace where the Royal Governors lived, the House of Burgesses in which the assembly met and the Raleigh Tavern, where the Phi Beta Kappa was formed."

The ball had already rolled well beyond these stated specifics and Mr. Rockefeller had agreed to finance the whole operation, even if the cost ran to four or five million dollars. Neither he nor anyone else could have realized that more than thirty years later the work of restoration would still be going on and that the cost would have soared to more than seventy million dollars.

It would be foolish to pretend that every Williamsburg householder looked upon the face-lifting project as the best thing that ever happened to him. There were some who liked the town the way it was and just wanted to be left alone to enjoy it—even though it was gently falling apart. Others began to see dollar signs blossoming on every crape myrtle, while those with a less mercenary outlook realized that Dr. Goodwin's faith in his dream had wrought a near miracle. The Association for the Preservation of Virginia Antiquities showed its support for the enterprise by deeding the site of the Capitol to the newly formed Colonial Williamsburg, Incorporated, on the understanding that the building would be reconstructed and completed within five years. Thus the State House that had been the first public building to be constructed in the original Williamsburg was to be the first to be archaeologically studied for reconstruction in the restored city.

The excavation of the Capitol's foundations revealed the entire outline of the western member of the H and only part of the eastern section, and, as was to be expected, the plan was that of the second Capitol and not of the first. But when the mid-eighteenth century builders remodeled the structure, they helpfully left behind traces of the apsidal end of the court room in the western section. As it was decided that the first Capitol and not the second should be recon-

26. Part of Duke of Gloucester Street as it appears
after restoration. View toward the apothecary shop
and Raleigh Tavern.

structed, this information was of paramount importance. Armed with
the archaeological data and with a wealth of contemporary documentary information, Mr. Rockefeller's architects, the able and respected Boston firm of Perry, Shaw and Hepburn, were able to rebuild
and appropriately furnish the massive structure in time to open it to
the public in 1934, just five years after they began. It was not, how-

87

ever, the first reconstruction to be completed; that distinction fell to
the historic Raleigh Tavern which was completed in 1932.

To pursue the story of the restoration of Williamsburg through
the following thirty years would carry us far from the theme of this
book. It must be enough to say that in 1963 a total of eighty-three
original buildings have been restored and more than four hundred
structures have been reconstructed from the ground up, the latter running the eighteenth century gamut from Palace to privy. Much more
pertinent is the history of the town's original conception and its progress through the eighteenth century, for not until the scene is set can
we watch the performances of the individual actors.

Just as the seasons of activity at Jamestown were governed by the
presence or absence of the Assembly, so the new town of Williamsburg was at first conceived as a center for housing and entertainment
when the Burgesses were gathered for their legislative sessions. When
these were completed, the gentry returned to their plantations and
the town went back to sleep. To that extent Williamsburg in its first
years was quite unlike any English country town where the residents
resided all the year round.

The Act of 1699 directing the building of the Capitol and the city
of Williamsburg carefully detailed the requirements for a state house,
but said very little about the planning of the town beyond naming it
and its main street. The land was to be laid out in half-acre lots, and
to hold these purchasers would have to build within two years ". . . one
good Dweling House containing twenty Foot in Width and thirty
Foot in Length . . . of tenn Foot Pitch and within six Foot of the
Street . . ." It is significant that no mention is made of the use of brick
so carefully specified for all Jamestown houses in the Town Act of
1662. Indeed, it would seem that in 1699, the Assembly was more concerned with building itself a home than with planning a town.

In October 1705, an amendment to, or rather a "continueing" of,
the Act of 1699, was somewhat more specific in its requirements for
acceptable houses on Duke of Gloucester Street. It stated that the
building of one house within the stipulated two years would be sufficient to hold two lots. That house was required to measure either fifty
feet by twenty or to be a "Brick or framed House with two Stacks
of Brick Chimney's & Cellars under ye whole House bricked forty

Foot long & twenty Foot broad." Unfortunately the extensive archaeological excavations in the town have unearthed very few traces of these buildings or their inhabitants, and it would seem that it was not until the second decade of the eighteenth century that Williamsburg really began to take shape. This negative archaeological evidence is somewhat supported by the *Journals of the House of Burgesses*, which record that in 1712 a certain Christopher Jackson was paid for "laying out the City of *Williamsburgh* and the Roads to the Ports belonging to the Said City." Nevertheless, when the Reverend Hugh Jones described it in 1724, he noted the existence of "rich stores, of all sorts of goods, and well furnished with the best provisions and liquors." He noted, too, that several good families lived there and that more did so "in their own houses at publick times"—shades of Jamestown. Describing the houses, he wrote that "Here, as in other parts, they build with brick, but most commonly with timber lined with cieling, and cased with feather-edged plank, painted with white lead and oil, covered with shingles of cedar, etc. tarred over at first; with a passage generally through the middle of the house for an air-draught in summer. Thus their houses are lasting, dry, and warm in winter, and cool in summer; especially if there be windows enough to draw the air. Thus they dwell comfortably, genteely, pleasantly, and plentifully in this delightful, healthful, and (I hope) thriving city of Williamsburgh."

In 1759, another reverend gentleman, Andrew Burnaby, vicar of Greenwich, was prompted to temper his enthusiasm with a modicum of reserve. He noted that the town "consists of about two hundred houses, does not contain more than one thousand souls, whites and negroes; and is far from being a place of any consequence . . . and although the houses are of wood, covered with shingles, and but indifferently built, the whole makes a handsome appearance."

In 1701 an Act had been passed to erect a public gaol, a feature that had previously been incorporated into the State House and that had been left out of the new Capitol. Five years later another Act was passed authorizing the building of a mansion for the Governor; in 1714 yet another ordered the construction of a magazine for the storage of the public arms. The spiritual needs of the city were catered for by the construction of a new brick church in 1711, while more temporal yearnings were satisfied by the appearance of a veritable toast of tav-

89

erns as well as the construction of the first playhouse in America, which opened its doors in 1716—and closed them again in 1727 when its proprietor hastily left town.

The city's attributes, so favorably described by Hugh Jones, still left it a far cry from the larger county towns of England. A visitor seeing Williamsburg through a somewhat jaundiced eye in 1736 found it "a most wretched contriv'd Affair for the Capital of a Country, being near three Miles from the Sea, is a bad Situation. There is Nothing considerable in it, but the College, the Governor's House, and one or two more, which are no bad Piles; and the prodigious Number of Coaches that croud the deep, sandy Streets of this little City. It's very surprising to me, that this should be preferr'd to *James-Town, Hampton*, or some other Situations I could mention."

It is unfortunate that most visitors who wrote descriptions of eighteenth century Williamsburg visited it at Public Times when the general court was in session and when the town's population had almost doubled. The man who, in 1765, cried, "I have been here three Days and am heartily sick of it," would doubtless have been equally unhappy on a market or fair day in any English town. Throughout most of the year the population of Williamsburg was no more than one to two thousand, but at Public Times it increased to five and even six thousand. In a town of, at best, three hundred houses, such a population explosion must have left vivid scars on the memories of visitors who were not conditioned to such congestion.

The total colonial population of Virginia increased steeply as the eighteenth century progressed. In 1670 the figure had been in the region of forty thousand including two thousand Negro slaves and six thousand white servants, the last category including an uncertain number of convicted felons. By 1715 the estimated figure had risen to seventy-two thousand white settlers and twenty-three thousand slaves, jumping to three hundred thousand Europeans and two hundred thousand slaves in 1774, representing a gigantic change in the white to black ratio in the course of a century.

Because Virginia's fortunes rested on her tobacco crops, there were no industries to make her towns grow and by the end of the eighteenth century Williamsburg was not much larger than it had been in 1730 or 1740. The town created no life of its own; like a theater's empty stage it waited for the players and the audience. While they stayed, it pulsated and glowed; but once the show was over, the music died, the lights went out, and the stage slept again—until the next time. But after the Assembly moved to Richmond in 1780, there were to be no more next times. No crowds of visitors flooded into town to fill the inns and ordinaries. The great plantation owners had decimated their fortunes in the Revolution and were hard put to keep their roofs in repair; there was little left over for spending at the miliner's, perukier's, goldsmith's, or cabinetmaker's shops of Williamsburg. By 1793 the town had a population of about fourteen hundred and two hundred houses "going fast to Decay." In that year Jedidiah Morse wrote in *The American Universal Geography* that "Every Thing in *Williamsburgh* appears dull, forsaken and melancholy—no Trade—no Amusements, but the infamous one of Gaming—no Industry, and very little Appearance of Religion." Three years later another visitor, Isaac Weld, passed through and subsequently described what he saw in his *Travels Through the States of North America*. The Capitol, he wrote, was "a capacious Building of Brick, now crumbling to pieces from Negligence. The Houses around it are mostly uninhabited, and present a melancholy Picture. . . . The Town contains about 1200 Inhabitants & the Society in it is thought to be more extensive and more genteel at the same Time than what is to be met with in any other Place of its Size in *America*. No Manufactories are carried on here, and scarcely any Trade."

Genteel decay was the watchword in Williamsburg through the nineteenth century. Once in a while a spark would fire the inhabitants from their lethargy as it did for two days in 1824 when General Lafayette returned to the scenes of his triumph. Other sparks set fire not to memories, but to the town's historic buildings. The Governors' Palace had gone in 1781, the Capitol followed it in 1832, then the main block of the College early in 1859, and the Raleigh Tavern at the end of the same year.

The Civil War began two years later, leaving its own corrosive stamp on the minds and property of Williamsburg's citizens. May 5, 1862, saw Generals Longstreet and Johnston quartered in a house near the site of the Capitol, but by the next morning, following the battle of Williamsburg, they had gone and their place had been taken by the Union commander, General McClellan. Throughout the rest of the war the town remained a Union base—except for one day in September 1862, when a Confederate force swept in and carried off the Union Provost Marshal. Probably in retaliation, Northern troops set fire to the rebuilt College, then the largest structure in the town. As the war progressed many other buildings suffered at the hands of Union soldiers, notably the brick advance buildings that had once flanked the approach to the Governor's Palace. These were pulled down to provide bricks to be made into chimneys for officers' huts at Fort Magruder, which lay a few miles outside the town.

The peace that followed the surrender at Appomattox was of the most bitter kind, bringing with it the scourge of Reconstruction. To the impoverished gentry of Williamsburg, the loss of their slaves marked the end of a way of life, and what was worse, they had few prospects of carving themselves a new one that offered any promise. Without the slaves to mow the lawns and trim the boxwood, the grass and weeds crowded up to conceal crumbling foundations and sagging sills, while fast-growing locust trees did their best to hide broken shutters and fallen shingles. In the eyes of some visitors, parts of the town slipped from being quaintly dilapidated and "olde worlde" into something approaching a rural slum. It was not until the years of the First World War brought a munitions factory into the neighbourhood that the city enjoyed a return to a measure of prosperity.

Opinions as to the true appearance of Williamsburg at the turn of the century are widely varied and often influenced by whether one's informant was raised in the town or came there later in life from some barbarous metropolis in the north. The former, perhaps with memory softly focused, recalls the Williamsburg of 1900 as a place of quiet and gentle charm, retaining much of its eighteenth century form. Its unquestionably hideous appearance in the 1920's is generally blamed on the advent of industry during the war. Although that industry did not last, the injection of fifteen thousand new inhabitants into the area brought a steep rise in property values, while improved road and railroad communications placed the city firmly on the map once more. The only drawback was that the hand of progress showed every inclination to put the past in its place—to bury it in the ground where it could not stand in the way of the future. But as we have seen (thanks to the vision of Dr. Goodwin) Williamsburg's future was to be quite different from that envisaged by the gas station proprietors and real estate dealers.

In a book that purports to be concerned with the archaeology as well as the history of colonial Virginia, the former is, I admit, conspicuously absent from this chapter. But archaeology deals with specifics; it finds the relics of single events, unearths the possessions of individuals, and fills in the details of history. To make use of archaeology's contributions we must first read the words of history and then allow the trowel and spade to add their punctuation.

They Dreamt
They Dug
in Marble Halls

IN THE WILLIAMSBURG of the 1920's, when Dr. Goodwin was dreaming of a day in which the colonial city would rise out of its own ashes, there were few citizens who knew anything about archaeology and a great many who probably could not pronounce the word if they saw it on paper. Nevertheless, in 1922 digging up the past suddenly leaped into the public eye when Lord Carnarvon and Howard Carter discovered one of the greatest archaeological treasures of all time—the tomb of Tut-Ankh-Amen. Jokes about Egyptology and mummies (some of them clean and a good many not), popular songs, and even a dance named after the Pharaoh, all contributed to the popularization of archaeology. Indeed, even today, as far as the public is concerned, a little of Tut-Ankh-Amen's glamour has rubbed off onto every archaeologist. Williamsburg was no hold-out against the craze of the moment, and when the first excavations began on the site of the Capitol, archaeology was already established in the shape of a sign on the rusted iron doors of a local garage reading "Toot-an-Kum-in."

On the strength of so obvious an omen it would have been little short of foolhardy not to have obtained the services of an Egyptologist to initiate Williamsburg's archaeological excavations. Sure enough, he was there; so, too, at different times were archaeological directors who had been previously trained as historians, architects, draftsmen, engineers, and building foremen. Not one, however, was trained in the very specialized discipline of historic archaeology, nor could he be, for no such animal then existed.

The techniques of archaeology, which all stem from an understanding of the principle of stratigraphy, are applicable to any site. It makes no difference whether we are excavating the remains of a Roman villa or a nineteenth century brewhouse, we are faced with the same practical problems of digging, recording, and preserving and we solve them in much the same ways. But there the similarity ends. The man who can identify and date a Roman amphora within fifty years would be somewhat out of his depth when called upon to pronounce on a yeast sieve made in Baltimore in 1854. Failure to identify the yeast sieve as such, might very well result in the loss of vital evidence. The same problem immediately presented itself in Williamsburg. The architects, who were primarily interested in uncovering old foundations and fragments of buildings, suddenly found themselves confronted with quantities of broken wine bottles, ceramics, tobacco pipes, buttons, shoe buckles, gun parts, kitchen hardware, and so forth, none of it having anything to do with the structures of the buildings, but having a great deal to do with the lives of their colonial owners.

Although immediate efforts were made to find people who knew something about these excavated artifacts, the sad truth dawned all too quickly; they just were not to be found. There were collectors and museum curators who specialized in the study of the fine and decorative arts of the eighteenth century. But a broken chamber pot hardly came under these categories, nor, indeed, did the majority of the objects that were being recovered. Quite apart from the quality of the items, the ability to recognize them on the basis of a single small fragment is an attribute that the majority of present-day curators do not need and so have not developed. Yet this ability is essential for any

95

archaeologist. Just as the classical excavator must be able to identify and date a south Italian vase of the fourth century B.C. when he sees an inch-square fragment of it, so the archaeologist working on an eighteenth century American site must be able to do the same for a piece of an English delftware punchbowl.

The basic difference between the study of objects of the classical age and those of colonial America is that there are so many more varieties of the latter. In a single day in Williamsburg we have recovered literally hundreds of eighteenth century objects ranging from jew's-harps, wig curlers, and sleeve links to corkscrews, upholstery tacks, and part of an iron corset. All these things called for speedy identification, for their age and the way they were lying in the ground had a bearing on the manner in which the excavation would be continued. If, for example, a fragment of nineteenth century pottery was found at the bottom of a house foundation, it would be imperative that the excavator determine there and then whether it got there before, during, or after the building's construction. On the evidence of that one fragment of pottery might hang the dating of the structure. If the excavator did not realize that the potsherd was of nineteenth century date until he showed it to a specialist months later, he would be unable to go back and determine exactly how the sherd came to be where it was, because the ground in which it lay would have been dug out in the course of the continuing excavation. In such a case a nineteenth century building might be mistaken for one of an earlier date.

With no archaeologists skilled in the excavation of colonial sites and few museum curators knowing much about the very mundane objects that were being found, the directors of the Williamsburg project were forced to create their own experts through the dangerous school of trial and error. Archaeology is essentially destructive; once the ground has been disturbed we can never put it back exactly as it was. Consequently, if we cannot do justice to the past when we dig, we are no better than the treasure hunters who tear up historic sites in search of loot, nor any less destructive than the builder who scours the land with a bulldozer. It is inevitable, therefore, that when archaeologists learn their craft by digging, lost fragments of history are the price of their tuition. Under the circumstances it was hardly surprising that in the early days of excavation in Williamsburg valuable information was lost. Much more astonishing was the remarkable amount of data that was retrieved, largely as a result of the architects' care and the excavators' common sense.

In the course of thirty years of excavation and study, Colonial Williamsburg has built up a collection of excavated eighteenth century artifacts that is unrivaled anywhere in the world. With this teaching material at hand and with so much experience behind it, Williamsburg is the ideal training ground for archaeologists specializing in the colonial period. Thus, out of its own necessity, Colonial Williamsburg has been able to ensure that it will never again be forced to undertake excavations without a fully trained staff to supervise them. It is unfortunate that the National Park Service, which undertakes more archaeological work on colonial sites than any other organization, still has not learned this basic lesson. Even today, fine archaeologists trained to excavate and study the cultures of the Southwestern Indians are sent to work on colonial sites in Virginia in the bumbling bureaucratic belief that a government archaeologist is the right archaeologist no matter where you put him to work. Through no fault of his own, an archaeologist trained in prehistory and suddenly transplanted to a colonial site today is little better than an Egyptologist was in Williamsburg thirty years ago.

The presence of a director trained in the history and objects of the period of the site to be excavated certainly strengthens the hand, but it is still far from a royal flush—unless of course, he is going to dig the entire site by himself. The problem of obtaining the necessary labor was immediately realized when the first sod was to be turned in Williamsburg. There was no alternative other than to make use of ordinary builders' laborers who knew how to wield a shovel but very little else. All that was required of them was to dig parallel trenches across the sites and to stop when they hit a foundation. They were further instructed to put any artifacts that turned up in their digging into wooden boxes provided for that purpose. Nine out of ten such laborers were no more interested in archaeology than they were in digging ditches. But every now and then one of them would discover that trying to identify the objects that they found and figuring out how they came to be where they were, made the digging less boring.

97

From such small beginnings archaeological excavators were born.

In Europe the problem of obtaining labor for archaeological work is not as acute, for there are eager volunteers waiting behind every bush, amateur excavators who can think of no more delectable way of spending their weekends and even entire vacations than being allowed to push a wheelbarrow. They come from all imaginable walks of life, yet work well and easily together, bound only by their interest in the past. In my own team working on London excavations were a radio commentator, a meat packer, a couple of civil servants, university students, a printer's apprentice, an artist, a timber merchant, and a Peer of the Realm. A more improbable crew would have been hard to imagine. Unfortunately this sort of enthusiasm has not yet been generated in Virginia; most applicants either want to be paid for their services or expect to be allowed to keep the artifacts that they find.

Just as the public must be conditioned and stimulated into buying Daisy Soap or believing that margarine is better than butter, so it has to be deliberately and continuously exposed to the fascination of America's colonial past. Many archaeologists still look upon the seventeenth and eighteenth centuries as too recent to be worthy of their notice and it is still a great deal easier to round up both amateur and professional excavators to dig a prehistoric Indian site than it is to find someone who wants to work on the site of an eighteenth century plantation. However, in recent years the public has shown an increasing interest in its past; so much so that in advertising, the claim that a product is "new and revolutionary" is no greater money spinner than the contention that it is "traditional and pre-Revolutionary." Every day of our lives we are asked to buy glass, china, furniture, even lipstick colors that carry us back to the wonderful days of the eighteenth century. Who can fail to have been enthralled by television commercials that show a crinolined cook offering the results of some delicious "mix" to a small boy in a tricorn hat? Regardless of the fact that we refrain from buying the "mix" on the grounds that nice boys take their hats off when they come in the house, the costume is now so familiar that it no longer provokes a twentieth century snigger. Instead we can expect a sigh of nostalgia for what we are pleased to suppose was an easier and more elegant life.

At first glance these may seem facetious considerations; yet if you ponder them for a while, you will be surprised to find how constantly the past is drawn to your attention in advertising modern products. In step with the times, newspapers have come to realize that quite sober accounts of colonial site excavations will appeal to a worthwhile percentage of their readers. This was not always so.

In the early days of Williamsburg's restoration the press looked upon the venture with the eye of Samuel Johnson, being amazed not so much at the way it was done, but rather that it was done at all. As the novelty wore off, the work of excavation and restoration continued to progress quietly and methodically with only occasional flashes of publicity-provoking drama. The resurrection of the Governors' Palace was one of the exceptions. Its dramatic history, the story of the research that made the reconstruction feasible, the excavations that gave the documents a third dimension, and ultimately the dramatic unveiling of the reconstructed Palace as modern buildings were pulled down from in front of it, all combined to excite the imagination as has no other Williamsburg project.

The idea that the Palace should be reconstructed was in Dr. Goodwin's mind as early as 1927 and possibly before. Consequently, the gathering together of all known documentary sources concerning it was one of the first tasks given to the architects for the restoration. The resulting report ran to more than three hundred pages, beginning in 1691 with the Assembly at Jamestown contemplating the building of a suitable house for the Governor, and ending with the Federal Army's 3rd Pennsylvania Cavalry using one of the Palace's advance buildings as its hospital in 1862. Between these terminals was crammed a mass of information on matters ranging from the cost of mending plaster in the billiard room in 1720 to the number of flat irons in the laundry in 1770, all of which was carefully studied and used as a guide to the proposed reconstruction and its furnishings.

Although the need for a new Governor's mansion had been realized before the Assembly moved to Williamsburg in 1699, it was not considered to be a priority requirement for the new city. In the first few years of the town's existence the matter was repeatedly raised and just as quickly set aside when someone asked where the money was to be found. With one hand on its pursestrings and the other tugging at its forelock, the Assembly humbly informed Governor Nicholson that "the Country at this time is not in a Condition to undergoe the Charge of building a House for the Govern^r." After Nicholson's recall, the new Governor Edward Nott brought with him a Royal command that the Burgesses should get on with "Building a House fit for the Reception of your Governor." Thus prodded, the Assembly passed an Act of April 1706, appropriating three thousand pounds for the job, to be defrayed by a duty of fourpence a gallon on rum and wine, a penny a gallon on beer and cider, and a pound a head on imported Negro slaves. In the preceding October the Burgesses had enacted that the house should be built of brick "fifty-four foot in length, and forty-eight foot in breadth, from inside to inside, two story high, with convenient cellars underneath, and one vault, sash windows, of sash, glass and a covering of stone slate, and that in all other respects the said house be built and finished according to the discretion of the overseer." The latter was Henry Cary, the man who had just completed the Capitol, and not unnaturally he was authorized to use bricks left over from the first job for the new Governor's mansion. Late in 1708 we find Cary petitioning the Assembly for more money and confessing that the building was not nearly finished. The following year found Cary still in trouble. Having followed the Assembly's instruction to cover the roof with slates, he had duly imported the necessary quantity from England only to find that a third of them arrived broken, and having got them he could find no workmen who knew how to lay them. The Burgesses sighed, wished Cary would stop bothering them, and instructed him to use wooden shingles instead.

With the arrival of Governor Spotswood in 1710, the building project acquired a new impetus. William Keith, in his *History of the British Plantations in America* (1738), noted that the new Governor was "so good a mathematician, that his skill in architecture, and in the laying out of Ground to the best advantage, is yet to be seen in Virginia, by the Building of an elegant safe Magazine, in the Centre of Williamsburgh, and in the considerable Improvements which he made to the Governor's House and Gardens." The improvements first entailed firing the unhappy Mr. Cary and instructing the Assembly to raise more money. This they reluctantly did, and continued to do as the years rolled by and the house still remained unfinished. In 1718 the Burgesses recorded a formal complaint against Spotswood's "construction of the law for finishing of the Governor's House, whereby he lavishes away the country's money contrary to the intent of the law." The net result was that Spotswood said he would have no more to do with the project and the Assembly thereupon enacted that Henry Cary's son should be given the task of completing the job.

A possible indication of the citizens' opinion of the opulent structure rising in their midst is to be found in the *Legislative Journals of the Council of Colonial Virginia*, wherein we read the entry for December 18, 1714, stating that "The Committee appointed Yesterday to wait on the Governor Reported that they had Accordingly waited on his Hon^r at the Palace." This is the first reference to the building as a "Palace" and it is possible that it was a slip of the pen, as the building continued for years afterward to be known officially as the Governor's House. Some writers have interpreted this passing reference as evidence of a derogatory popular sobriquet that may have been circulating in the colony at that time. Indeed, it may be. On the other hand, we do know that the word "palace" was sometimes used in the eighteenth century, with no snide implications, to describe a large and imposing residence. But no matter how it started, the name stuck and was widely used, without any derisive connotation, throughout the life of the mansion.

The building, furnishing, and landscaping was finally concluded in about 1720, and four years later Hugh Jones informed his readers that "From the Church runs a street northward called Palace Street; at the other end of which stands the Palace or Governor's House, a magnificent structure, built at the publick expense, finished and beautified with gates, fine gardens, offices, walks, a fine canal, orchards, etc. with a great number of the best arms nicely posited by the ingenious contrivance of the most accomplished Colonel Spotswood. This likewise has the ornamental addition of a good cupola or lanthorn, illuminating with most of the town, upon birth-nights, and other nights of occasional rejoicings."

It is hard to imagine that Governor Gooch could have been referring to the same building when he wrote twenty-three years later that it was "so old and decayed it would require an annual repair of at least £100." Nevertheless, such was the case and the Governor's Council noted "the ruinous condition of the Governor's House" and ordered that its own estimate of the cost of repairs be made. Although the conjectured cost of more than twelve hundred pounds must have given the Council a momentary seizure, the repairs were approved and work eventually began. The records of the costs show that very little was spent in 1750 and 1751; but in 1752 the bill came to more than eight hundred pounds, and in 1754 another massive sum of more than nine hundred pounds was spent. The latter sum sent the price of the repairs over the two thousand pound mark and well out of range of the original estimate. It is believed that by this time the work had gone beyond "repairs" to include new construction in the shape of a handsome ballroom and supper room that extended some seventy-five feet beyond the north face of the building as originally constructed.

Fortunately our knowledge of the structure of the Palace is augmented by considerable documentary data concerning its contents, much of it being derived from the household inventories of two of the colony's Governors, Fauquier and Botetourt, both of whom died in office, the former in 1768 and the latter in 1770. In addition there is a further inventory of the Palace's contents made during the Revolutionary war in 1779, one that doubtless includes many items that had been left behind by the last British Governor, Lord Dunmore, when he fled from the building in 1775. We may note, for example, that when Lord Botetourt died there were in the hall "Arms and Colours. 2 looking Glasses—6 fine leather Buckets, 1 step Ladder—1 step Ladder," (sic) these last presumably being pieces of fire-fighting equipment. In the inventory of 1779 there is no reference to the step ladders, but we do find listed "6 leather water buckets," probably the same ones that had hung in the hall in Lord Botetourt's day. We do not know whether they were still there in December 1781, but if they were their presence was of little avail; for the building, which was then serving as an American military hospital for the sick and wounded from Yorktown, caught fire and was totally destroyed.

Just how the fire began will never be known, although a wide range of possible explanations was put forward. George Washington was informed that the disaster was an "accident . . . laid into the lower rooms, where no sick were, by negroes or disaffected persons . . ."

The *Royal Gazette* for December 29, 1781, published in Charleston during the British occupancy, reported that "Last Saturday night about eleven o'clock the palace in the City of Williamsburg, which is supposed to have been set on fire by some malicious person, was in three hours burnt to the ground." In July of the same year the French General de Lauberdière stated that "This fine building, as well as one of the pavilions of the University was burned down in the course of the Winter owing to the negligence of a few American soldiers who had been transported thither wounded or sick, after the siege of York."

Just to ensure that the blame should be lodged in almost every conceivable direction, we have the statement of Johann David Schoepf, in his *Travels in the Confederation 1783-1784,* that "The palace of the one-time Governors also on the north side of the principal street, lies in ruins; this was a large and handsome building— but through the negligence of the American troops quartered there after the siege of York was set afire, although there are those who say it was done by the Loyalists." So, loyalists or disaffected persons, American soldiers, Negroes—we can pick our arsonists; yet considering the fact that the building housed wounded persons at the time of the fire, it would be just as reasonable to pin the blame on a spitting log or a candle flame in a gust of wind.

Regardless of how the fire started, the fact remains that the Palace was gutted so completely that it was never to be repaired. On May 13, 1782, it was reported to Virginia's Council of State that "Many people are taking away the bricks belonging to the Palace," and Governor Benjamin Harrison was advised to authorize the sale of all the bricks for the best price that could be obtained for them. Later in the month the Governor wrote to the Speaker of the House of Delegates telling him that "The Governor's house at Wmsburg. is burnt down and many of the walls have tumbled. The Executives have given orders for the sale of the Bricks the only method by which they could be saved to the public: the outhouses are going fast to destruction and will soon be in ruins." This melancholy scene was observed by a classically minded Alexander Macaulay in 1783 who told posterity that "on the spot where you see these ruins, formerly stood the Palace which far exceeded the Temple of Diana at Ephesus, or that of the Sun at Palmyra."

27. An engraving of about 1740, which depicts, among other things, Williamsburg's College buildings, the Capitol, and Palace. From a copperplate presented to the late Mr. John D. Rockefeller, Jr., by the Bodleian Library of Oxford, England.

But posterity was not particularly impressed and the site was put up for sale in 1785 and sold to Edmund Randolph who hired a local contractor to patch up the surviving offices and outbuildings; he was paid in part with "250 old Bricks from ye Palace."

The fate of the outbuildings in the Civil War has already been mentioned, and there is no need to explore the subsequent history of the site other than to recall that when Mr. Rockefeller first became interested in Williamsburg the back wall of the local grammar school was sitting firmly and implacably on the front foundation of the Palace. All that remained above ground were the occasional old bricks that had been re-used in the walls of the school.

Fortunately, two very important pieces of pictorial evidence survived that provided information regarding both the appearance and plan of the building. The first took the shape of an engraving in copperplate of 1740, identified by a Williamsburg research worker in the Bodleian Library at Oxford, England (Fig. 27). It showed perspective elevations of the College, Capitol, and Palace, the last complete with outbuildings, garden walls, and even indications of the formal gardens themselves. The Palace building was only shown from the south front, but this was enough to show the placing of the windows, iron balcony, main doors and steps, roof pitch, chimneys, ballustrade, cupola and weather vane, most of which could not be accurately conjectured from the documents and which were unlikely to be revealed by excavations.

The second key piece of pictorial data was provided by a measured ground plan of the Palace drawn by Thomas Jefferson (Fig. 28), now in the collection of the Massachusetts Historical Society. Jefferson had been Governor of Virginia from June 1779, to November 1781 and so had resided for a time in the Palace. It was not, he noted, "handsome without; but it is spacious and commodious within, is prettily situated, and, with the grounds annexed to it, is capable of being made an elegant seat." In odd moments Jefferson made numerous sketches for possible improvements that never came to anything, and although these drawings survive, they were by no means as informative as his very rough plan of the building as it actually was.

The excavation of the Palace foundations began in June 1930 (Fig. 29), and soon it was realized that much of the interior as well as sections of the walls had collapsed into the cellars. It was probably at this point in the story of Williamsburg's archaeology that the significance of stratification was first appreciated. The strata here, however, were not an indication of a time span but rather of the stories of the building. The fire, so the documents tell us, started on the lower floor and burned upward; thus the first floor would have collapsed into the cellars first, followed by the floors of the second and third stories as the flames roared up. Anyone who has seen a burning building knows very well that the rooms and their contents do not drop neatly down as though cut out with a blow torch, and it is not to be supposed that any such phenomenon occurred at the Palace. Such things as marble mantelpieces may very well have remained suspended on the walls for some time after the floors had plunged downward. Nevertheless, there was evidence that the building had fallen in a reasonably orderly manner, and a great deal ended up in the cellars where much of it remained undisturbed for a hundred and fifty years. The documentary evidence quoted above shows that the local citizens carried off some of the bricks and it is probable that they pulled through the rubble close to ground level in the hope of recovering anything useful or valuable. Had the Palace burned in its more prosperous days, all sorts of treasures would have lain buried in the ruins encouraging any amount of burrowing and digging. But with the Governor gone and the interior virtually stripped, little remained beyond the fabric of the building itself and the ashes of one soldier who perished in the fire.

The remains of four marble mantelpieces were found in the debris, the pieces somewhat scattered, indicating that in all probability they had not fallen as single units but had either come to pieces on the walls or had hit something on the way down. On the basis of the burned fragments, one of the mantelpieces was copied and installed in the entrance hall in the position indicated by the Jefferson plan. A second mantel contained a finely carved central marble plaque depicting deer standing in a rural setting. This panel was so well preserved that it has been put back into the reconstructed mantel of the parlor (Figs. 30 and 31), beneath which it was found. The style of this mantel is closely paralleled by one in England at Eltham Lodge in Kent, a house built in the third quarter of the eighteenth century. We may reasonably suppose, therefore, that the Palace mantel is of similar date and so could not have been in the building as first conceived. A study of the history of the Palace thus suggests that the mantel was added when the expensive repairs were in progress in the years 1750-54, a piece of deduction that graphically illustrates the value of the closest liaison between the archaeologist, historian, and architect.

Many other features of the Governor's Palace were derived from archaeological evidence, notably the walnut paneling of the hall; the precedent for this was provided by charred fragments of that wood found in the debris. Similarly, the hall's floor of white and black marble slabs is based on excavated fragments, the ratio of black to white being determined by the number of fragments of each color

106

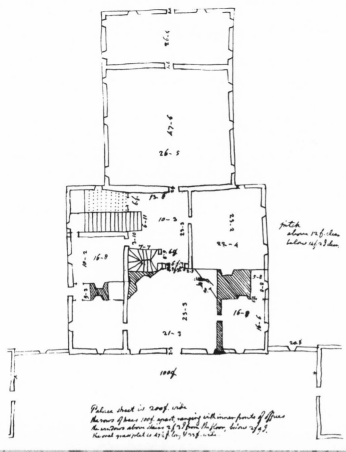

28. A measured drawing of the Governor's Palace made by Thomas Jefferson about 1779.

29. The foundations and cellars of the Governor's Palace as exposed in 1930. View to the north toward the ballroom and supper room.

30. The parlor of the Governor's Palace with the original marble mantel ornament found in the excavations.

31. Restored marble mantel ornament found in the excavation and used in the reconstructed parlor mantel.

that was found. The identification of the types of marble enabled the restoration architects to obtain their materials from the same sources as the originals. Delftware fireplace tiles were also found in the excavations, some decorated with pastoral scenes in blue and others with biblical motifs in purple (Fig. 32). Six of the purple were put back in a fireplace on the first floor, while two of the blue were incorporated into the fireplace of the Governor's bedroom. In addition, a quantity of plain white delftware tiles was discovered on the site of the kitchen, suggesting that the interior may have had a somewhat clinical appearance.

Much more dramatic than the recovery of marble or tile fragments were the remains of the Palace cellars themselves; for these were found to be in a remarkable state of preservation, with steps, doorways, stone-paved passages, and even the brick-walled boxes in the "Binn" cellar still surviving. Anyone who hoped to find a hoard of bottled wines was destined for disappointment; the cellars were empty. It was not always so, and we know that when Lord Botetourt died in 1770, they contained a goodly array of wines and kitchen supplies. His inventory named eight different cellars: the "Rum Cellar," which no one will be surprised to know contained a hogshead of rum; the "Stone Cellar," (presumably so named because it possessed a stone floor) containing among other things, broken pots of sweet meats, pickled mangoes, three boxes of candles, and a bottle of gin; and next the "Cooks Cellar," housing bottled gooseberries, currants, brown sugar, rice, and three pots of lard. In the "Binn Cellar" was a stock of hock, Madeira, claret, Burgundy, porter, and small beer that comprised a total of more than nineteen hundred bottles. Eleven brick-walled bins were uncovered in the excavations and eleven were listed in the Botetourt inventory, each one devoted to a specific wine or beer. Next in the list was the "Vault," wherein the bottles were not stored in bins but were presumably stood on shelves or laid in wooden racks. The wines there included claret, white, arrack, Madeira, and champagne, as well as peach brandy, honey, French brandy and "old Spirits"—a total of around three hundred bottles. The "Cydar Cellar" was home to a barrel of peach brandy, forty-one bottles of English cider and two and a half gross of Virginia cider; while the "Strong beer Cellar" held a stock of rum, spirits, strong beer, and "3 doz 9 Bottles damaged ale." Finally, the "Madeira & Cheese Store" contained, somewhat predictably, six pipes of Madeira and two double Gloster cheeses. Although the Palace cellars were undoubtedly as well stocked when Governor Dunmore beat his hasty retreat in 1775, the privations of the war years coupled with the tenancy of Patrick Henry and Thomas Jefferson ensured that little or nothing remained when the Palace was made into a military hospital. It would have been pleasant to have envisaged the patients repairing to the cellars and there drinking their troubles and pains away. But had they done so a large number of empty bottles would undoubtedly have been found by Colonial Williamsburg archaeologists.

Even if we cannot find archaeological evidence of the heroes of Yorktown celebrating their victory in the Palace cellars, the setting is still one of the most evocative that survives from Virginia's colonial centuries. The reconstructed Palace today rises upon those same foundations and visitors can make their way down the same steps and along the same stone-flagged passages that were trodden by countless slaves carrying wines to titillate the palates of all the great figures of eighteenth century Virginia. Cellars at any time possess—at least for me— an inescapably romantic aura, and these with their worn brick and stones lit only by occasional lanterns, produce a feeling of being one with the past that cannot be beaten by walking the streets of Pompeii or entering the tomb of Tut-Ankh-Amen. The palace cellars, incidentally, provide one of the few places in restored Williamsburg where the visitor can see the reconstruction actually resting on the old brickwork. In most instances the colonial foundations were too decayed and fragmentary to permit them to take the weight of the rebuilt structures.

The art of the landscape architect was as important to the final appearance of a building in the eighteenth century as it is today. The planning of terraces and the careful cutting of trees to expose attractive vistas was a feature of most of the great Virginia plantations, and it was only to be expected that the Governor's Palace would rival the best of them. Much of the initial inspiration for the layout of the Palace gardens came from Governor Spotswood, who prided himself on his taste and talents in that direction, and the records show that he was still adding improvements as late as 1720. As we have seen earlier, Spotswood's extravagance had made him thoroughly unpopular with the members of the Assembly, and in such an atmosphere even the smallest irrita-

32. A manganese-decorated delft "scripture" tile. One of six found at the Governor's Palace and re-used in a reconstructed mantel.

tions were quickly magnified. Not the least of them resulted from the Governor's landscaping beyond his own property. In an irate letter, the wealthy merchant John Custis related that Spotswood had asked permission "to cut down some trees that grew on My Land to make an opening, I think he called it a vista and told me he would cut nothing but what was only fitt for the fire. . . . As to the Clearing his vista he cut down all before him such a wideness as he thought fitt. amongst which there was two very good oak Timber Trees, that my Tenant had reserved to cover my Tenement . . ." This was no way to win friends and influence the local gentry, but from the historian's point of view it was a most fortunate occurrence. Had Spotswood cut only those trees that he had agreed upon, Custis would never have written the letter that tells us of the Governor's vista.

Although there are numerous passing references to the Palace gardens scattered through the records, none is particularly informative. The best source is the previously mentioned copperplate from the Bodleian Library which shows the positions of paths and flower beds immediately in front of and behind the Palace. Much more information was to be gleaned from the archaeological excavations which revealed practically every major feature, except for the planting schemes, that the visitor sees today. The courtyard walls, fruit-garden walls, the three flights of steps leading to the north garden, as well as flights leading down the west terraces to the canal, all were exposed in the course of the digging. In addition, the excavators recovered numerous fragments of garden equipment in the shape of broken earthenware flower pots, stone pots, and glass bell jars to cover young plants.

The 1768 inventory of Governor Fauquier listed thirty-two bell jars and three hundred and thirty-two earthen pots, all of which were taken over by his successor, Lord Botetourt. When the latter's inventory was made in 1770, the total had shrunk to twenty-two bell jars and a hundred and sixty-two flower pots, suggesting, perhaps, the Governor had had some very clumsy slaves among his gardners. Stretching imagination almost to the breaking point, we might be able to read into this a declining efficiency after Christopher Ayscough ceased to be head gardner in 1768. He had held the job for ten years, during which time his wife Anne had been housekeeper at the Palace, an association that was recalled in the course of the excavations when a silver spoon bearing their initials was found in the garden (Fig. 33).

More pertinent to the history of the gardens was the recovery of numerous fragments of green glass bell jars and as many pieces of broken flower pots. Some of the pots were decorated with applied clay ornament in the shape of the heads of cherubs, which, by a remarkable coincidence, closely resemble the features of Lord Botetourt as we see them on his weathered statue that stands at the College (Fig. 34). The report on the 1930 excavations lists the discovery of "Fragments of large stone vases," and although these pieces cannot now be found, it is possible that they may have been included among the "12 Leaden & six stone flower Potts" listed in the Botetourt inventory as being in the garden.

An opportunity to associate excavated objects with documentary history is a satisfaction that is rarely enjoyed by classical archaeologists and never by those who concern themselves with prehistory. But in

33. Silver teaspoon possibly made by the Williamsburg silversmith James Geddy for Christopher and Anne Ayscough, who were head gardener and housekeeper at the Palace.

34. Statue of Lord Botetourt now in the College of William and Mary.

35. A conjectural reconstruction of the first brick church in Bruton Parish. About 1685.

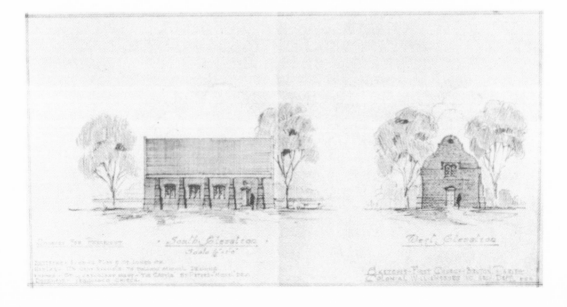

historic archaeology it happens all the time. When the pieces of the puzzle fit snugly together, one acquires the self-satisfied grin that is worn after checking the answers to a magazine quiz and finding that one's score is not merely "excellent" but "brilliant." On the other hand, when the archaeology fails to complement the history, the discrepancy is patently obvious, an embarrassment that is unlikely to be visited on the prehistorian whose findings cannot be referred to an answer sheet. I do not propose to argue the heresy that the archaeologist who excavates on colonial sites must be more skillful than his colleagues working in the field of Indian archaeology. Yet should you ever care to consider it, you might find that the argument has some merit.

Houses That Tobacco Built

VIRGINIA's tobacco economy created a way of life quite different from that lived in the Northern colonies where urban development relied on varied industry and trade. Her towns were small and their tradesmen and craftsmen were mainly dependent on business given to them by the great plantation owners. Consequently, Virginia never acquired a large and wealthy middle class. The plantation owners generally made their purchases in England where they acquired money from the sale of their tobacco, and only fell back on credit at their local stores in moments of emergency. Dubious though the value of their custom may have been, the fact remained that a large proportion of the colony's townspeople lived to serve the plantations. This being so, it is time to pause and take a look at the plantations and their owners before contemplating the tradesmen who were dependent on them.

Tobacco, being the life blood of the colony and the only commodity that was likely to make a man rich, ensured that anyone who

115

could acquire a piece of land, did so. The fifty acres a head that had been given to each of the first settlers at Middle Plantation was a most desirable asset, particularly to men many of whom had lived their lives in England owning little more than the clothes they stood up in. In Virginia in the seventeenth century land was cheap, plentiful, and readily accessible from the many rivers and creeks that spread like arteries through Tidewater. At the close of that century the majority of Virginia's farmers possessed holdings of a hundred acres or less, and the historian Thomas J. Wertenbaker has estimated that only one Virginian in fifteen owned more than a thousand acres. A plan of part of the Governor's Land in the vicinity of Green Spring Plantation made in 1683 shows sixteen tenants, all with rented holdings ranging from twenty-five to two hundred and fifty acres.

At the beginning of the eighteenth century the farmers began to realize that the constant planting of tobacco on the same land was rapidly wearing it out. It is hard to understand why it should have taken them so long to discover this, as the theory of the rotation of crops had been the cornerstone of English agriculture since the early Middle Ages. The Reverend Burnaby, describing the treatment of the land in the Southern colonies in 1759, explained that first the trees were felled "two or three feet above ground, in order to let in the sun and air, leaving the stumps to decay and rot, which they do in a few years. After this they dig and plant, and continue to work the same field, year after year, without ever manuring it, till it is quite spent. They then enter upon a fresh piece of ground, allowing this a respite of about twenty years to recover itself . . ." It has been estimated that it would take about seven years of tobacco growing, with each crop being inferior to the last, before a field would be worked out. Once this fact was appreciated, those who could afford to do so began a race to acquire more land. Tenant farmers and small holders soon fell by the wayside, while those with already substantial acreage acquired thousands of acres more, many of the holdings in counties far distant from their home plantations. Not unnaturally, the acquisition of large and scattered land blocks or "quarters," as they were called, raised labor problems that had not existed in the days of the small farm that could be run by one family. The problem was solved by a vast increase in the slave trade (see Chapter IV, p. 90), and as even damaged slaves were not cheap, the initial cost of this labor further widened the gap between those who could and could not afford to expand their holdings. Eventually, of course, when the plantation owner's slaves were established he was able to recoup on his original investment by breeding his own. It is perhaps surprising the Virginians did not send out more of their own slave traders, for the market was so great that in 1736 the planter William Byrd II commented that he feared that the colony would eventually be called New Guinea. No doubt many a nineteenth century Virginia plantation owner grimly recalled that it was not the Southern planters who made fortunes out of the slave trade, but the merchants of the Northern colonies. Be this as it may, Virginia's plantation economy could not have survived without its slave labor.

Handsome plantation houses and beautiful fan-fluttering women have become part and parcel of the popular Virginia image, and every year thousands of tourists pay their dollars to enter Virginia's stately homes. The finest series of colonial examples is to be found along the north bank of the James River; Shirley, Westover, Berkeley, and Carter's Grove, all of them restored to a lesser or greater degree, but all retaining much of their eighteenth century grandeur. Unhappily, some of the most magnificent of Virginia's colonial mansions are now nothing more than archaeological sites, and consequently bear names that mean nothing to the visitor: Green Spring on the James, Rosewell on the York River, and Corotoman on the Rappahannock are three that have received archaeological attention. Therefore these merit discussion here much more than do the mansions that still survive.

On the assumption that Williamsburg's Governor's Palace is still fresh in the reader's memory, I propose to discuss Rosewell first, even though it was the last to be built and the most recently destroyed. Rosewell was one of the finest brick structures ever erected in English America (Fig. 36), and its checkered history provided an excellent example of the trials and even hardships of an eighteenth-century Virginia planter. The mansion was begun by the wealthy Mann Page I soon after 1721 when his old house burned down. The Pages had long possessed interest in Williamsburg and it will be recalled that Mann's grandfather, John Page, had owned a house that had been pulled down when Duke of Gloucester Street was laid out. Mann Page had watched the slowly unfolding splendor of the Governor's Palace, and appar-

36. Rosewell as originally conceived. A conjectural
reconstruction by the late Thomas T. Waterman.

ently undaunted by the knowledge of its vast cost, decided to build a
palace of his own, preferably one even better than the Governor's. As
it turned out, Rosewell not only rivaled the grandeur of the Governor's Palace, but also paralleled its unfortunate history. Nine years
after work had begun, Mann Page died leaving to his widow estates
that included "his dwelling house, with all outhouses thereto belonging, where he then lived, and the mansion then building, with all
lands thereto adjoining."

Rosewell was next inherited by Mann Page II, who continued to
work toward the completion of the mansion as his father had conceived it, a great pile three storys high above an English basement, the
windows and doors ornamented with elaborate details in stone and
rubbed and ground brick, and a great deck-on-hip roof surmounted
by not one but two cupolas from which the Pages could enjoy a magnificent view across the York River. The mansion was flanked by two
brick advance buildings very reminiscent of those before the Governor's Palace, and surrounded by gardens and vistas that would have

118

made Governor Spotswood green with envy. The cost of all this was phenomenal and in 1744 Mann Page II sold off twenty-seven thousand acres to pay his inherited debts. We do not know how much, if any, of the money was spent on the completion of the house, but we do know that he had married in 1743 and had presumably moved his bride into the mansion.

Mann Page II was constantly in debt and like most of his class relied on the sale of his tobacco to keep him from bankruptcy. It appears that even that let him down from time to time, as it did in 1773 when his agent wrote in a letter that his tobacco "stunk like a dunghill and is not worth a farthing per cwt. . . . his Rappa. tobo. [Rappahannock tobacco] is likewish Trash." By this time Mann Page II had moved out of Rosewell, and having failed to learn from experience, he had proceeded to build another great house, Mannsfield, near Fredericksburg. This house was destroyed in the Civil War and its site was subsequently excavated by the National Park Service in 1934.

After Mann Page's departure, Rosewell was lived in and the plantation managed by his son, John Page, who was later to become Governor of Virginia. Like the Palace twenty years after its completion, Rosewell was badly in need of repair; and John Page wrote in 1771 that he was engaging a man to "put it in a saving Condition next Spring." Like his father, John Page was frequently in debt as a result of poor crops, as is attested by a letter to his agent in which he explained that "no Body hates the Thought of being in Debt more than I do: but the Great Scarcity of Money here, the Shortness of my Crops for four Years past, & the necessary Expenses of an encreasing Family joined to the Commencement of Housekeeping in a large House, have forced me to submit to it for a while." But if John Page's finances were in poor shape, his status in Virginia was as sound as a Spanish dollar. He held many high offices in the state besides the Governorship and a seat in Congress; he was also a close friend of Thomas Jefferson, a relationship which, according to tradition, provided Rosewell with its principal claim to a place in American history.

It is said that it was in one of the cupolas on the roof of the mansion that Jefferson sat with John Page on a June day in 1776 and there read over and discussed the first draft of the Declaration of Independence. Unhappily, like a number of other pieces of Virginia's treasured "lore," the story has grown over the years until the original kernel of truth has been mislaid. It was, in fact, a physical impossibility for Jefferson to have visited Rosewell in June as he spent the whole of that month in Philadelphia, having returned there early in May following a six-week illness at Monticello. Indeed, on arrival in Philadelphia, he found a month-old letter from John Page awaiting him, clearly proving that the two men had not seen each other for some time. However, we do know that after the adoption of the Declaration in its somewhat edited, and, in Jefferson's view, mutilated form, he sent copies of his draft to certain friends for comparative purposes. Some historians are of the opinion that of the three known copies, one may have been sent to Page, in which case this could have been the acorn from which the Rosewell legend grew. But even if the Declaration association is fictitious, the mansion's roof did possess another better documented claim to fame; for it was there that John Page made the first American experiments in the measuring of annual rainfall.

After the death of John Page in 1808 and that of his widow thirty years later, the much run-down mansion was sold to a promoter named

37. The interior of the hall of Rosewell as it was after its desecration in the mid-19th century.

Thomas Booth, a name that the architectural historian Lawrence Kocher has said "should rank high in the annals of vandalism." Having purchased Rosewell for the sum of twelve thousand dollars, Booth began to tear it apart, ripping off the historic lead roof, stripping the paneling from the walls, and removing the marble paving from the hall and the mantelpieces from the principal rooms (Fig. 37). Not content with desecrating the mansion itself, he turned his attention on the gardens, cut down the avenues of stately cedars, and removed the bricks from the walls of the Page graveyard. All this material he sold for the then princely sum of thirty-five thousand dollars. Having completed this violation he disposed of what was left of the great house to the Deans family of Gloucester for another twenty-two thousand dollars. Booth had thus made a profit of forty-five thousand dollars on his original investment and enjoyed as well the satisfaction of having destroyed one of the finest examples of colonial architecture in America.

The new owners did what they could to repair the house and to turn it into a pleasant home, but even in 1855 they did not possess the unlimited means that were needed for the job, and when the Civil War was over they were as impoverished as every other Virginia plantation owner. In March 1916, nearly two hundred years after the first Page home had been destroyed by fire, Rosewell burst into flames and was consumed before help could be summoned. Had its owners then been able to afford to build a new roof over the shell, the structure might have been saved and subsequently restored. But as it was, the site was abandoned and the gaunt walls were slowly embraced by a creeping jungle of vines and trees that grew up around it.

When I first saw the ruin in 1956, the south wall had already collapsed, but the remainder still towered up, thrusting its stone-capped chimneys defiantly above the tops of the trees (Fig. 38). Covered with trailing vines, embossed with moss and lichens, and inhabited by small brown lizards, Rosewell had for me much the same impact as had the Mayan ruins of Chichen Itza for the famous American archaeologist, Edward Thompson. "Pen cannot describe," he wrote, "or brush portray the strange feelings produced by the beating of the tropic sun against the ash-colored walls of these venerable structures. Old and cold, furrowed by time, and haggard, imposing, and impassive, they rear their rugged masses above the surrounding level and are beyond description." Such was my first impression of Rosewell.

121

38. The mansion of Rose-
well as it appeared in 1957.

39. Wine bottle seal of
Mann Page II found at
Rosewell.

There are those who claim that the ruins are haunted, and if ever there was a setting designed as a backdrop for the supernatural, Rosewell is undoubtedly it. A number of people who have visited the site have experienced an unaccountable feeling of depression and one Williamsburg architect came away with a color photograph of the ruins that contained curious white, fog-like images that could not be explained away as photographic blemishes. For my part I have experienced nothing more than a great sadness at seeing the ravages that time, fate, and vandalism had wrought. If Rosewell does have a ghost, it must surely be that of Mann Page I, who may be unable to sleep easily in the mutilated graveyard for his anger at Thomas Booth's treatment of his great architectural achievement. Thoughts of ghosts were afoot in Rosewell long before it burned, for in 1876, Ann Page Saunders, the daughter of Governor John Saunders wrote a short Christmas story entitled *Leonora and the Ghost* which used Rosewell as its setting—thus providing the only extant description of the mansion before Booth set to work on it. Additional help is derived from an insurance policy of 1802 which shows the plantation's five buildings; the mansion measured sixty-two feet by seventy-two feet, three stories high and covered with lead; the two advance buildings were described as "A brick Kitchen 60 feet by 24 feet—one story high—cov^d with wood," and "A brick Dwelling house" with similar measurements and details. Also listed were a wooden barn and "A brick Stable—120 feet by 24 feet one story high covered with woods," this last being an unusually large and remarkably substantial structure.

On our visits to Rosewell in 1956, my plan was simply to try to locate as many of the outbuildings as could be found—particularly the remains of the circular brick icehouse that was known to have been virtually intact in the early 1930's. This was eventually located and found to have collapsed into itself, its interest somewhat further reduced by the fact that the standing brickwork appeared to be of nineteenth century character. Also located were the sites of the two advance buildings and an open brick-lined well, into which one of the party very nearly stepped. Deep in a heavily wooded section some sixty-three yards west of the mansion, a burrowing ground hog had thrown up into the scree at the mouths of its tunnels quantities of oystershells, bricks, and fragments of bottle glass. An examination of these artifacts suggested that the animal had dug into a rubbish pit dating from the mid-eighteenth century. As most such pits measure five or six feet in diameter and are three to five feet deep, it was decided that it would be a useful and simple matter to excavate it. Accordingly, permission to do so was obtained from one of the owners, Miss Nellie Deans Greaves and from the late Colonel G. A. Greaves, who very nobly offered his assistance.

The site of the pit lay on the upper edge of a small valley, at the bottom of which rose a fresh-water spring known locally as Pocahontas Spring in the belief that the Rosewell acres were the site of chief Powhatan's Indian capital when the first colonists landed in 1607. Not knowing the exact size or location of the rubbish pit, it was resolved to dig a trial trench down the slope with the intention of cutting a section through the filling. But right from the start nothing went according to plan. The jungle of trees and thick underbrush had spread a mantle of roots two or three inches below the surface as tightly knit and as easy to dig through as steel chicken wire. As a result a much larger area was laid out than anyone thought would be needed and the whole span was laboriously denuded of its vegetation both above and below ground, in the course of which I managed to slice open the top of my thumb with a machete and thus wasted most of the first day chasing round the countryside in search of a doctor.

When the first trench twenty-eight feet long was dug, we found that we were not dealing with a small five foot pit but with a vast hole that extended from end to end of the trench and still went on down the slope. Another test cutting bisecting the first showed that the hole was some seventeen feet wide and more than five feet deep. It was perfectly obvious that the laboring force of three, one of them my wife, was sadly inadequate for the job in hand. Nevertheless, we plowed on, working mostly on weekends for a period of almost two years. Although the spectacularly informative results made the project well worthwhile, there were times along the way when the smell of mutiny hung in the air.

The prospect of finding an archaeological "treasure" in the tabloid sense of the word was raised when six inches from the surface of the first test trench emerged a large and perfectly preserved silver coin of Louis XV of France dated 1719 (Fig. 40). This half-écu seems to

40. Silver half-écu of Louis XV found in excavations at Rosewell.

be the coin of the highest denomination yet found in colonial Virginia and I confess that we had visions of finding a buried hoard of them further down. Fortunately, from an archaeological point of view, this early promise was not fulfilled. I say "fortunately" because had the pit contained a treasure of silver, Rosewell's owner would have had to be immediately informed and before long the story might have leaked to the newspapers. Previous bitter experience has shown that almost before the ink is dry, eager treasure hunters will converge on the site from all points of the compass, turning a formal archaeological excavation into something resembling the Somme in 1917.

Although the pit held no treasure in the popular sense of the word, it did contain a mine of valuable information as well as a great quantity of intrinsically important artifacts. Among the items were fragments of more than three hundred glass wine bottles, plates, bowls, chamber pots, and cups and saucers in English earthenwares, German stoneware, and Chinese export porcelain; also various gun parts, tobacco pipes, buttons, silver sleeve links (Fig. 41), wine glasses, pins, and fish hooks. The key to the date of the deposit was a pewter shoe buckle found at the bottom of the main artifact-bearing layer; it was molded with an ornament of two hogsheads and the words NO EXCISE. This was a political slogan popular in 1763 when a large section of the English public was appealing against the imposition of an excise tax on cider. The slogan was coupled with other cries favoring the radical John

125

Wilkes, whose attacks on the government of Lord Bute in the same year found much favor in the American colonies. On the evidence of the buckle it was deduced that the pit had not been filled with rubbish until after 1763.

Further evidence was found in the upper layers of the refuse in the shape of fragments of black and white marble flooring slabs, bricks with mortar attached, vast quantities of iron nails of all sizes, and much window glass, many of the pieces scored with a glazier's diamond. The fragments of marble paralleled the flooring slabs found at the Governor's Palace in Williamsburg and were unlikely to have come from anywhere other than the mansion of Rosewell itself. The same was true of fragments of mold-decorated window glass of a type that had only been found once before, and then in a rubbish pit of about 1730 discovered in Old Jewry in the City of London. The presence of mortar attached to the bricks left no doubt that they had been used, as also had the nails, many of which had had their ends clenched over. These last clues precluded any contention that the objects represented unused materials left over after the building of the house. Thus, if they could not have been associated with a building going up, then they had to have come from one on the way down.

Knowing that John Page sent to England for supplies in 1771 to enable him to put his house "in a saving Condition next Spring," and in view of the fact that the relics had to have been thrown away after 1763, there was reason to suppose that the pit contained debris from repairs to Rosewell begun in the spring of 1772. In support of this contention, we also had the fragments of diamond-scored window glass, and we know that among the supplies ordered by John Page in 1771 was "A Glaziers Diamond of 20/ value."

Rosewell's original brickwork was created from bricks made from clay dug on the site and there is documentary evidence that the surplus was sold to Carter Burwell to help in the building of Carter's Grove on the James River. If bricks were needed for John Page's 1772 repairs to Rosewell, it is reasonable that he would have followed in his grandfather's footsteps and have made them on the spot, an operation that results in the digging of large holes. Furthermore, it is fair to suppose that as he was planning well in advance for his spring repairs, he would have made his bricks in the summer of 1771. Now it so happened that

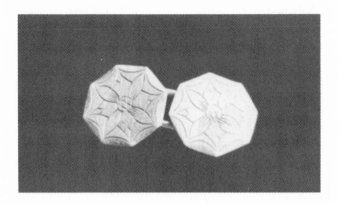

41. Silver sleeve links of about 1740
found in Rosewell excavations.

the great pit excavated in 1957 contained some twenty inches of primary silt washed from the banks and it was at first assumed that such a deposit would have taken considerable time to accumulate. In the winter of 1958-59, however, approximately two feet of silt washed into the completed excavation, leaving no doubt that the twenty inches of primary silt could have accumulated in a single winter. On this evidence it was presumed that the pit had been dug to obtain clay for brickmaking in the summer of 1771, that it partially silted up during the following winter, and was filled with trash in the spring of 1772. It seems, however, that in the course of the winter a group of Indians lit a cooking fire in the lee of the east face, scorched the bank, and left behind meat bones and broken pottery. The Indians' pottery included cord-impressed wares of types hitherto attributed to the Late Woodland or early Contact Period. But as they were deposited over the pit's primary silt which contained eighteenth century bottle fragments, there was every reason to suppose that traditional Indian pottery forms continued in use long after the Indians had acquired a taste for European wares.

Among the many unusual objects found in the pit was a large lump of unshaped stone streaked with veins of copper ore, a combination of malachite and hematite. The stone was not indigenous to the area, and although there was evidence of some brass working on the site, it seemed highly improbable that copper ore would have been smelted at Rosewell. Since no satisfactory explanation for its presence

127

was forthcoming, the lump was duly catalogued and put aside in the not very serious hope that an answer would ultimately turn up. Some months later, while doing research on quite another facet of Rosewell's history, the following information was found in the *Virginia Magazine of History:* "In 1728 'King' Carter, his sons Robin and Charles, and his son-in-law, Mann Page of Rosewell, organized the Frying Pan Company to mine copper in the cuprous sandstone formation on the present boundary of Fairfax and Loudoun [counties]." It would take more evidence than this to infer that the Pages did smelt copper at Rosewell, but it is possible that the excavated lump was a specimen or souvenir brought back from the mine.

One of the most fascinating and at the same time the most frustrating aspects of historical research is that you constantly find scraps of information that look as though they ought to fit into the picture, yet you cannot for the life of you think where. This is true of a notice in the *Virginia Gazette* in 1767 stating that on January 13th, the ship *Sally* then lying in the York River was cleared for passage to London "with 394 hhds. of tobacco, 14 casks and 1 box of gensing, 4 hhds. and 8 casks of snake root, 3 hhds. of deerskins, 5 casks of copper ore, 20 tuns of pig and 19 tuns of bar iron, 15,000 staves, and 3,000 feet of plank." Somebody, therefore, carried five casks of copper ore to the York River in 1767, a year that fell within our period of 1763-72. I cannot help wondering whether there might be some connection between that shipment and the Rosewell ore. This will, of course, remain mere idle speculation until some substantiating evidence is found. On the face of it, the odds against its doing so are a million to one; but in this profession one is constantly surprised at the frequency with which those long shots come up.

The Rosewell pit not only contained copper ore and fragments of brass scrap but also yielded evidence of local blacksmithing in the shape of waste iron and roughly made tools. Alongside these were items of horse furniture, harness and carriage buckles, horseshoes, and spurs. A small cache of brass harness ornaments was found in the leaf and twig-lined nest of the ground hog whose burrows we had so callously disturbed. While we are busily drawing conclusions from the artifacts, it might be reasonable to suppose that the ground hog was an antique collector! More useful speculation centered around the horse furniture in general, for its presence in the pit seemed to indicate that the massive brick stable mentioned in the 1802 insurance policy might have stood nearby. Working on this theory a careful search through the jungle north of the pit revealed part of a brick foundation as well as traces of a paved area to the south of it. It is possible, therefore, that these were part of the stables and that, on archaeological evidence, the unit may have included a forge for shoeing horses and repairing and making tools for use on the plantation, as well as for the maintenance of horse and carriage harness.

The supposed traces of the Rosewell stables were not excavated, nor, indeed, were the sites of the advance buildings, well, or icehouse. The purpose of the project was only to excavate the one refuse pit and to try to determine from it something of the life and history of the plantation. The surviving walls of the great mansion will one day come tumbling down, sooner rather than later, if current vandalism on the property continues, and it will then be ripe for careful archaeological investigation. At present, however, the occasional falling bricks would make work in the immediate vicinity of the ruin a hazardous and fool-hardy operation. In any case, the site is worthy of a full scale archaeological investigation that would take much time and cost a great deal of money; anything less would do more harm than good.

Mann Page I, who started the building of Rosewell, had taken as his second wife the daughter of Robert Carter, a man of great wealth, who had recently built himself a magnificent house on the north shore of the Rappahannock in Lancaster County. Unlike Rosewell, the cost of building Corotoman, the Carter mansion, did not beggar its owner, but neither did the house have anything like the long life of the Page home. This last factor makes Corotoman a potentially more important site than Rosewell as the building was destroyed at the height of its splendor and prosperity. Consequently, anything that survives in the buried remains can be closely dated within the period of the life of the mansion. The exact date of Corotoman's construction is not certain, although it is known to have been erected early in the eighteenth century. The date of its destruction, on the other hand, is established as having occurred in late January or early February 1729. No descriptions or plans of the house survive, and were it not for the evidence of archaeology, the supposed grandeur of Corotoman would be based

129

largely on assumption. It would be argued that Carter was one of the richest men in the colony, the owner of a thousand slaves and three hundred thousand acres of land, and that such a man could have afforded the best. It would be further pointed out that he built the surviving Christ Church in Lancaster County, one of the finest pieces of ecclesiastical architecture in Virginia, and that his children by birth and marriage built such great houses as Rosewell, Berkeley, Nomini Hall, and Sabine Hall. Carter's will, made in 1726, referred to his "mansion Dwelling," and when the house burned, the *Maryland Gazette* of February 4th, 1729, described it as "The fine large house of Col. Carter."

The site was partially excavated in the 1930's by Mr. James Wharton, a local antiquary who dug into the rubble-filled cellars with a small team of Negro laborers. The approach was not particularly scientific, but the results were spectacular. Having dug down through a mass of brick rubble, the excavators found themselves in one of the wine cellars from which they extracted more than a hundred unbroken glass wine bottles as well as huge quantities of fragments. Carter prided himself on his wines and his letters to agents and friends in England are full of requests for wine coupled with rude comments on the quality of those that he had already received. A shipment of brandy he described as "Stark naught. Such I never met with that bare the name French brandy," while most white wine he found to be short lived; "It turns brown and loses the briskness of its taste." He was better served, however, by his purchases of spa waters from Bristol and Germany, all in bottles, and by English Dorchester ale, although there is some doubt whether he personally liked it. "I find your Dorchester ale," he wrote to his agent, "is so pleasing to the company I am forced to give entertainment to that instead of one hogshead of it I desire you to send me four hogsheads well and carefully bottled and safely packt up." James Wharton in his published essay *King Carter, The Man* has noted that this order alone would have brought nearly two thousand bottles to Corotoman.

It was common practice in the eighteenth century for the gentry to order their wines drawn from the wood and shipped in bottles bearing a seal on the shoulder ornamented with their shield of arms, crest, rebus, or initials. Thus one might have expected that many of the

130

bottles in Carter's cellars would have borne his seal; but although four fragments bearing the seal "R C" have been found elsewhere on the site, not one was recovered from the cellar excavations. Of the Carter seals that were found, all save one are of the cheapest variety, perhaps reflecting the man's parsimonious if not miserly attitude that shows itself so frequently in his letters. Governor Francis Nicholson's opinion of "King" Carter creates a similar picture; he thought him a man "of extraordinary pride and ambition. He is likewise famed," wrote the Governor, "for his covetousness and cowardice. To people that will flatter, cajole and as it were, adore him, he is familiar enough, but others he uses with all the haughtiness and insolence possible." In all fairness, however, it must be added that Nicholson was naming some of his own traits, and in any case, there was personal animosity between the two men; one would have been unlikely to have seen any good in the other.

Among the bottle seals found in the general vicinity of the house site was one bearing the legend "R Willis," a discovery that was of interest in that its owner Richard Willis (b. 1656, d. 1700) was survived by his wife Elizabeth, who almost immediately married Robert Carter. She brought with her not only a handsome inheritance of nearly three thousand pounds sterling, eighty-four head of cattle, six horses, and miscellaneous servants and slaves, but also a bonus attraction in the shape of the contents of her late husband's cellar.

Although no Carter seals were actually discovered in the Corotoman cellar, Wharton did recover two seals, one of them on an intact bottle bearing the initials RH over a merchant's mark, and the other attached to a fragment and bearing the inscription THOMAS GREAT • COLCHEST • around what appeared to be a pair of turned bed posts. Mr. M. R. Hull, curator of Colchester Museum in England reported that a bottle of about 1720 with a similarly ornamented seal had been found at Colchester (Figs. 42 and 43). The late Lady Ruggles Brise in her book *Sealed Bottles* identified that seal as coming from a tavern called the "Two Twisted Posts" on High Street and links it with a "Mr. Great of Colchester," who was in business as late as 1761. Mr. Hull has traced Mr. Great to a Red Lion Tavern but could find nothing to link him with the Two Twisted Posts. Be this as it may, there is no doubt whatever that the Colchester bottle and the Corotoman seal came from

42. Bottle seal of tavern keeper Thomas Great of Colchester, England. Found in the wine cellar at Corotoman.

43. Wine bottle made for Thomas Great and found in Colchester, England.

the same tavern and belonged to the same Thomas Great. Tavern bottles were generally adorned with seals to deter patrons from carrying them off—in contrast to the privately owned sealed bottles which were frequently intended as "personalized" gifts. A case of wine given as a Christmas present would be a welcome addition to a friend's cellar, and when, later, the servants brought that wine to the table the seal would recall the source of the gift. But it seems highly improbable that "King" Carter would have been on such terms of friendship with the proprietor of a Colchester tavern, and so the presence of such a bottle in the Corotoman cellar still remains a mystery.

Unfortunately, no records in the shape of drawings, measurements, or photographs were made of the Corotoman excavations and we must rely on James Wharton's happily excellent memory for clues to the appearance of the structure. He estimates that the building measured something in the region of eighty feet by twenty-five feet and that the basement floor was reached at a depth of less than five feet, indicating that the house had only a half basement with the

132

ground floor consequently raised three or four feet above the land surface. The floor of the cellar was paved with stone slabs and all that could be removed were taken up and sold in Washington. At the time of the excavation, the mansion lay partially on one property and partially on another, the boundary running more or less through the center of the building. Fortunately, only one property owner would agree to the site being excavated and, therefore, when Wharton and his men reached the dividing line the project had to be abandoned. Thus half the site still survives and will do so, one hopes, until it can benefit from careful excavation by skilled archaeologists aided by experienced architectural consultants.

It seems that the cellar or the part thereof that was cleared, contained brick bins not unlike those found at the Governor's Palace in Williamsburg. A local legend that was instrumental in inciting Wharton to dig on the site told of a smaller cellar separated from the main block by an iron grill behind which wine bottles still stood in neat rows on the shelves untouched by the fire. At one time the grill had been partially exposed and local inhabitants had been able to reach in and extract those bottles that were closest to the entrance. There are all manner of obvious objections to this story. But at present only one thing is certain—the wine bottle treasure house did not come to light in Wharton's excavations. For the benefit of anyone having visions of a further assault on the site, I must mention yet another local legend that concerns secret tunnels leading into or out of the main cellar that are inhabited by a guardian snake of great age and prodigious size. I do not know of anyone who has actually seen the snake (some say it measures nearly thirty feet in length), but at least one tunnel exists, although its purpose was almost certainly drainage rather than a secret entrance to the mansion.

Although no marble mantelpieces were carefully extracted and pieced together as they had been in the Palace excavations at Williamsburg, numerous items of builder's hardware were recovered and have been carefully preserved by Mr. Wharton. These include rim locks from interior doors (one with its key fused in place) and hinges of various sizes ranging from six inch H hinges to giant HL varieties measuring seventeen inches in length. These last are very similar to those used on the great doors at Christ Church built by Carter in

1732. It might be conjectured, therefore, that similar doors provided the entrance to Corotoman. If we argue that the church indicates Robert Carter's architectural taste, it could be construed that other details of Corotoman besides the size of the doors may have manifested themselves in this surviving building. There is certainly no denying that there are easily discernible traces of Christ Church in the brickwork of Rosewell, notably the west doorway of the church and the south door of Rosewell, and the great arched windows in the east and west pavilions of the house that copy the similarly shaped windows of Christ Church. By projection it could be reasoned that if Rosewell has similarities with Christ Church, then it may have had even closer similarities with Corotoman. An opportunity to test this theory will be forthcoming only when the site of Corotoman is excavated and the ground plans of the two mansions can be compared.

Two further items of hardware are worthy of comment. The first is an elaborate ornamental strap hinge cast in bronze that was found to the west of the house and is the property of Mrs. Joseph Childs, who owns that part of the site. The hinge is seven inches long and too large to have been used on an item of furniture. It almost certainly comes from one of the more important interior doors of the mansion, and when polished such hinges would have contrasted magnificently against a dark wood. However, it appears that they did not do so, as the hinge bears traces of white paint both on its upper surface and seeping under the edges of the back. There is no doubt that the door was painted and the hinges too; which leaves us wondering why under the circumstances such fine hinges were used at all. Iron H or HL hinges of the types found in Wharton's digging would have served equally well and would have been considerably cheaper.

The second significant object is the iron frame from a casement window (Fig. 44) found in the course of Wharton's digging within the cellar. Two feet seven inches in height, the window hung on pintle hinges and was opened by means of an ornamental wrought-iron latch. It was pierced with holes to attach it to a wooden frame that held the camed quarrels (leaded panes of glass). Just such a window—though perhaps a little more decorative in its latch—was found at Jamestown and it dated from the seventeenth century (Fig. 45). To have used a window of this type at Corotoman seems out of char-

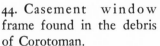

44. Casement window
frame found in the debris
of Corotoman.

45. Casement window frame
found at Jamestown.

acter with the supposedly grandiose conception of the mansion. The
new sash window with its larger panes of crown glass represented a
great improvement over the old casement with its multitude of small
panes divided by unsightly strips of lead. The historian, Marcus
Whiffen, notes that the earliest known use of the counterweighted sash
window in England occurred at Whitehall Palace in London in 1685.
Although the College when first built in Williamsburg in 1695 is believed to have had casement windows, the 1699 Act of Assembly
directing the erection of the Capitol specifically stated that "the windows to each Story of the s^d Building shall be Sash Windows". Robert
Beverley, in his *History and Present State of Virginia*, written in 1705,
discussed the appearance of both public and private buildings and

135

noted that the private were being built with "their Stories much higher than formerly, and their Windows large, and sasht with Cristal Glass . . ." Such windows were used at the Governor's Palace at Williamsburg, at Carter's own Christ Church, and at his son-in-law's Rosewell (see also p. 190). Therefore, the presence of a window casement at Corotoman is unexpected, to say the least.

It has long been assumed that casements were used in some of Williamsburg's earlier buildings, but it is only recently that substantial archaeological and documentary evidence has been forthcoming to support this belief. The study of the accounts of a Williamsburg builder, James Wray, has shown that in 1732 Colonel Thomas Jones ordered repairs to his house and was subsequently billed:

To 4 foot of New Glass & Lead at 1/-	–. 4. –
To 18½ foot of old Glass sett in New Lead at 6ᵈ	–. 9. 3
To putting In 49 Diamond panes of Glass at 2ᵈ	–. 8. 2
To mending a Light In a Iron Casement	–. 1. 3
To 6 square panes of Glass at 3ᵈ	–. 1. 6

The continuing accounts show that in 1735 Jones paid for repairs to both casement and sash windows, but it does not necessarily follow that both were in the same building.

As for the archaeological evidence, mention has already been made of the leaded windows found in the cellar of a house on Nassau Street (Chapter IV, p. 78), and although these were the most intact examples yet found, they were by no means alone. On every early eighteenth century site that we have excavated in the last six years, we have found fragments of quarrels and pieces of lead cames. On the other hand, the excavation of a well on the site of Williamsburg's new United States Post Office in 1961 yielded part of an iron sash weight and a finely preserved brass pulley wheel from the frame of a sash window. This well had been filled with rubbish prior to about 1730. Unfortunately, very little is known of the history of that site as it lies in the James City County section of Williamsburg whose colonial records were destroyed in the Civil War. As the well was not in the immediate vicinity of a public building, it might be conjectured that the weight and wheel came from a private residence. Another possible explanation is that the land was occupied by a craftsman working in the building trade, a theory suggested by the presence in the well of part of a saw blade, a plane iron, a large ladle, lumps of waste lead and metallic slag. But regardless of whether or not the weight and wheel came from a house on the Post Office site, they provide irrefutable archaeological evidence that sash windows were in use in Willamsburg before 1730.

On the basis of these various pieces of evidence, it seems highly improbable that casement windows would have been used in any of the principal windows of Corotoman unless the construction date of the house was much earlier than we suppose. However, we know from Robert Carter's inventory made at the time of his death that the old seventeenth-century family residence was still standing when the big house burned and that he moved back into it for the last three years of his life. It is possible that this "Old House" had been remodeled and that iron casements and other old hardware from it had been removed and stored in the cellars of the new mansion—doubtless for the express purpose of confounding the archaeologists of the twentieth century.

While no structural information resulted from the Wharton excavations beyond that gleaned from the iron hardware, the present owners of the site have recovered fragments of black and white marble flooring slabs that suggest that the building may have possessed a hall whose paving resembled those at the Governor's Palace and Rosewell. Sizable lumps of badly burned lead were also found and presumably came from the roof, although there is no knowing exactly how it was used. One small piece resembles a stalagmite and was created in much the same way, the lead dripping down as the house burned, the drops hardening as they reached the ground and piling up one upon another.

Unfortunately, "King" Carter's published letters tell us nothing about the house in its days of glory, while his brief comment on its destruction is more tantalizing than helpful. Writing to a friend in London in 1729, he merely remarked that "The terrible disaster I underwent by fire, of which you will hear, among many other great destructions, consumed all my stock of old wines of which I had a pretty good store." He also lost a tea service in the new English white

137

salt-glazed stoneware, a ware whose first recorded appearance in America would seem to have been in 1724 in Boston. We know of this tea service not through Carter's correspondence, but from James Wharton's excavation, in the course of which he found three cups and a small milk jug (Fig. 46), all badly burned, but still recognizable and now the earliest "documented" examples surviving from colonial America.

The third significant plantation site began its life before Robert Carter was born and continued after his mansion-building children were dead. To find it we must return to James City County and the vicinity of Jamestown, to a bubbling fresh-water spring about a mile from the James River named Green Spring. On this site stood the finest house of seventeenth century Virginia, the home of Governor Berkeley and, for a short while after the burning of Jamestown in Bacon's Rebellion, the seat of the colony's government. The site had been partially excavated by Mr. Jesse Dimmick, the owner of the tract in 1929, and then more thoroughly by Mr. Louis R. Caywood for the National Park Service in 1954 and 1955 (Fig. 47). Both excavations revealed that there were two adjacent houses on the site, but until 1954 it was generally supposed that the westerly ell-shaped building was the earlier of the two. Caywood's excavations clearly showed that this building cut through and overlay the eastern foundations and so had to be a later structure. The Park Service archaeologist's excavation report designates the east structure as "The Old Manor House" and the ell-shaped building as the "Mansion House," names which we can usefully retain here (Fig. 48).

Historical evidence is scant, thanks largely to the loss of the James City records, and no early descriptions of either house survive. Sir William Berkeley came to Virginia as a firmly Royalist Governor in 1642 in the dark days of England's own Civil War. The following year he acquired the nine hundred and forty acre tract known "by the name of Green Spring," a holding that had been enlarged to more than a thousand acres by 1661, at which time a further thousand was added. In addition, Berkeley had the use of a narrow belt of land extending along the north bank of the James River to the Chickahominy River, some three thousand acres known as the Governor's land which conveniently adjoined his own property. The Old Manor House is

46. Rare early English white saltglaze cups and pitcher found in the ruins of Corotoman, which burned in 1729.

believed to have been built between 1643 and 1649 and resembled a typical small English brick country house of the period; on the east face it was adorned with a pair of buttress-like "towers" that probably provided deeply recessed mullioned windows for the principle rooms. Between these flanking rooms was a larger entrance hall.

It was here that Governor Berkeley sat in judgment on the ringleaders of Bacon's Rebellion in 1676, and it was here that special commissioners were sent the next year to look into the whole unfortunate episode—one in which Berkeley himself showed to but poor advantage. When the unwelcome guests finally departed, Lady Berkeley arranged that they should leave in a carriage driven by the public hangman, and the Commissioners subsequently complained that she "went into her Chamber and peeped through a broken quarrel of the glass to see how the show looked." The comment graphically recalls the fact that although the green broad glass quarrels used in seventeenth century windows let the light in, they were far too uneven, colored, and bubbled to permit anyone to look out through them.

139

47. The mansion of Green Spring in course of excavation in 1955.

48. A simplified plan of the Green Spring "Manor" and "Mansion." A and B indicate areas in which the later house and garden-wall footings overlie the earlier foundations.

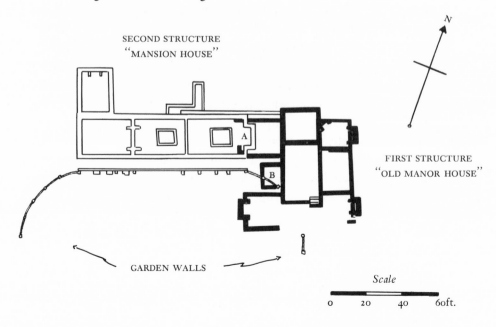

SECOND STRUCTURE
"MANSION HOUSE"

N

FIRST STRUCTURE
"OLD MANOR HOUSE"

A

B

GARDEN WALLS

Scale

0   20   40   60ft.

The southern face of the Old Manor House would appear to have been E-shaped with two large and one small wing extending from the main block. In comparison with the great Tudor and Stuart houses of England, this house was small, measuring in all no more than about sixty feet by sixty, with its largest room being only thirty by twenty feet. Berkeley had stated that after the rebellion he had two hundred men living in his house, a feat that would have shamed a professional sardine packer. Undoubtedly, however, he meant that they were quartered in outbuildings and tents in the immediate vicinity of the house and not actually in the residence itself.

The 1954 archaeological excavations revealed quantities of burned brick and plaster in the area of the house, suggesting that all or part of it had been destroyed by fire. Berkeley died in 1677 and in the following year his widow wrote that Bacon's Rebellion had left the house looking "like one of those the boys pull down at Shrovetide, & was almost as much to repair as if it had beene new to build, & noe signe that ever there had beene a fence about it, in soe much that it has cost above £300 to make it habitable, & if I had not bestowed that money upon it, the Plantation had not beene, worth £100, & as it is I thinke it the finest seat in America & the only tollerable place for a Governour..."

In 1680 Lady Francis Berkeley remarried and the Green Spring estate thus passed into the hands of the influential Ludwell family. However, it was rented to Governor Culpeper in 1680, to Lord Effingham in 1684, and was used as the seat of Assembly in 1691 as the fourth State House at Jamestown was then so out of repair that it could not be used. One might reasonably suggest, therefore, that the original Green Spring Manor House was still standing into the last decade of the seventeenth century. As there are numerous references to the great activity at Green Spring in the second decade of the eighteenth century, it could also be supposed that the Old Manor House disappeared and the new Mansion House was built at about the turn of the century.

If it seems that I am overconcerned with the relationship between the two buildings, I should perhaps stress more strongly that here is a case where the archaeological evidence was completely at variance with the opinions of architectural historians who have published accounts of Green Spring Plantation. Mr. Jesse Dimmick published an account of his excavations in the *William & Mary Quarterly* in 1929, and he there put forward his belief that the Manor House predated the ell-shaped Mansion House. Three years later the well-known historian of Virginia architecture, Thomas Waterman, wrote that the theory seemed improbable, as the foundations followed no known seventeenth century plan, whereas the ell-shaped building had its parallels in seventeenth century England. Documentary evidence supported Waterman at least to the point of showing that even in the late eighteenth century there was a tradition that the Mansion House was Berkeley's seventeenth century residence. In 1796 the famed architect Benjamin Latrobe visited Green Spring with a view to designing a new house for its owner, William Ludwell Lee. Latrobe subsequently wrote in his diary that "The principal part of Greenspring house was erected by Sir William Berkeley . . . It is a brick building of great solidity, but no attempt at grandeur. The lower story was covered by an arcade which is pulled down. The porch has some clumsy ornamental brick work about the style of James the first . . ." Latrobe had studied in England, and although Greek revival was his particular forte, there is every reason to suppose that he would recognize early Jacobean style when he saw it. Certainly, in Latrobe's mind, there was no doubt of the building's antiquity, for he described it as the "oldest inhabited house in North America" and noted that "Many of the first Virginian assemblies were held in the very room in which I was plotting the death of Muskitoes." Yet in spite of these authoritative opinions, the fact remained that the eastern end of the Mansion House cut into the foundations of the Old Manor, while part of the handsome, curving eighteenth century garden wall actually passed through one of the Manor's rooms. The history and the archaeology were, it seemed, hopelessly incompatible.

So much research has been devoted to the documentation of early American history both in this country and in Europe that one might be forgiven for supposing that all the libraries, old bookshops, and dusty attics have been scoured from end to end and that little or nothing still remains to be found. But the truth of the matter is that new pieces of documentary evidence are constantly being discovered, while many that are already known are found to contain facts that

142

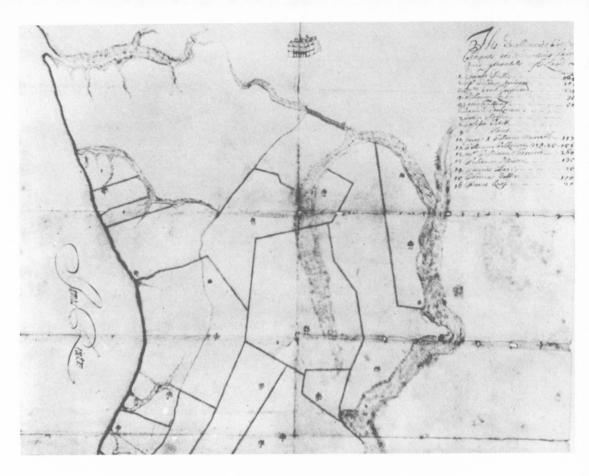

49. A survey of part of the Governor's Land west of Jamestown in 1683. It provides the only known drawing of 17th
century Green Spring and also shows Edward Challis as the
tenant of the site on which evidence of potting was discovered
in 1961.

were not thought important by previous researchers. In 1957, a land
survey made for Virginia's governor Lord Culpeper in 1683 was found
in the William Salt Library, Stafford, England (Fig. 49). The plat not
only listed sixteen of the governor's tenants and showed the positions
of their houses near the James River west of Jamestown Island, but
also included a sketch of His Excellency's mansion at Green Spring.
The house is shown from the east, and although it does not conform too closely to the excavated plan of either the Old Manor
House or the Mansion House, it does show a five-arched arcade. While
this discovery does not change the irrefutable fact that the Manor
House predated the Mansion House, it does link the building that
existed in 1683 with the arcade mentioned by Latrobe. It may, there-

143

50. Two bricks, dated 1666, from a brick trough containing a thick bed of green glass. Found in the woods near Green Spring.

fore, be construed that at least part of the Mansion House was in existence by 1683.

If I am accused of cheating by holding back the Salt Library's plat until I have floundered through the rest of the very confusing evidence, I confess that I did so deliberately—for two reasons. First, because the 1683 drawing was not known when most of the historical and archaeological work was being done, and secondly to show how scraps of key evidence can still turn up to throw new light on old problems.

The artifacts from the Green Spring excavations were not particularly impressive and comprised typical domestic trash, much of it of eighteenth and nineteenth century date, derived from contexts that are not specified in the published report. Among the earlier and more unusual objects was a small brass clock face, slightly more than three and a half inches in height, which provided five different categories of time, the hours of the day, days of the week, days of the month, and two more that cannot now be identified. Significant though this was to the horological history of colonial Virginia, of more obvious importance was Caywood's discovery of a potter's kiln to the east of the house, which he concluded had been in operation during Governor

Berkeley's ownership of the site. Some years before this discovery was made, evidence of glassmaking had been found in the low-lying woods even further to the west toward the edge of Powhatan Swamp; the principal exhibit was a narrow brick trough coated on the inside with dark green glass and bearing on two of the bricks the incised legend "H.A.L." and the date "Aug. 6. 1666" (Fig. 50). I shall return to these important relics of early Virginia industry in Chapter VIII.

Turning now from a site where the archaeology clouded the history to one where the history was pieced together entirely as a result of archaeology, we come to a comparatively small and unimpressive house at Tutter's Neck that lies on a tributary of College Creek only three miles or so from Williamsburg. The plantation appears on no map and the house figures in no surviving document. Tutter's Neck plantation might very well have vanished forever from Virginia's history had it not been for the groping blade of a bulldozer that plowed into the building's foundation one day in the summer of 1959. The machine thrust its way through the debris of two buildings pushing quantities of bricks, mortar, and domestic trash before it to create windbreaks for the protection of young fir trees that were to be planted on the site. Unfortunately it was not until the following spring that Colonial Williamsburg archaeologists heard what had happened and hurried to the site to see whether anything of the buildings had escaped. It was soon apparent that although the important upper soil levels had been entirely stripped, the two bottom brick courses of each building survived. Subsequent excavation revealed most of the ground plan of a long narrow house measuring close to forty-three feet by nineteen and having at either end massive chimneys each more than nine feet wide (Fig. 51).

To the north of the residence lay the foundations of a much smaller building, little more than twenty-five feet long and sixteen and a half feet wide but having a great chimney ten feet in width at its base. This building was assumed to have been a kitchen, and it was from beneath and around its foundations that most of the clues to the history of the entire site were derived. Partially beneath the kitchen chimney lay a refuse pit measuring nine feet in diameter, into which had been thrown more than a hundred wine bottles whose shapes identified them as dating between about 1690 and 1710. Five of the

145

bottles bore seals with the initials F ♰ and one was stamped Richard Burbydge 1701—the earliest dated wine bottle so far found in Virginia (Fig. 52). The proportion of five F ♰ seals to one Burbydge suggested that in the long run the F ♰'s would be of greater significance in piecing together the history of the site. On the other hand, the dated seal was helpful in that it showed that the rubbish pit could not have been filled prior to 1701 and consequently the kitchen building had to date even later. The existence of the pit beneath the foundation further indicated that the site had been occupied before the kitchen was built, thus suggesting that the residence was older.

The next step was to go through all the surviving documentary sources of the first quarter of the eighteenth century in search of an individual bearing the initials F ♰ who owned land in the appropriate section of James City County. The clue was eventually found in a record of 1732 contesting the will of one James Bray whose mother had earlier purchased from Frederick Jones "one messuage, plantation, piece or parcel of land," known as Tutties Neck, "three hundred acres, more or less, lying and being in the parish of Bruton." Further corroboration was provided by a letter of 1721 from Frederick Jones to his brother about the latter's merchandise being "marked by mistake F ♰." Thus it was to be inferred that Frederick did identify his own property in that way and it was therefore reasonable to suppose that his wine bottles were similarly marked.

Having once established that the tract was known as Tutties or Tutter's Neck and that it was once owned by Frederick Jones, it was possible to pursue its history through the documents—although the loss of the James City County records balked many a good lead. While references to the site went back to 1632, no artifacts were recovered that suggested any occupation prior to about 1690 or 1700. We know that Frederick and his brother Thomas (Colonel Jones of the casement windows, see p. 136) came to Virginia in 1702 after the death of their father, Captain Roger Jones. He had come to the colony with Lord Culpeper in 1680 and was given the job of stamping out piracy in the Chesapeake Bay. Jones found, however, that collusion was less effort and infinitely more profitable, and as a result of his labors he amassed a sizable estate. Unfortunately he was unable to hide his activities forever, and in 1692 the Council of Virginia wrote to the Secretary of State in

51. An artist's impression of the residence and kitchen at Tutter's Neck. About 1740.

England accusing Jones of "adviseing, trading with and sheltering severall Pyrates and unlawfull Traders, instead of doeing his duty in sieing them. By which means ye sd. Jones laid ye foundation of his p'sent great Estate." The devious Captain Jones thereupon packed up and went home to London. After his death his sons, who already owned interests in ships trading with Virginia, came over as settlers to claim their inheritance—three hundred acres in James City County apparently being part of Frederick's share.

The Jones brothers may already have had additional interests in North Carolina, for as early as 1702 they were joint owners of a tenton sloop the *Otto of Carolina*. In 1703 Frederick was indulging in a lawsuit in that colony and in 1707 he received a grant of more than 4,500 acres there. At some time around this date he moved down there, but retained close ties with Williamsburg for some years to come. He rose to become Chief Justice of North Carolina succeeding Tobias Knight, who had resigned after being too closely associated with

147

Blackbeard the pirate. It would seem that Jones plunged into his new job with an enthusiasm that would have gladdened the heart of his late father. In 1721 he was accused of appropriating court money given into his hands for safekeeping. Five days after the charge was tabled, Jones made his will and conveniently died before he could be called to account. This phase of Frederick Jones's life did not have any bearing on Tutter's Neck, but it does show that the site had once belonged to a man of enterprising character though doubtful morals.

After Jones sold the Tutter's Neck acres to Mrs. Bray, the property was absorbed into the much larger neighboring plantation of "Little Town," the home of the Bray family. Archaeological evidence suggested that the excavated site became a quarter, farmed by a handful of slaves under the supervision of a white overseer. The clues to this supposed decline in Tutter's Neck's fortunes were found buried in a series of rectangular rubbish pits, all lying beneath the kitchen building. A wine bottle in one pit was of a type not manufactured before the late 1730's, thus indicating the date after which the pit was in use. Yet all the European pottery associated with the bottle was of types that one would expect to have found in use at the turn of the eighteenth century. Table knives had been broken and resharpened;

52. Wine bottles from Tutter's Neck bearing seals of Frederick Jones and Richard Burbydge, the latter dated 1701.

a seventeenth century brass spoon had seen such service that half the bowl had worn away. Our impression was that these things either belonged to an extremely poor family or had been supplied for the use of the slaves, their original owners having no further use for them. The rubbish pits also contained numerous fragments of pottery made by the local Pamunkey Indians who copied European forms. Such wares were extremely common on plantation sites and also in eighteenth century Williamsburg. In view of the fact that the Indian products were of such low quality that one cannot imagine even the poorest white colonists having any personal use for them, one must look elsewhere for the extensive market that the ware enjoyed. That market was almost certainly to be found in the slave population, and thus the pottery's discovery at Tutter's Neck pointed to the presence there of quartered slaves.

The fact that the rubbish pits were all grouped together under the kitchen indicates that before the building was erected this was an area deliberately set aside for the burial of trash. It is then odd that the same ground should subsequently have been chosen as the kitchen's site. One would have assumed that the builder would have realized that such loose soil would lead to trouble—which indeed it did, the foundation of the chimney having settled into the early circular pit.

I do not know whether I am particularly prone to lucky coincidence (it certainly is not true when I indulge in small wagers), but it seems that in archaeology I have enjoyed more than my fair share. Some eight or ten years ago while walking on the foreshore of the River Thames at London, I picked up the base of a delftware salt decorated on the inside with a portrait of a Carolian gallant wearing a full wig and an equally full mustache. Although the river shore was littered with thousands of pieces of broken pottery, I retained this piece largely because the painted face caught my fancy. Through the years I showed the fragment to museum curators and specialists in English delftware, but I was never able to find a parallel for the salt or meet anyone who had ever seen anything like it. But a parallel did exist, and it was waiting to be found in one of the rubbish pits at Tutter's Neck (Fig. 53). Although the Virginia example is less well preserved than the one from the Thames, there is no doubt that they came from the same factory and were probably painted by the same hand.

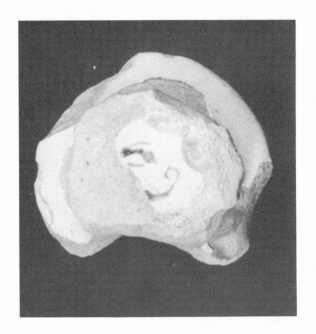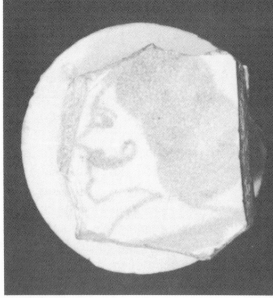

53. Interior bases of rare and identical English delftware salts decorated in blue with profiles of Carolian
gallants. Left, from Tutter's Neck. Right, from the
River Thames at London.

The artifacts from Tutter's Neck were not as varied as those
from Rosewell, but like the Rosewell collection they were found in
closely datable deposits and as such throw valuable light on the personal possessions of Virginians in the eighteenth century. They do
not, however, tell us very much about the Tutter's Neck buildings,
beyond the fact that the residence possessed casement windows that
made use of both rectangular and diamond-shaped quarrels. Other details, if they existed, had been swept away by the bulldozing. Thus the
reconstructed drawing was based only on the evidence of the ground
plan and on data derived from other contemporary buildings of similar
proportions.

Although we frequently try to describe archaeology as a detective
story, the analogy is never entirely appropriate. The formula for a
good mystery story is to present the reader with a set of characters,
let one of them commit a crime, then scatter a nice mixture of clues
and red herrings, leave them around for two thirds of the book, and
then quickly and neatly drop them all into place at the end. In archaeology we have our actors, our mysterious event, and our clues; but
when the last shovelful of earth has been thrown back into the excava-

150

tion, there is always something left over that will not fit into the story. At Tutter's Neck we were left with one of our actors still standing around waiting for a part to play. To be left with a handful of unused clues is one thing, but to wind up with a loose, named player is quite another, particularly when that player happens to bear a name close to that of the most famed actor of the Elizabethan stage, Richard Burbage.

While Frederick Jones readily came back to us after his wine bottles were found, Richard Burbydge continued to be little more than a name molded in glass. He appears in the records only once, in a list of James City County residents who inspected the *Jamaica Merchant*, a vessel lying at anchor in the James River in 1710. But the name Burbydge is one that readily lends itself to misspelling, and it is just possible that he was the Richard Burbridge, master of the hundred-ton vessel *Johanna of Gosport* that dropped anchor in the James in the spring of 1702—the same year that Frederick Jones arrived in Virginia and only a few months after Richard Burbydge had his name and the date stamped on his wine bottle. Were I a novelist, it would be tempting to see Jones as a passenger aboard the *Johanna of Gosport* telling the captain of his inherited estates and urging Burbydge to try his own luck ashore. As a result, perhaps, Burbydge settled in James City County, swapped the wine of friendship with Jones, and lived on in Virginia in health and prosperity. It would be only natural that when, years later, Governor Spotswood had a ship to be examined, the choice should fall on that respected retired sea captain Richard Burbydge. But fortunately or unfortunately—depending on your point of view, we are concerned only with facts; so Richard Burbydge must give up his parrot and his wooden leg and be remembered merely as the owner of a bottle that found its way into Frederick Jones's trash pit.

Matters of Life
and Death

"AFTER DINNER we came back to Williamsburg," wrote a French visitor in 1765. "Never was a more disagreable Place than this at Present. In the Day Time People hurying back and forwards from the Capitoll to the Taverns, and at Night, carousing and drinking in one Chamber and Box and Dice in another, which continues till Morning commonly, there is not a publick House in Virginia but have their Tables all batered with ye Boxes which shews the extravagant Disposition of the Planters."

The taverns of Williamsburg, and the Raleigh in particular, were the temporary homes of the majority of visitors to the city at Public Times. They served as places of business and tended as well to the needs of those who came to eat, drink, or gamble away their money, their tobacco crop, and even the land on which they grew it. In short the taverns or "ordinaries" as they were more frequently termed, were

152

centers of *life* in colonial Virginia. They existed in every town and village and were stationed along the roads for the benefit of travelers and their horses. Some, like the Swan Tavern at Yorktown and the Raleigh in Williamsburg, were as well known in Virginia as were London's Boar's Head, Mermaid, or Rose taverns in England. Indeed, it has been claimed that the Raleigh on Duke of Gloucester Street in Williamsburg was the most famous tavern in the South, ranking alongside the noted City Tavern in Philadelphia or Fraunces' Tavern in New York. Many other hostelries were important in their own areas, but the amount of documentary research in this field has been very limited and few tavern sites outside Williamsburg and Jamestown have been archaeologically explored. The major exception is the reconstruction of the Swan Tavern at Yorktown by the National Park Service, a structure that is now leased as an antique shop. Excavations on this site revealed the foundations of the story-and-a-half tavern building that had been in existence as early as 1722, as well as those of the kitchen, stable, smokehouse, and privy, all of which have been reconstructed.

Although the Swan was the most important of Yorktown's taverns, there are few clues to its original appearance. The best are to be found in the inventory of landlord James Mitchell who died in 1772 "in his sixty eighth year; a Man who was as generally esteemed as any in the Colony." From this inventory we learn that there were six beds in "the Rooms Upstairs," which suggest that lodging facilities were somewhat limited. Although we do not know the size of the beds, there is ample evidence from other sources to show that tavern visitors frequently shared beds at rates advertised as "for lodging in clean sheets, one in a bed, sixpence; if two in a bed, threepence and three farthings; if more than two, nothing."

The Swan's principal room on the first floor was furnished with twelve leather-bottomed chairs, and walnut and mahogany tables, one of these being "for Cards lined." Like most eighteenth century taverns of any standing the Swan had its billiard room, while the room next to it housed two pairs of backgammon tables and a chessboard with two sets of men. The room described as the "Chamber" was almost certainly the public eating and drinking room, for besides its tables and chairs it contained a goodly array of "blue and white china plates . . .

red and white china plates" and a variety of bowls, teapots, tea cups, coffee cups, glass decanters and wine, cider, and punch glasses. The National Park Service excavations resulted in the recovery of large quantities of broken glassware and ceramics, some of the stoneware tankards being ornamented with a swan in high relief. However, as far as I can discover no serious attempt has been made to study the mass of artifacts and to try to equate them with the inventory, or to look upon them as anything more than an interesting collection of odds and ends.

An English visitor to Yorktown in 1736 noted that "The Taverns are many here, and much frequented," which was hardly surprising in a town that was a major port and a haven for carousing seamen. Fortunately for its more genteel inhabitants, the town lay on two levels: the stores, warehouses, and more disreputable places of relaxation close to the shore (Fig. 54), and the better homes ranged along the bluff behind. Of the former nothing remains but one small restored house, the Archer Cottage, whose foundations are of ballast stone. These undoubtedly date from the heyday of Yorktown when ships bound for England unloaded their ballast there before taking on cargoes of tobacco, staves, shingles, corn, cotton, or pig and bar iron, deerskins, ginseng, and snakeroot. Many of these commodities were doubtless stored in the immediate vicinity of the Archer Cottage, probably in barrels similar to one found imbedded in sand in the cellar beneath the building. Little is known of the history of the cottage, although archaeological evidence suggests that the colonial frame structure may have been destroyed by a fire that did much damage in Yorktown in 1814. The cottage's position indicates that the reused colonial foundations are possibly those of an ordinary run by shipwright Abraham Archer "under the Hill at York Town" in the mid-eighteenth century.

Although there were undoubtedly many drinking places and brothels on Virginia waterfronts that were disreputable enough to make a colonial dame swoon, the majority of taverns were as respectable as the trade permitted. Tables of rates and prices were set by the county courts and these were required to be displayed in the public rooms. In addition, the tavern keepers were required by statute to refrain from permitting on the Sabbath Day "any person to tipple and drink any more than is necessary," a pleasant regulation which, while

154

mindful of the solemnities of Sunday, was equally cognizant of the colonists' need to quench their thirst on a hot summer day and to warm their vitals on a cold winter's night. An excellent idea of the range of the liquid fortification available in eighteenth century Yorktown or Williamsburg is to be found in the list of rates authorized by the York County Court in March 1709-10. In it we find that "Wine of Virginia Produce" was the most expensive you could buy, selling for five shillings a quart, while "Virginia Beer & Cyder" were the cheapest and were dispensed at threepence three farthings a quart. Among the imported lubricants were "Canary & Sherry, . . Red & White Lisbon, . . Western Islands Wines, . . French Brandy, . . French Brandy Punch or French Brandy Flip, . . Rum & Virginia Brandy, . . Rum Punch & Rum flip" and English beer. In the following year an addition to the list tabled "Roger's best Virg[a] aile" at a rate of sixpence a quart, half the price of English beer and twopence farthing more expensive than the Virginia beer and cider. This entry would not be particularly noteworthy were it not for the fact that this is the earliest reference yet found to William Rogers, brewer of Yorktown and operator of an extremely important potting factory (see Chapter VIII, p. 221) where he appropriately manufactured tavern mugs and jugs.

54. An artist's reconstruction of part of the Yorktown waterfront as it may have appeared during the Revolution.

55. Rhenish Westerwald tavern mugs bearing the ciphers of Queen Anne and George I or II. Found in Williamsburg.

56. Items like these from Williamsburg excavations were common on the tables of every colonial tavern.

While wines and spirits were generally served in glasses, most taverns dispensed ale, beer, and cider in pewter or pottery mugs; of the latter the blue and gray stoneware tankards from the Rhineland were the most common with mugs of English brown stoneware in second place. The German tankards were made to hold standard quantities and marks of capacity were usually painted on the sides in cobalt. The English mugs, on the other hand, were not so marked, but they were made to rigid standards of capacity and were required to be impressed with an official stamp to distinguish them from those that did not contain accurate measures. The majority of the brown stoneware mugs were of half-pint capacity, but some were of massive proportions and held one or even two quarts. An inventory in the letters of William Beverly listing goods to be sent from England to Virginia in 1740 were "gallon Stone Juggs" and "pottle Stone muggs upright sides"—a pottle being two quarts. A fine example of one of these huge mugs was unearthed some years ago in a field at Lightfoot, a village a few miles from Williamsburg. Another slightly smaller mug of brown Nottingham stoneware was found in an eighteenth century context at Jamestown, a reminder that Americans were not always as rude about English beer as they are today.

Unfortunately there is little documentary evidence to tell us of the activities and character of the taverns of seventeenth century Jamestown. In marked contrast are the hostelries of Williamsburg whose histories are well known, and any one of them could be used as a typical example of the eighteenth century. But as I have already intimated, the Raleigh was the most famous of them all, not because its liquor or its cuisine were particularly outstanding but because it held a status in the town that was virtually that of a public building. Legislators repaired there to continue their debates after leaving the Capitol, and when in May 1774, Governor Dunmore dissolved the House of Burgesses for objecting to the closing of the port of Boston after the tea party, eighty-nine of the members met in the Raleigh's "long room" to form an association to ban imports from Britain. In happier times the Governor's Council undertook its official entertaining at the Raleigh; the Phi Beta Kappa Society is believed to have been founded there in 1776; and two years later Governor Botetourt entertained there after the oath-taking ceremony at the Capitol. It was in the

Apollo Room of the tavern that young Thomas Jefferson danced with his Belinda and afterward wrote to his friend John Page of Rosewell that "Last night, as merry as agreeable company and dancing with Belinda in the Apollo could make me, I never could have thought the succeeding Sun would have seen me so wretched . . ."

Mingling with the echoes of the minuet and the bark of table-pounding politicians the psychic among us may hear the sounds of commerce, land sales being transacted, crops sold, and servants hired, while outside on the steps or porch everything from slaves to ships was sold by auction.

Although the Raleigh was the most famous of Williamsburg's colonial taverns (Fig. 57), there is no documentary evidence to show that it was among the earliest of them. The first known reference to the tavern by name does not occur until the mid 1740's, and when the site was excavated in 1930, the techniques of historic archaeology were not sufficiently developed for the construction date of the foundation to be determined. Like the Governor's Palace, the Raleigh cellar foundations and walls were extremely well preserved and it was possible therefore to reconstruct the building on top of them.

Along with the rest of Williamsburg, the Raleigh fell on hard times in the early Federal period and passed through numerous hands before being largely remodeled in the 1840's. It was turned, somewhat ironically, into a seminary for young ladies in the 1850's and finally burned to the ground in 1859. Through all its changing fortunes, the bust of Sir Walter Raleigh retained its place of vantage above the entrance, looking down with the same dignified amusement on raucous colonial tipplers and studious, giggling young ladies alike. In 1816 the bust was described as being of brass "with a fine forehead and right reverent beard." But when Benson J. Lossing visited the tavern in 1848 and made the drawings on which much of the reconstruction is based, he noted that ". . . the front part of the old Raleigh tavern had been torn down, and a building in modern style was erected in its place . . . The leaden bust of Sir Walter Raleigh, which graced the front of the old inn, now ornaments the new building." A few years later the bust was "not very artistically painted to make it more realistic," the hair and beard being colored a reddish brown. Local tradition has it that the bust was salvaged from the flames and was later

158

57. A busy day at the Raleigh Tavern in Williamsburg.

taken to Richmond, but what became of it after that is a mystery. It is
certain, however, that the head was parted from its stone base as
that remained in Williamsburg (Fig. 58). After being many years in
the safekeeping of the Association for the Preservation of Virginia Antiquities, it was presented to Colonial Williamsburg in 1933 and now
resides in the archaeological museum. The stone, with its archaically
spelled inscription SIR WALTER RALEGH, is certainly no object of beauty
and nine out of ten visitors pass it by without a second look. Nevertheless, it is one of the most historic relics surviving from eighteenth century Williamsburg, for beneath it passed all the leading actors in
the drama of Revolutionary Virginia. The fact that the stone pedestal
survives gives some credence to the belief that the Raleigh bust may
also have been saved from the fire. If it was, then there is perhaps a

slim chance that it may still be hiding in an attic or serving as an ornament in some Richmond garden.

When we try to envisage the way in which the colonists entertained themselves and each other, archaeology tends to let us down. It is true that we can unearth occasional gaming pieces, simple children's toys, and huge quantities of broken wine bottles; yet somehow these things are no more evocative of excitement, laughter, and happiness than is morning sunlight falling on the full ash trays and empty glasses of last night's party; the magic has departed. Yet it lives on in the pages of history. From an announcement in the *Virginia Gazette* for December 7th, 1739, we can obtain a lively impression of the kind of "diversions" that passed the daylight hours in Williamsburg at Public Times:

> AND for the Entertainment and Diversion of all Gentlemen and others, that shall resort thereto, the following PRIZES are given to be contended for, at the Fair, *viz.*
>
> A good Hat to be cudgell'd for: and to be given to the Person that fairly wins it, by the common Rules of Play.
>
> A Saddle of 40s. Value, to be run for, once round the Mile Course, adjacent to this City, by any Horse, Mare or Gelding, carrying Horseman's Weight, and allowing Weight for Inches. A handsome Bridle to be given to the Horse that comes in second. And a good Whip to the Horse that comes in third.
>
> A Pair of Silver Buckles, Value 20s. to be run for by Men, from the College to the Capitol. A Pair of Shoes to be given to him that comes in second. And a Pair of Gloves to the third.
>
> A Pair of Pumps to be danc'd for by Men.
>
> A Handsome Firelock to be exercis'd for; and given to the Person that performs the Manual Exercise best.
>
> A Pig, with his Tail soap'd, to be run after; and to be given to the Person that catches him, and lifts him off the Ground fairly by the Tail.

To the modern sophisticate these may seem but simple rustic amusements; yet in their proper setting of cheering, wagering spectators, contestants competing steamy-breathed in the brisk winter air, and tavern keepers ready with hot drinks and good food, such honest pleasures had much to commend them.

58. The stone base of the bust of Sir Walter Raleigh that was mounted over the tavern door.

59. The reproduced base and bust of Sir Walter Raleigh as visitors to the tavern see it today.

There were, of course, more intellectual entertainments for those who desired them and from time to time visitors to the Raleigh could witness such wonders as a "Microcosm—the World in miniature—an intricate piece of mechanism" or attend a "Lecture upon Heads" complete with "exhibits."

Then there was the theater—the first to open its doors in English America—where the citizens of Williamsburg could watch local talent romping through the *Beaux' Stratagem* or revealing another brand of Virginia ham in the *Tragedy of Cato*. The theater was erected in 1716 by William Levingston who entered into an agreement with a dancing master and his wife, Charles and Mary Stagg (previously Levingston's indentured servants), that together they would obtain a "Patent or a Lycence from ye Governour of Virg^a for ye sole Priviledge of acting Comedies, Drolls or other Kind of Stage Plays within any Part of ye s^d Colony . . ." The chosen lot on Palace Green east of the Governor's Palace was readily granted to Levingston by the trustees of the City at a rent of "one grain of Indian Corn" per annum, and the theater was promptly erected.

In their agreement with Levingston, Charles Stagg and his wife had compacted that they would "not only act in ye s^d Stage Plays (Sickness & other reasonable Accidents excepted) but . . . also use their best Endeavours to teach & instruct others in ye Way & Manner of acting according to ye best of their Skill . . ." It is not hard to imagine Levingston and the Staggs bubbling over with the same excitement that still surrounds the birth of every theatrical venture from a Broadway musical to a women's club skit. Perhaps they had visions of bringing the magical if bawdy atmosphere of Drury Lane to Virginia. But whatever the intention, the outcome was simply that William Levingston took his place in the annals of American theater as the first "angel" to ape the fate of Icarus and plunge into bankruptcy. By 1727, Levingston had sold his theater and left town. Eight years later it was bought by the apothecary, Dr. Gilmer, and during his ownership a few plays were performed there. Then, in 1745, Gilmer disposed of it to the city which remodeled the building and used it as a Hustings Court until its demolition in about 1770.

Very little is known of the appearance of the theater; archaeological digging revealed only fragmentary traces of a foundation measuring eighty-six feet six inches in length and thirty feet in width, a structure quite large enough for a small playhouse. But the only artifacts to be found that had any association with the building were in a pit dug into the clay inside the area of the foundations that was filled with shattered bottles dating from the 1740's, pharmaceutical glass, and broken delftware ointment pots and jars. These were almost certainly relics of Dr. Gilmer's ownership, and one must suppose that shortly before he disposed of it, the building was in such poor shape that his servants had no compunction about burying his trash inside it. The brick foundations were only thirteen and a half inches in thickness (one and a half bricks) and the building was presumably, therefore, of timber resting on brick foundations. Four square holes running in a line down the middle of the center section of the building perhaps indicate that the long auditorium roof was at some time supported by upright timbers.

The documentary clues are even more slight. We have Levingston's agreement with the Staggs that he would "cause to be erected & built at his own proper Costs and Charge in ye City of *W^{ms}burgh* one good substantiall House commodious for acting such Plays as shall be thought fitt to be acted there." In 1724 the Reverend Hugh Jones in his *Present State of Virginia* noted that not far from the public magazine was "a large area for a market place; near which is a play house and good bowling green." In short, beyond proving that the theater was built and in use by 1724 the documents so far discovered tell us nothing. One can only hope that further details may yet be found or that a re-excavation of the site might yield additional evidence, although it is hard to imagine what possible form the latter could take.

Soon after Dr. Gilmer disposed of the first theater, another was built on Waller Street at the east end of Williamsburg beyond the Capitol, and although archaeological evidence is lacking, the records show it to have been a more elegant structure than its predecessor. It opened in 1751, with a production of Shakespeare's *Richard III* presented by a professional cast known as the "Company of Commedians" starring Walter Murray and Thomas Kean. In the prosperous years prior to the Revolution, the second theater was a great success and was regularly attended by "a numerous and polite audience." But when the war ended it seems that the theater had ceased to function, the tinsel and the glitter having been banished along with the gilt and gingerbread of Williamsburg's colonial prosperity.

Although the setting for the colony's make-believe dramas have vanished virtually without trace, the scene of some of its most poignant real-life comedies and tragedies still survives in the shape of the colony's Public Prison in Williamsburg. Just as there had been prisons at Jamestown adjacent to the General Court, so, when the Capitol was erected in the new city, a gaol was one of the first requirements (Fig. 60). An Act of Assembly of 1701 decreed that the building should be of brick measuring thirty feet by twenty feet, with one room on the first floor plus an apartment above for the use of the gaoler, one room upstairs for the confinement of petty offenders and two more below for "Gaols for the Criminals of both Sexes to be underlaid with Timbers under Ground to the Foundations to prevent Undermining . . ." In addition there was to be a twenty-foot-square yard surrounded by a ten-foot wall in which the prisoners could be exercised. The act concluded its list of requirements by stating that the committee overseeing the project should send to England for all necessary materials including iron bars and bolts. In about 1711 the gaol was enlarged to include an annex for debtors. Then in 1722 further alterations were made that entailed the erection of a separate keeper's house. Various other changes occurred during the eighteenth century, but as they are not itemized in the records there is no knowing exactly what they may have comprised. However, it is generally supposed that the principal features remained approximately the same until the Civil War, at which time much of the brickwork went the same way as the Palace advance buildings—loaded on Union carts and hauled out to help build quarters at Fort Magruder. After the war the buildings were patched up and continued to serve as the city jail until the end of the nineteenth century. Part of it still survived when the restoration of Williamsburg began and has been incorporated into the reconstruction whose plan is based on substantial archaeological evidence.

The excavations of 1934 revealed the original outline of the colonial gaol complex with cell plans, yard walls, cesspool vaults, and alterations of various dates. The most interesting of these features were two pits to the west of the yard, brick-walled, and measuring six feet

164

by six feet and descending the same distance into the ground. Both had been filled with rubble comprising bricks, mortar, and burned wood, this last being supposed to be the remains of wooden flooring that had burned. However, there is no record of the buildings being damaged by fire. At a depth of three feet below the present ground surface a human skeleton was found, its head resting on a ledge caused by the falling away of a section of the brick wall. Just how the man came to be buried amid the rubble we shall never know, but some clue as to *when* is provided by twenty brass buttons found with the bones (Fig. 61), one of which was marked with the word GILT. According to the *Encyclopaedia Britannica* gilt-button manufacturing was developed by Mathew Boulton in Birmingham's Soho works in 1767, while William Hone in his *Every-Day Book and Table Book* of 1831 quotes a Birmingham historian, William Hutton, as giving the credit to one John Taylor who died in 1775. I have been unable to discover the date of Taylor's supposed discovery, but it might have been as early as the mid-eighteenth century. On October 3, 1757, the *Boston Gazette and Country Journal* advertised "Best double gilt Regimental Coat and Breast Buttons, and a Variety of a cheaper Kind for the Country Sale . . ." There is no doubt, therefore, that gilt buttons were in production during the third quarter of the century. On the other

60. The restored public gaol at Williamsburg.

hand, the late Mr. W. L. Calver of the New-York Historical Society examined the button from the gaol and on the basis of its mark assumed that it dated no earlier than 1780 and probably not before 1790.

To a person who has no interest in historical or archaeological research the lengthy arguments and profound discussions that have surrounded this one small object over the years seem to confirm their belief that we are ripe for the psychiatric couch. Nonetheless, the date when the gaol skeleton was thrown into the pit was of paramount importance in determining when part of the building was destroyed—and it all hinged (and still does) on a single word on the back of a brass button.

The rubble filling of the square pit continued for a further three feet below the skeleton and terminated on a clay floor, on which were found two pairs of leg irons (Fig. 62), a massive padlock, and an even larger key. An identical pit to the north containing similar rubble also yielded a pair of iron leg shackles. Although the two box-like structures were initially believed to have been subterranean dungeons, there is little doubt that they were actually cesspits—an even more curious place to find a human burial.

Contemporary opinions of the gaol range from a "strong sweet Prison" to "a vile jail," and although much depended on whether you were confined therein or merely passing by, the available evidence shows that it was no sanitarium. In 1738 the colony reimbursed a Williamsburg citizen for the loss of a Negro slave "who being committed for Felony, and thereof acquitted, by a long Confinement in Prison, became so exceedingly Frost-bitten, that a Mortification ensued, whereof he died." Such cases were not uncommon, but even so the gaoler was not permitted to provide blankets, clothing, or access to a fire without a special authorization. In the summer the tortures of the climate were equally unattractive, as a certain Royalist Josias Rogers discovered in 1776. He found that "The vault of the prison was full [presumably one of the three found in excavations beneath the main block] and began to overflow: the weather became intolerably hot, the airhole was small, their food only bullock's lights and water; they were covered with vermin; an inveterate itch broke out among them, and the jailfever began to appear. For the safety of the town it was now thought proper to pay a little more attention to the jail."

166

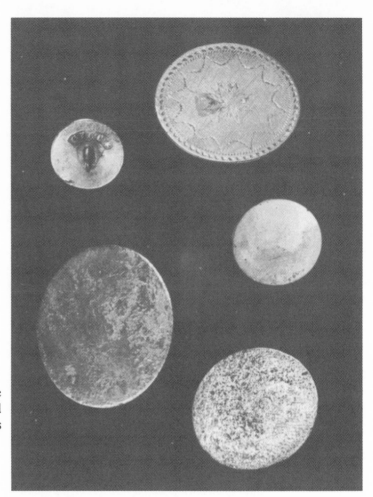

61. Brass buttons from the coat of a skeleton found buried in one of the cesspits at the gaol.

Although the vault was cleaned, and the floors washed with vinegar and strewn with wild mint, it was still no bed of roses when the prison's most famous guest arrived in June 1779.

The much detested British General Henry Hamilton, Governor of the Northwest Territory, was captured and brought to Williamsburg, where he languished in the gaol for more than a year. Known to most supporters of the Revolution as the "Hair Buyer General" because he used Indians to attack non-military objectives, and supposedly paid them for American scalps, his treatment in Williamsburg was deliberately more harsh than a prisoner of his standing ordinarily deserved. His importance to the history of the gaol, however, is not that he suffered in it, but that he subsequently wrote about it and described features that tied in with the archaeological evidence. He described his cell as being a place whose only light was admitted through a grating

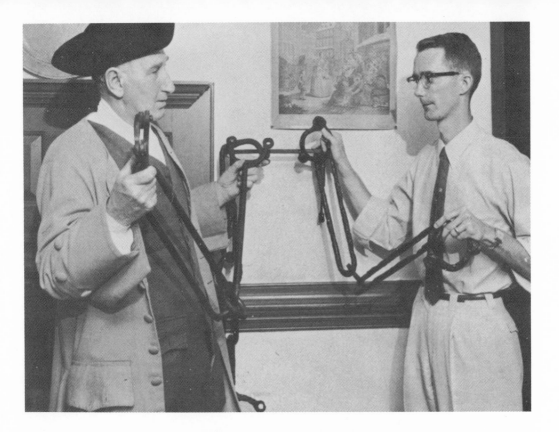

62. Reproductions and original leg irons found at the gaol are
compared in the gaolers' quarters.

in the door. "The light and air were nearly excluded for the bars of
this grating were from three to four inches thick. In one corner of this
snug mansion was fixed a kind of Throne which had been of use to
such miscreants as us for 60 years past, and in certain points of wind
rendered the air truly Mephytic—opposite the door and nearly adjoining the throne was a little skuttle 5 or six inches wide, through
which our Victual was thrust to us." Parts of one of these iron-
clamped wooden toilets were found in the surviving section of the
building and provided evidence for the dimensions of the reconstructed throne, a feature of the gaol whose once germ-laden and
lethal potential is forgotten amid the jokes and merriment that it
evokes from the majority of modern tourists.

A wry humor has always grown fungus-like upon adversity and
grim jests about jails are legion. No doubt the guests residing in the
Williamsburg gaol would have derived some amusement from the
petition of the Rev. William Bland who served as chaplain at the gaol
during the Revolutionary years and who, in 1779, appealed to the

168

House of Delegates for a salary increase. Describing himself as "Ordinary of Newgate," he explained that he suffered heart-rending anguish through being ". . . obliged to be a frequent Spectator of the distresses of those unhappy Persons who are sentenced to die . . . an attendance on those, & the disagreeable necessity of following them from the Prison to the place of execution would wound the feelings of the hardest Heart . . . and has often so deeply affected your Petitioner, that he has frequently determined to resign his Office." He therefore requested that the House should ". . . take his case into their consideration, and grant him such an addition to his salary as their Wisdom shall think meet . . ." It seems that the House did—though the extent of their wisdom is not recorded. More interesting than the Rev. Bland's mealy-mouthed petition is the reference to his title: Ordinary of Newgate. What did it mean?

Bland's petition turned up while I was searching the colonial sources relating to the gaol, and the reference to Newgate seemed to demand an explanation. Recalling that in the early nineteenth century, London's grim Newgate Gaol was often derisively described as "Akerman's hotel" after its gaoler William Akerman, I wondered whether Bland's title suggested any comparable sobriquet. But as an ordinary was a name used to describe not only the proprietor of a public eating house but also a clergyman employed to administer to condemned criminals, that explanation was quickly abandoned. The question still remained, why Bland, chaplain at the gaol in Williamsburg, should have the title of Ordinary of Newgate. Was it to be inferred that this gaol was known in the colony as Newgate? As far as I could discover, there were no other documents to support such a theory. I had long since given up hope of solving the problem when I was reading a dictionary of 1737 in search of something quite different and I came across a description of an ordinary which read: ". . . also the bishop's deputy, who gave criminals their neck-verse to read, as the ordinary of Newgate did not many years since." Now it may be that nine out of ten people know what neck verses were, but I did not. Turning to another page of the same dictionary I learned that they were "a verse or two in a *Latin* book of a *Gothic* black character, which a person convicted of several crimes (especially manslaughter, for which he otherwise should suffer death) was former put to read in open court; and if the ordinary of *Newgate* said, *legit ut Clericus*, i.e. *he reads like a Clerk*, he was only burnt in the hand and set at liberty. But now this practice of reading the neck-verse is quite left off." It was possible then that the title of "ordinary of Newgate" might have been given to any clergyman who read neck verses. If this was correct, one question was replaced by another: was the practice of reading neck verses (which had been abandoned at Newgate prior to 1739) used in Virginia at the time of the Revolution? The answer was that they were not. The ancient law governing Benefit of Clergy (permitting the mitigation of sentences for those able to read) continued in use in Virginia until 1796, although the actual literacy test of reading from the fifty-first psalm had been abandoned in 1732. Thus the neck verse and Newgate association collapses, unless, of course, the title went back to the days when the Virginia General Court did require the verses to be read.

I am fully cognizant of the fact that this line of research has nothing whatever to do with archaeology. Yet it serves as an example of the fascinating uncharted seas that remain to be explored in the world of historical research, and how, once we have embarked, there is no knowing which way the currents of the past will carry us. Every time we start to correlate the archaeology and documentary history of a colonial Virginia site, we hear the voices of the Sirens coaxing us away into new, exciting—and often entirely irrelevant channels.

The gaoler at Williamsburg's Public Prison at the time that the Rev. Bland was doing whatever it was he did, was a certain Peter Pelham who combined his somber profession with that of organist at Bruton Parish Church. Although he was once accused of laxity in the former role, in the latter he was without peers. A visiting merchant who heard him in 1783 wrote: "There's the Church fam'd for its noble Organ of one hundred tones, touch'd by the modern Orpheus—the inimitable Pelham." Fifteen years earlier he had been musical director for the first Williamsburg production of John Gay's *The Beggar's Opera*, which, appropriately for Pelham, was set in Newgate Gaol. By a strange coincidence one of the sets of leg irons found in the Williamsburg prison excavations was identical to those worn by Macheath, the highwayman, in William Hogarth's famous painting of the opera's trial scene.

170

Municipal gaols of the eighteenth century, be they as large as Newgate or as small as that at Williamsburg, were not penitentiaries in the modern sense of the word; their purpose was simply to keep the accused in cold storage until they could be tried and sentenced. Terms of imprisonment were not common in the eighteenth century; instead the felons were "transported" from England to America, or from one colony to another, to work out their sentence. In addition to being temporary quarters for those waiting trial at the General Court, Williamsburg's "Publick Prison" was a repository for runaway slaves or indentured servants waiting to be claimed by their masters, prisoners of war, the mentally deranged, and debtors who remained there until either their debts were paid or their creditors relented. The lengthy sojourns of some unfortunate debtors was almost as much of a headache to the gaolers as the inevitable surfeit of Negroes. In 1772 the first problem was alleviated when an act of the General Assembly decreed that henceforth creditors should pay the full expenses (which were then tripled) of their debtors' imprisonment. It thus became cheaper to let bad debts be bad debts. The Negro problem was less easily solved because each runaway slave belonged to someone and was waiting to be claimed. From time to time owners were glad to be rid of their recalcitrant property and so never came forward to retrieve them; some slaves then languished there until they died of cold or disease. On one occasion in the early days of the Revolution the House of Delegates ordered that all the Negroes then in the gaol should be delivered to a gunpowder manufacturer "for the purpose of making saltpetre," but this was an unprecedented action occasioned by the difficulties of the times.

Punishments in the colonial era were much more severe than they are today; the death penalty was inflicted for a variety of crimes from murder, piracy and treason, to forgery, horse stealing and petty theft. The belief that the fate of miscreants should serve as a warning to others resulted in the infliction of most punishments in public, while some of the lesser penalties were even designed to use public opinion as part of the punishment. In 1705 an Act of Assembly ordered "the Building and Maintaining of Prisons, Pillorys Whipping Posts Stocks and Ducking Stools in Every County." One Virginia county had dutifully supplied all this grim equipment before it discovered to its

171

embarrassment that it had no water deep enough to duck its ducking stool. While documentation is lacking, it is probable that the psychological effect of these devices was no different from that which they enjoyed in England, the less industrious elements of the public looking upon them not as awful warnings but as a form of entertainment with audience participation. It may be that the fun of pelting the occupants of stocks and pillory with rotten vegetables occasioned the Governor's Council to demand, somewhat testily, that "the Pillory and Stocks set up in the Court of the Capitol, be forthwith removed, it being placed there without the direction of any Person having authority for that purpose and in a very unfitt place." There is no archaeological or documentary evidence for the exact position of the reconstructed stocks and pillory in front of the gaol, but there is little doubt that they stood in that general vicinity. Archaeology has played a small part in the reconstruction, in that the massive padlocks that secure them are copied from the one found in the cesspool. In the same way, the two large locks on the gaol gate behind the pillory are reproduced from an example found in the excavations.

Digging in Williamsburg has largely been confined to the heart of the city now know as the Restored Area, but had the excavations continued to the north along Capitol Landing Road, the graves of numerous criminals would probably have been found; for it was there that the colony's principal gallows stood. This structure was undoubtedly of the same pattern as London's celebrated "Tyburn Tree" comprising three vertical posts supporting a horizontal triangular frame which enabled four or five criminals to be neatly suspended from each of the three sides at one and the same time. The *Virginia Almanack* of 1771 laughingly referred to it as "the three cornered tenement on the road to the Capitol Landing." This popular device should not be confused with the vertical post and braced right-angled member, the gibbets on which the bodies of criminals were left to hang in chains as a warning to others. These grim reminders were common sights in England into the early nineteenth century, but we do not know how plentiful they were in colonial Virginia. They were certainly in use in 1700 when three pirates were tried before an admiralty court at Elizabeth City. The men were found guilty and placed in the custody of the sheriff of Queen Anne County who was instructed to "hang the said John Hoogling upon a Gibbett to be erected by you for that purpose up by the Neck till he be dead, dead, dead and there let him remain and hang . . ." The sheriff was further directed to set up two more gibbets "of Ceedar or other lasting wood" on which to suspend the other pirates and to "leave 'em hanging in good strong Chaine or Rope til they rott and fall away . . ." Much later, Mr. Dejean, Justice of the Peace of Detroit, who was confined in the Williamsburg gaol with General Hamilton, was said by the latter to have "had as delicate a sense of danger as either Sancho or Partridge and now Gibbets and wheels presented themselves to his fancy in all their horrors."

More unpleasant than the suspension of the entire criminal was the barbarous penalty for high treason that entailed drawing, hanging, and quartering. The luckless victim was drawn on a hurdle or ox hide to the place of execution, there hanged and let down alive to see his entrails burned before his eyes before his head was cut off and his body quartered. Afterward these five pieces were displayed in selected public places. By the eighteenth century, disemboweling was generally omitted or preceded by beheading, although the penalty in its most horrible form was inflicted in England on the ringleaders of the Jacobite rebellion of 1745. As far as I know there is no documentary evidence that this gruesome sentence was ever imposed in colonial Virginia; yet there is possible archaeological support for it in the shape of a human leg and half a pelvis found down a well at Jamestown (Fig. 63) that had been filled in at the end of the seventeenth century. It is hard to find any other explanation for the presence of a quarter

63. Human bones of a left leg and half a pelvis found in the filling of a well at Jamestown. Perhaps a relic of a colonist executed for high treason.

of a human body in so unseemly a grave. The well lay close to the Jamestown foundation known as the "row house," part of which had been used as a jail prior to 1680 and which was then included in a lease to Phillip Ludwell comprising "the two houses . . . now lyeing in ruins, the One that house where the gaole was kept And the other that next adjoyning . . ." There is good reason to suppose that the buildings had been laid in ruins during Nathaniel Bacon's Rebellion of 1676, an event that resulted in the ringleaders being tried for treason. The records show that Governor Berkeley passed sentences of great severity and it is possible that at least one, perhaps William Drummond (Chapter III, p. 75), was quartered after hanging. If so, the most logical place to display one of the segments would have been outside the ruins of the jail that he had been instrumental in destroying. As the bones were found only four feet from the top of the well, it could be construed that after the row house was destroyed its well became a repository for domestic trash and therefore a fitting place for the rebel leg after it had served its cautionary purpose.

The relics of human conflict seem to hold a greater fascination for the general public than do those of pleasure or industry. As a result, it is much easier to encourage legislators to protect a battlefield from becoming the site for a housing development than it is to do as much for the remains of a colonial residence. I often wonder whether it is really more important to make a shrine out of an empty field where men died, than it is to preserve the places where those same men had spent all except the last day of their existence and where many had made a lifetime of contribution to the emerging greatness of this nation. The fact remains that modern Virginia has raised a fine crop of battlefield (predominantly Civil War) souvenir hunters, but pathetically few serious antiquaries of the caliber of those to be found, say, in the ranks of the New-York Historical Society.

It must be admitted, of course, that battlefields, as such, do not commend themselves to careful archaeological study. They do not, as a rule, pose questions that cannot be answered through documentary research but can be resolved by digging. On the other hand, military camps which were garrisoned and subsequently stormed (or even abandoned) can be extremely rewarding to the archaeologist. Like the cargoes of wrecked ships, they contain objects that ended their life on a known date and are free from contamination by other items that had been thrown away over long periods of habitation.

The only colonial military site in Virginia to have been extensively excavated is at Yorktown where the National Park Service has carefully reconstructed the British defenses around the town as well as those thrown up by the Continental Army during the siege of 1781. In the winter following the battle, troops who remained quartered at Yorktown busied themselves dismantling the siege lines and redoubts, tearing down the earthworks, and filling in the ditches so that the land could again be farmed. The main British defense line, however, being situated so close to the town, was left to slowly erode away during the following century until parts of it were incorporated into the ramparts thrown up during the Civil War.

Although hard to escape from, Yorktown should, by the rules of the game, have been readily defensible, having the natural protection of a creek and marsh to the west and the York river to the north. Only the south and east lay open to an assault in force, and consequently it was in that area that the British defenses were the most substantial. These comprised a main defense line of rampart and ditch with artillery-bearing redoubts spaced along it. Beyond this line to the east, on rising ground commanding both the landward and river approaches to the town, were two separate fortifications—redoubts numbers Nine and Ten. At the commencement of the siege the French troops advanced from the west and then swung to the south to avoid the marsh, leaving only artillery to bear on the western end of the town and on the British shipping in the river. The American troops meanwhile moved in from the east. Together they threw up the first siege line from the river at the east almost to the marsh at the west, and when this was completed, they prepared to move forward to dig in on a second line. Five days later the "second parallel" was established within storming distance of the main British defense line; but instead of reaching to the river as had the first, it was forced to bend back on itself to avoid enfilade fire from the heavily manned redoubts Nine and Ten. Thus these two defensive islands held the key to the gates of Yorktown and, as it turned out, to the success of the Revolution.

The attack on these redoubts was launched under cover of darkness on the night of October 14, the French making the assault on

175

number Nine and the Americans on Ten. Both were taken in less than half an hour of brisk fighting.

Redoubt Nine was a five-sided earthwork with gun platforms at the corners. It was protected all around by fraises (sharpened stakes), a ditch with a smaller ramp of earth beyond it, plus a perimeter defense of trees and brushwood known as an abatis. Count William de Deux-Ponts, who commanded the attack, recalled that "We lost not a moment in reaching the abatis, which being strong and well preserved, at about twenty-five paces from the redoubt, cost us many men, and stopped us for some minutes, but was cleared away with brave determination; we threw ourselves into the ditch at once, and each one sought to break through the fraises, and to mount the parapet." After scaling the earthwork the French were able to increase their fire power, "making terrible havoc among the enemy, who had placed themselves behind a kind of intrenchment of barrels, where they were well massed, and where all our shots told."

The Park Service excavations revealed the outline of the British ditch and yielded numerous small relics of the engagement ranging from gun parts and shoe leather to buckles and buttons, some of these last bearing the insignia of the 18th Regiment of Foot, one of the British units defending the position. Two gun barrels were found in the ditch along with a bayonet and ammunition comprising four eighteen-pound solid shot and one eight-inch mortar shell. The assault had cost fifteen French lives, some of which were probably represented by eight skeletons that were found in the ditch and in the interior of the redoubt. The most informative of the burials was a group of three discovered inside the fortification (Fig. 64); one had two lead shots in the left side of the chest, another had his skull smashed in at the top and left side, perhaps as the result of being clubbed with a musket butt while scaling the parapet. The archaeologist directing the excavation kept a careful record of the positions of the artifacts associated with this skeleton and from it we can obtain some idea of the uniform that the soldier was wearing. Archaeologist Thor Borresen's report includes the following details: ". . . traces of cloth uniform on and around the bones; 10 brass cloth covered buttons down center of chest, four from left side of chest, 3 at each shoulder, 6 at each elbow, 3 at each wrist; an iron buckle below each knee; 2 brass suspender eyes in

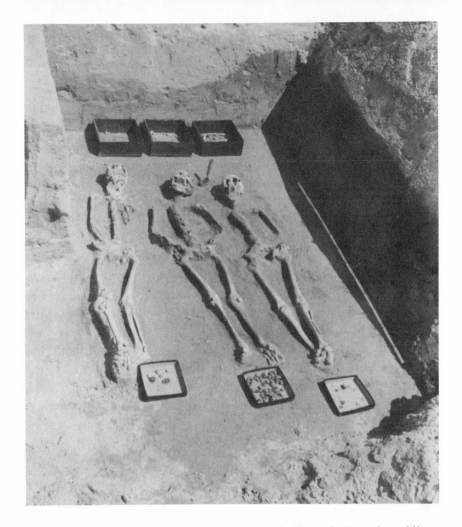

64. Three skeletons, probably of French soldiers, found interred inside redoubt number Nine.

lumbar region." It was to be hoped that a careful study of the placing of the buttons might reveal something about the type of coat the man was wearing. But as far as I can see the only clue that is easily spotted is provided by the groups of six buttons at each elbow which had almost certainly collected there when they fell away from the tops of large pockets just below the waist. But unhappily such pockets were common features of many eighteenth century coats. It is unfortunate that the buttons were cloth-covered and not of ornamental types that would identify the man's regiment. But it seems reasonable to deduce from his injury that he was attacking rather than defending the ground in which he was ultimately buried.

The majority of the objects found on the battlefield were confined

177

to occasional pieces of military hardware and relics of those minor dramas in which exertions not listed in the drill book caused soldiers to pop their buttons. One of the most unusual and certainly the most unexpected item to be found turned up in redoubt number Eight at the northeastern end of the British main defense line. It was a small wooden barrel containing black powder and lead musket balls (Fig. 65). The excavator, Edward B. Jelks, identified it as a budge barrel, a powder container described in *The New World of Words* (1671) as "a little tyn barrell to carry Powder in for fear of fire." A later English dictionary (1749) defines it as "a Tin Barrel to hold Gunpowder, containing about 130 *lb.* having a Purse, or Case of Leather made fast over the Head, to prevent the Powder from taking Fire; used on board of Ships."

Although the barrel was not made of tin, it was bound with brass hoops, indicating that it was deliberately manufactured from components that could not strike a spark and so ignite the contents. Each of the hoops was stamped with the broad arrow that identified it not only as British Government property but also showed that it was not expendable as were ordinary powder barrels. Thus, even though no leather top was found, the budge barrel identification seemed sound. Furthermore, the dictionary reference to such objects being used on

65. A brass-hooped British ammunition barrel containing black powder and musket balls found in the excavation of redoubt number Eight at Yorktown.

178

66. National Park Service reconstruction of the gun deck of the British frigate *Charon*, which uses cannon and other objects recovered from the York River.

ships, coupled with the broad arrow marks, could suggest that the barrel came from a British naval vessel. Taking this reasoning a stage further, it might be tempting to link the barrel with armament that the British commander, Lord Cornwallis, removed from the frigate *Charon* and added to his defensive artillery prior to the siege. The British military authority Mr. Charles Ffoulkes has stated that until the last quarter of the eighteenth century powder for loading cannon was kept in budge barrels, and the fact that the Yorktown example was set upright in the ground would seem to suggest that this was its purpose. A further stab at the validity of the naval connotation is provided by the presence of budge barrels in the inventory of the public arsenal at Middle Plantation in 1685. The fact that the Yorktown barrel also contained musket balls seems to be an inexplicable contradiction. We can only wonder whether the balls may actually have been cannister shot

179

whose container had disintegrated in the course of time after having fallen accidentally into the barrel during the battle.

The discovery of the ammunition barrel in redoubt Eight was an unexpected bonus, for most of the objects made from organic materials had disintegrated. Nevertheless large quantities of wooden relics have come back to us from the battle, not from the earth but from the bed of the York River where they lay in the wrecks of British ships until salvage operations were begun in 1934. This project was jointly sponsored by the National Park Service and the Mariners' Museum at Newport News, the latter providing the divers and equipment. Since that was, of course, some years before the invention of the aqualung, the divers were hampered by the conventional deep sea suits and helmets, but they managed to recover a wide range of objects from ship's timbers to wine bottles that provided useful data concerning the equipment of British vessels.

Before the siege of Yorktown began, Lord Cornwallis was supported by a small fleet comprising four major ships and a miscellaneous collection of transports and other smaller craft lying at anchor in the York River. The principal naval vessels were the forty-four gun *Charon*; a twenty-eight gun frigate, the *Guadeloupe*; another, the *Fowey* of twenty-four guns; plus the sloop *Bonetta* with fourteen guns, and two small fireships, one appropriately named the *Vulcan*. Because it was realized that these vessels were more of a liability than an asset, most of them were removed to the comparative safety of the River's north shore off Gloucester Point where they could usefully command any approach up the York from the sea. On September 21, the *Vulcan* was sent on its combustible way down-river in an abortive attempt to ignite the French vessels lying at the mouth. The allied bombardment began on October 10 and French batteries shelling the *Charon*, still anchored off the Yorktown shore, set it afire along with an indeterminate number of other vessels. A contemporary observer recalled that "The ships were enwrapped in a torrent of flame, which, spreading with vivid brightness among the combustible rigging, and running with amazing rapidity to the tops of the several masts, while all around was thunder and lightning from our numerous cannon and mortars, and in the darkness of the night, presented one of the most sublime and magnificent spectacles which can be imagined." It is not hard to see which side this graphic chronicler supported.

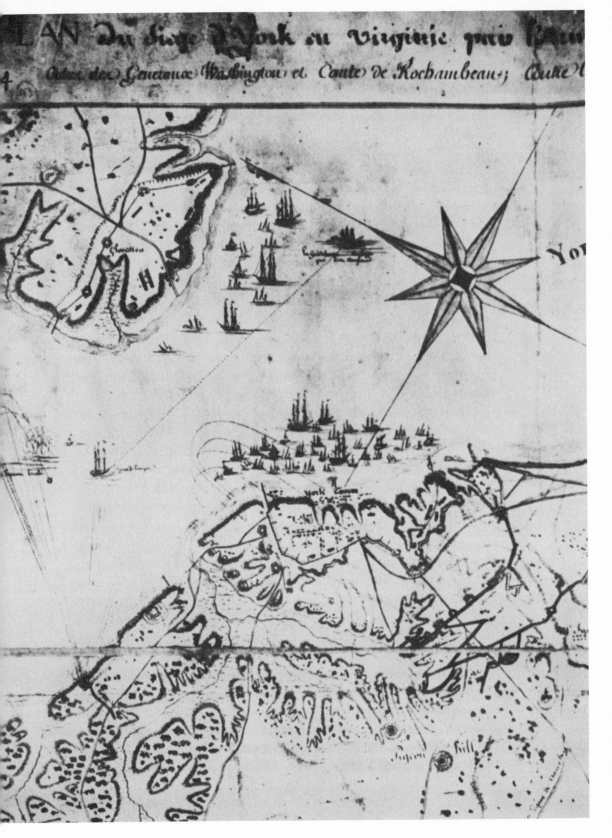

67. A French map of the siege of Yorktown, made in 1781.
It shows the positions of British ships scuttled and sunk in the
York River.

Many small vessels were deliberately sunk by Cornwallis below the town to prevent the French fleet from attacking him from the rear (Fig. 67). He later scuttled the *Guadeloupe* off Gloucester Point and the *Fowey* on the Yorktown side to prevent their falling into American hands. The *Bonetta* became a prize of war as also did some twelve transports and other lesser vessels, but it would seem that the best part of the small British fleet wound up on the bottom of the York River, with considerable variation in the condition of the vessels when they landed there. The French tried to raise the *Guadeloupe*, but we do not know whether they were successful. Then, in the mid-nineteenth century a resident of Gloucester County attempted to salvage some brass cannon that he thought were lying in a wreck that he estimated to be an "English frigate of large class." Although nothing much more was done for nearly a century, during that time oystermen occasionally dredged up old wine bottles which may or may not have come from the wrecks of 1781. Such finds continue to be made today, and Miss Emily Janney of Gloucester has a collection of bottles from the river, one of them of the Revolutionary period adorned with a worn but once handsome seal bearing a stag's head surrounded by an infuriatingly illegible inscription. The fact that old bottles are known to be readily saleable may make it seem that these are the only important objects to be dredged or tonged from the bed of the York River; whereas in truth it is possible that all sorts of objects have been pulled up and many of them thrown back as worthless. I have been able to track down only one ceramic item (Fig. 68), a small Rhenish Westerwald jug ornamented with the initials of George the First or Second, now owned by Mrs. Lloyd Bullock of Richmond, Virginia. When it was found more than thirty years ago it was covered with barnacles and was adhering to a piece of lead, which suggested that it may have come from a wreck—though not necessarily one of Revolutionary date.

In the summer of 1934, dragging operations up and down the York River off both the Yorktown and Gloucester shores pinpointed numerous obstructions which were subsequently investigated by the divers. As a result, two wrecks were found lying close together in mud, both in an advanced stage of disintegration. The mud was pushed away with a fire hose and a large quantity of objects ranging from innumer-

68. Rhenish Westerwald stoneware mug with the cipher of George I or II, dredged up by oystermen from the York River.

able wine bottles (Fig. 69) to barrel staves and mast wedges were found lying close to the keels. In 1935, the scene of operation was moved from the Yorktown shore to comparatively shallow water off Gloucester Point where another wreck was located. From this were recovered several small pieces of ordnance, some bar shot, and a miscellaneous collection of broken pottery and glass. The catalogue of items recovered from the entire salvage operation ranges from six-pound cannon to the head from a barrel of salt pork inscribed "Shaw June 22 '80."

There is no doubt that the divers found wrecks of the Revolutionary period and it may reasonably be presumed that they date from the days of the siege of Yorktown. On the other hand, there is some indication that a few objects of earlier and later date may have become mixed with the material from those wrecks. One has only to walk the shores of the York at very low tides to find artifacts dating from the seventeenth century onward, and as already intimated, it is quite possible that wrecks of other dates as well as trash from ships that anchored in the river are all to be found preserved in the York's muddy treasure chest.

69. Wine bottles salvaged from a British wreck in 1934.

70. An earthenware storage jar, 3 feet high, on the deck of the dredger immediately after recovery from the bed of the York.

In 1954 Chief Warrant Officer Eugene F. Moran, head of the diving section at Fort Eustis, reported that he had located the wrecks of eleven wooden ships on the bed of the river near Yorktown and he claimed that the timbers were well preserved. This revelation did not prompt either the Park Service or the Mariners' Museum to undertake any further investigation. There is, nevertheless, every reason to suppose that the York still holds valuable information and with luck it will keep it until a large scale examination of the wrecks can be made and their relics carefully tabulated and preserved. Fortunately the York is sufficiently muddy to make salvage work far less attractive to treasure-hunting amateurs than is skin-diving for Spanish gold in the comparatively clear waters of the Caribbean.

While the advent of the aqualung made submarine archaeology possible, it also brought with it an army of looters whose only interest is recovering relics that can be sold or admired by their friends. Just as pot hunters are the bane of the terrestrial archaeologist's existence, so the treasure-seeking scuba diver is an anathema to the web-footed historian. Like the Roman city of Pompeii which was suddenly buried in the midst of life, so scores of colonial Virginia merchantmen were cut off and interred just as precipitously. They rest now on the sea bed together with cargoes whose careful study can tell us more about the day to day objects of colonial life than can the artifacts discovered through years of digging on land. It is to be hoped that states whose shores are a playground for divers can see their way to restricting the exploration of wrecks to those professional organizations and institutions that are able to extract and preserve the wealth of information that they contain.

The study and interpretation of artifacts in relation to their environment is the principal reason for an archaeologist's existence, and he uses his clues to build up a picture of past events in much the same way regardless of whether the relics come from beneath sea or soil. A graphic example of this research in relation to the relics of Revolutionary Virginia was provided during the 1930 excavations in the gardens west of the Governor's Palace in Williamsburg where a forgotten cemetery came disconcertingly to light (Fig. 71). In it were a hundred and fifty-eight skeletons, only two of them female. For some reason that has since been forgotten, it was at first believed that the

71. The Revolutionary War cemetery at Williamsburg
in course of excavation.

cemetery was a tragic relic of the Civil War, and it might very well
have been written off as such had it not been for the presence of many
pewter buttons in the graves (Fig. 72). A careful study of these small
and often much decayed objects revealed that some of them bore the
insignia of British regiments, notably the 80th Foot (the Royal Edinburgh Volunteers) and the British Provincials, a colonial force loyal to
the Crown, both of them units in the army of Lord Cornwallis. But
these buttons were only found in association with examples bearing the
initials U.S.A., indicating that the graves were of American soldiers
who had made use of a few British buttons. The fact that the American
specimens were marked "U.S.A." irrefutably associated the cemetery
with the Revolution and not with the War of 1812, for by the latter
date the American general service button bore only the letters "U.S."

Documentary evidence was subsequently produced to show that
the Palace had served as a military hospital following the siege of
Yorktown. Although the war in Virginia was over, the wounded and
sick still had much to endure, not the least of their hardships being their
quarters in the once elegant Governor's Palace. Winter was fast ap-

186

proaching, and in a letter to Governor Nelson, the Quartermaster General confessed that he found "the American sick in a suffering Condition; and I fear it will not be in my Power to yield them adequate Releif—Wood and Straw are most wanted at Present, and the Means of procuring them are hardly attainable . . ." He went on to urge that stoves moved to Richmond should be brought back with all possible speed. The records do not show whether they ever arrived, but if they did, their service was short. Six weeks later fate, with fiery tongue in cheek, decreed that the chill rooms of the Palace should be transformed into an inferno. Fortunately all save one of the soldiers then in the building were able to escape.

The combination of historical and archaeological evidence left little doubt that the Palace cemetery was filled between October and late December of 1781. The identity of the men will probably never be known, although there is a possibility that one particularly large skeleton may be that of Colonel Scammel, Washington's former Adjutant General who was killed at the beginning of the siege of Yorktown. Another of the graves contained not only a series of decayed "U.S.A." buttons, indicating that the man had been buried in his military coat, but also a sleeve button or cuff link set with glass "stones," and a small lead bullet which may have caused his death. One of the men was found to have undergone a trepanning operation (Fig. 73), and it was satisfying to discover that the Williamsburg apothecary, Dr. Galt, was the owner of a set of trepanning instruments and also the official surgeon to the military hospital. The evidence of trepanning was not the only remarkable feature of this last skeleton as we discover from its description in the archaeologist's field notes. "Skeleton No. 151 . . . 1 upper arm bone shows amputation about 3″ below elbow. 1 lower arm bone shows amputation just above wrist. Lower leg bones of both legs show amputation just below knees. However, lower leg bones of both legs were found buried on top of arm bones and back bone. Skeletons Nos. 152 and 153 were found below skeleton No. 151." It is hard to imagine how this extraordinary state of affairs came about, although it is certain that the remains were dumped into the top of an open grave that had already received two, more formal interments. The only possible explanation seems to be that the unfortunate soldier died on the operating table and remained there to become a student surgeon's

187

chopping block. Later, the pieces may have been bundled into a sheet and dumped ignominiously into the nearest open hole.

Although most of the archaeological clues from the Palace cemetery fitted snugly between the pages of documentary history, after thirty years one mystery resolutely remains unsolved—the identity of the two women who lie alongside the hundred and fifty-six men. Were they simply camp followers, as some have suggested, or were they patriotic women of Williamsburg who went to the Palace to nurse the wounded and remained to die, perhaps, of smallpox? It is doubtful that we shall ever know. But the very fact that after all the digging has been done and all the historians have finished their research, questions like this still remain unanswered, reminds us how quickly and easily time eradicates. Thus an event of less than two centuries ago has become just as deep a mystery as any that surround interments that occurred hundreds or thousands of years earlier. When we realize this, the value of archaeology in the study of colonial America can be more readily appreciated.

The excavation of colonial graves, whether they lie in public cemeteries or solitary holes, invariably causes a furor far greater than their archaeological importance. On the one hand, the sensation-seeking elements of the public want to gape at the bones, while, on the other, religious groups and would-be descendants are outraged that the remains should be disturbed. It is pointless to argue that over the years it has been the churches and their sextons who have been the greatest desecrators of graves or to debate the motion that the bones left behind by a departed relative are any more sacred than the legacies that the family was so ready to squabble over before Uncle Charlie was cold in the ground. The fact remains that any attempt to disturb the soil in or around the foundations of a colonial church results in the uncovering of human bones, and this invariably leads to trouble. Immediately the unfortunate archaeologist sets foot in the graveyard he is liable to be looked upon as a reincarnation of Burke, Hare, and Dr. Knox all rolled into one. This is probably one of the reasons very little archaeological research has accompanied the restoration of Virginia's more important colonial parish churches.

The Association for the Preservation of Virginia Antiquities undertook the most careful archaeological work on a church site to date

72. Pewter buttons from the Revolutionary War cemetery at Williamsburg: 1. Continental general service; 2. Rhode Island Regiment; 3. The Royal Edinburgh Volunteers (80th Foot); 4. The Royal Provincials; 5. An unidentified regiment of dragoons.

when they explored the foundations of the seventeenth century church at Jamestown. Although this is undoubtedly one of the most famous of the colonial churches in America, the extent of its archaeological investigation was rivaled by those at one of the smallest and least known. In the summer of 1934, Mr. Joseph W. Geddes excavated around the little brick Episcopal church at Hickory Neck in James City County and gathered a wealth of valuable information that clearly indicates the value of such work. He was able to show that the present structure is merely a small northerly addition to a much larger eighteenth century church that had long-since been destroyed. Excavation revealed most of the foundations of the earlier structure, which was found to have an interior measurement of sixty feet by twenty-six feet, information that was confirmed by the church's vestry book which was fortunately preserved in the library of the Episcopal Seminary at Alexandria, Virginia. In this book were found the original specifications agreed upon by the vestry in December 1733. As they provide an excellent idea of the kind of church that an average eighteenth century Virginia parish could hope to possess, it seems reasonable to quote them in detail. The building was to be:

"... fifteen foot from the flooring of the Pews to the Plate; the flooring of the Pews one foot from the high part of the ground; a compass ceiling [i.e. barrel vaulted, a segment of a circle]; the Aisles to be laid with white Bristol stone; the walls to be three bricks thick up to the water table, and two bricks and a half from the water-table upwards; a Gallery twelve feet long. Six windows in the body of the church; and two in the East end in proportion to the pitch of the walls; the windows to be decked with sashes to be glazed with sash glass and to be hung with leads and pulleys; wainscot shutters and wainscot pews. The front of the pews, pulpit and desk to be quarter-round and raised panels Modillian Eave with plain gable ends: and single Cornice the roof to be covered with plank and shingled on that; the doors and doorcases and window frames to be twice primed, first with Spanish brown and then with white lead; and a Compass alter with rails and banisters and a table and font as usual; to be a complete finished Church ..."

The price: four hundred and twenty pounds.

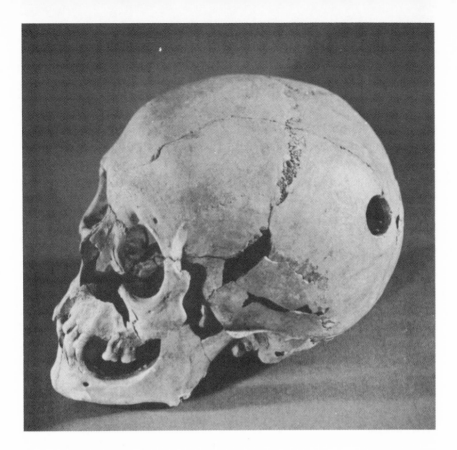

73. Trepanned skull from the hospital cemetery at Williamsburg.

It seems that the vestry had trouble with the builders and the job that should have been completed in one year took five. In 1742 a brick wall was erected around the churchyard, and although no signs of it were to be seen above ground in 1934, the foundations were uncovered in the course of the excavation and proved to enclose an area a hundred feet square. The northerly addition to the church was ordered in 1773 and completed three years later. The date at which the main body of the church was destroyed is not known and apparently the archaeology gave no clue. Yet it is clear that only the 1773 addition was standing in the early nineteenth century, and records show that it became a parish school in 1834 with the imposing name of Hickory Neck Academy. A ten-foot extension was then added to the south overlying the foundations of the main church and old bricks derived from it were reused.

The excavator and architect Joseph Geddes outlined his discoveries and interpretation at the church's bicentennial celebration in 1934 and urged that the original brick building should be reconstructed. But

191

the modern congregation is small and it realized that the rebuilding of the sixty foot church would cost a lot more than the four hundred and twenty pounds of 1733. Consequently the foundations were quietly covered over and discreetly forgotten.

The value of archaeological work on church sites depends, not unnaturally, on what one hopes to learn from it. If, as in the case of the Hickory Neck church, we are looking only for the ground plan of vanished structures, excavation can be eminently informative. But if we hope to be able to determine the date when the church was erected, we are almost certainly destined to be disappointed. Unlike most secular structures where domestic trash is helpfully scattered around, church sites yield little but bones and building rubble, neither of which can be closely dated. There is, of course, always the remote chance that a dated brick might be found and (providing it had not been reused from an earlier building) this would certainly make the digging worthwhile. Evidence of this kind was revealed in the late nineteenth century at St. Luke's Church near Smithfield, Virginia, when a brick was found bearing the date 1632. This was not discovered as a result of archaeology but was dramatically exposed when part of the roof fell in. In any case, it does illustrate the fact that such dated bricks might be found in the course of excavations. St. Luke's, incidentally, is one of the finest examples of seventeenth century church architecture in the United States—regardless of whether or not all the experts are agreed that the 1632 brick gives the true date of construction. It was this church that provided precedent for the style of the church at Jamestown when the latter was reconstructed by the Colonial Dames of America in 1907.

Next to the Jamestown church the most historically important are those that stood at Middle Plantation and in eighteenth century Williamsburg. The surviving Bruton Parish Church has received virtually no archaeological attention and, indeed, none is needed. It was designed in cruciform plan by Governor Spotswood in the winter of 1710 and was in use five years later. This now famous church replaced an earlier brick church erected in 1683 which stood to the northwest of the present building. The foundations of this structure were discovered in 1938 more or less by accident in the course of one of the most bizarre exploits in the history of Virginia archaeology.

In the spring of that year a minor sensation was created by the arrival in Williamsburg of Mrs. Maria Bauer, a well-known philosophical and cryptographic student who claimed that the vicinity of Bruton Church hid the key to the authorship of Shakespeare's plays as well as proof of Francis Bacon's right to the throne of England. She explained to a slightly surprised Vestry that this all came about because Elizabeth the Virgin Queen was not all that she seemed, having secretly married the Earl of Leicester. The son resulting from this union was adopted by Lady Ann and Sir Nicholas Bacon and grew up as Francis Bacon, rightful heir to Elizabeth's throne. It was further explained that Bacon was the father of twins, Mary and Henry Blount, and that when James I set the Stuart line on the throne of England, Henry Blount was sent to Virginia with Bacon's documents and manuscripts in his safekeeping. Blount changed his name to Nathaniel Bacon and later interred the precious papers, sealed in copper cylinders, beneath the foundations of the first brick church in Bruton Parish. This information was derived in part from a book of cryptic poems written in 1635 (forty-eight years before the church was built) and also from the "Shakespeare" plays. As for Shakespeare himself, the citizens of Williamsburg learned that he was one of Elizabeth's lovers and that the false poet and immoral queen were finally united in a single grave. A plan of Bruton churchyard was subsequently published with the tomb of Governor Nott inexplicably marked SHAKESPEARE, a confusion that has since sired a variety of rather astonishing conclusions.

Even if some of their visitor's deductions were a little startling, the Vestry of Bruton Parish broadmindedly agreed to allow an exploratory excavation to be opened up inside the tower of the present church. But when the hole was nine feet deep and nothing had been found, the Vestry very properly decided to quit before the tower settled into it.

Mrs. Bauer had hitherto supposed that the eighteenth century church stood on the same site as the earlier building, but after a careful study of anagrams supposedly hidden in the wording of tombstones in the churchyard she realized that she was wrong. Particularly informative, apparently, was the stone of James Nicolson who died in 1773, for its inscription was cunningly worded to indicate the position of the tower of the first brick church and also that of the vault that held the copper cylinders. A second request for permission to dig was received by the Vestry with diminished enthusiasm and after careful consideration it was refused. Being unwilling to abandon the hunt when such eloquent clues had been provided by the tombstones, Mrs. Bauer proceeded to probe around the churchyard with an iron rod and finally encountered part of the brick foundation of the seventeenth century building. Early one August morning she appeared in the churchyard with a small band of helpers and proceeded to dig herself an unofficial hole. By the time a passing vestryman noticed the flying dirt, the excavators had uncovered part of the north wall and one of the buttresses of the old church. A halt was immediately demanded, but nothing could alter the fact that the church had been found. A few days later, the City of Williamsburg and the Vestry agreed to appropriate sufficient funds to defray the cost of exposing the entire foundation. This was hastily accomplished, but because of the embarrassing publicity surrounding the whole affair, the foundation was just as quickly covered up again.

The building was found to have internal measurements of sixty by twenty-four feet with walls seemingly reinforced outside by five brick buttresses at the north and south (Fig. 35). It seemed, therefore, that the structure was of the Jacobean style adopted by the builders of the Jamestown and Smithfield churches. There was no indication of a tower or of Mrs. Bauer's "Great Virginia Vault." A rough drawing made by the Swiss traveler Franz Ludwig Michel in 1702 provides the only known picture of the building. This shows it to be of brick and covered with slate (?), with Jacobean curvilinear gable ends, three arched windows in the south wall and two more over a door at the west end. Michel showed no tower, nor, for that matter, does he show any of the buttresses whose foundations the excavations clearly proved to have been there. There is a record, however, that the building of "a steeple and a ring of bells" was being considered by the Vestry in 1685. As for the buttresses, we know that the original contractor, George Marable, was replaced in 1681, at which time certain unspecified changes were made in the plan. It is just possible, therefore, that the buttresses might have been omitted even though their foundations were laid.

It is to be hoped that one day it will be possible to re-examine the

194

foundations of the church and its surrounding wall in an attempt to answer some of the many questions that are still not resolved. Unfortunately even now, one has only to stop and read the inscription on a Bruton tombstone for someone to suspect that he is a secret Baconian. So before the church can be archaeologically studied for its own sake, it may be necessary to discover a signed affidavit by Shakespeare that will settle the Bacon controversy once and for all. Failing that, we have no alternative but to suggest that the plays were actually written by Bacon for Richard Burbage who gave the manuscripts to his grandson who fled to Virginia (cleverly changing his name to Burbydge) and passed them to Frederick Jones. Jones, in turn, took them to North Carolina and there sold them to a ship's captain bound for London. While the Baconian students are chasing this hare, a future archaeologist may, perhaps, be able to do some careful work on the early Bruton Church—unless it is discovered too soon that the ship's captain got no further than Yorktown.

VIII

How Doth the Little Busy Bee?

ONE OF THE principal thoughts in the minds of the shareholders in the Virginia Company was that they should obtain a profit on their investment. Most of them doubtless expected to see a speedy return in the form of gold, but failing that, the profit could be acquired the hard way—by shipping home timber, and any other natural resources that the colony might offer. Early in 1608 the first samples of ships' masts and clapboard were shipped to England along with a barrel of "Gould oare" which, to everyone's embarrassment, turned out to be iron pyrites. This unhappy experience was but a foretaste of the disappointments that the Company's stockholders were to suffer throughout its life. As every smoker knows, Virginia was destined to yield only one profitable commodity, and once this potential was realized all ideas of even encouraging other enterprises quickly dwindled. Indeed, in the eighteenth century the English Board of Trade took

196

the opposite view to the old Virginia Company, seeing the colony as a market for British exports rather than as a source of varied and useful imports. As a result of this policy Virginia never developed any worthwhile industries and consequently the archaeological record is slim.

In the fall of 1608, Captain Christopher Newport arrived at Jamestown with the Second Supply, bringing with him a group of carefully chosen artisans and craftsmen among whom were a group of eight "Dutchmen and Poles," the former almost certainly being Germans rather than natives of Holland. Some of the eight were glassmakers and when Newport returned to England late in the year, he took with him "tryals of pitch, tarre, glasse, frankencense and sope ashes, with what clapboard and wainscot could bee provided." The craftsmen, it seems, were new brooms who swept comparatively clean; the ability to set up a glass factory and to produce a "tryal" of glass before Newport sailed for home was no mean feat.

Considering the uncertain temper of the local Indians, the site chosen for the glasshouse "in the woods neare a myle from James Towne" would seem to have been a little foolhardy. Nevertheless, the workers built themselves a "goodly howse . . . with all offices and furnaces thereto belonging" and in the spring of 1609 they produced another test sampling. What they had been doing all winter is not recorded, but it is quite possible that they were kept busy preparing their raw materials and manufacturing the clay siege pots in which the components were melted together in the furnace. It would be nice to be able to add that after the completion of the spring "tryal" the glassmakers went on to make bottles and glasses that rivaled the best products of Europe. But the sad truth is that there is no evidence that they did anything beyond turning up at a convenient moment one day while John Smith was being attacked by Indians near the glasshouse. On "perceiving two of the Poles" the Indians took to their heels and thus enabled the two glassmen to leave their inadvertent mark on a page of history.

The winter of 1609 brought with it the horrors of "The Starving Time" when hopes for most of the colony's projects were buried along with the majority of its settlers. Nothing more was heard of the Poles or their glasshouse. In England table and window glass were becoming increasingly important commodities and the first quarter

197

of the seventeenth century saw a vigorous scramble for patents whereby single companies could obtain monopolies on the entire industry. In 1621, when the English glass business was in the hands of a company headed by Sir Edward Zouche, an enterprising gentleman named William Norton applied to the Virginia Company for a similar patent to "make all manner of Beads and Glasse" in the colony. The patent was granted and Norton set sail for Virginia with a gang of six Italian glassmakers and a letter commending him to the council at Jamestown. The letter urged that the "Glass Worke" should be established "neare some well inhabited Place, that neither his Gange be subject to Surprise, nor the Commodities of Glasse and Beads be vilified by too common a Sale to the *Indians*." As it turned out the Virginia Company need not have bothered itself about the sale of the products, for it is highly likely that there never were any.

Everything that could go wrong did so; a storm blew the glasshouse down, the Indian massacre of 1622 temporarily closed it, Norton died, and the Italian glassmakers fell sick and wanted to go home. The Virginia Company treasurer in the colony took over the management of the factory and tried to get production under way. But the Italians made one excuse after another "that they might by that Meanes be dismissed for *England*." Treasurer George Sandys was not a man to give up easily, and when the Italians explained that they could not mix their glass because the sand would not run, he sent to England for a supply of sand that would do so. In 1624, the year that the Virginia Company lost its charter and Virginia became a Crown Colony, Sandys gave up the struggle, and America's first glass industry was abandoned.

The land on which the glasshouse stood was situated at the western end of the narrow neck joining Jamestown "Island" to the mainland. A quarter of a century after the factory closed its metaphorical doors, the site was still known as "the Glass house" and the headland was later named "Glass House Point." It remained so when Mr. Jesse Dimmick (the owner and first excavator of Green Spring) obtained the property. In 1931 he was exploring the heavily overgrown promontory when he came upon stones and lumps of vitrified slag. Thus encouraged, he undertook limited excavations on the site and uncovered the remains of three furnace-like structures as well as

74. The Jamestown glassmaking complex in course of excavation in 1948. The main furnace is in right background.

fragments of siege pots with traces of glass still adhering to them. Realizing that here was a discovery of major importance Dimmick reburied the structures and erected a protective fence around them.

It was not until 1948 that any further work was undertaken on the site, this time under the aegis of the National Park Service and the direction of J. C. Harrington. The entire site was carefully excavated (Fig. 74), not only for the purpose of studying the structures but also in the hope that examples of the products would be recovered. As the latter were expected to include small glass beads it was essential that every ounce of soil be painstakingly examined. But when all was done, not one bead had been found, nor had a sufficiently large fragment of glass been unearthed to indicate the shape of any vessel. It is true that a heap of glass fragments was found to the south of the furnaces, but this was undoubtedly cullet (waste glass) that was added in the mix to basic ingredients of sand, lime, soda, and potash. Many of the pieces were typical bits of glasshouse debris, runs, trails, and drops,

199

with at least one piece bearing the marks of the pincers that had gripped it.

Cullet could be obtained either from old household glass or, when a factory had been in operation for some time, from its own waste. The heap of pieces found by Harrington perhaps came from the latter source, and it could be construed as evidence that the Jamestown glasshouse had been at work long enough to produce its own cullet. On the other hand, it could equally well be argued that knowing that glass would be extremely scarce in the young colony, the glassmakers brought a supply of factory cullet with them.

Before trying to deduce what the Jamestown glassmakers did or did not make, it is necessary to take a look at the furnaces and see what clues can be extracted from them. The largest was almost circular in plan and had a diameter of about nine feet; this had presumably been the main working furnace that contained the siege pots filled with the precious molten glass. The domed roof was probably built from boulders packed around with clay and had ports or working holes above the pots. Through these the blowers would insert their rods and extract the gathering of molten glass to be blown. The ports were framed with a pottery ring having a square or rectangular exterior edge, and fragments of these were found in the excavations.

To the south of the working furnace were two smaller furnaces set back to back, and these Harrington has identified as fritting and annealing furnaces respectively. The first was used for the preliminary fusing of the ingredients, while the second served to provide the slow cooling process that was necessary to prevent the finished products from shattering. Yet another furnace lay to the east of the group and this Harrington believed was used to bake newly made siege pots. The only other significant features were a barrel-lined well and a rectangular pit north of the main furnace which had probably been dug to obtain clay for constructing or repairing the furnaces. The fact that this hole was lined with furnace debris indicates that it was dug after at least one furnace had been dismantled. That evidence was used in J. C. Harrington's published report on the site to support the belief that the furnaces as found were relics of the second glassmaking venture and that the same site served both factories. It could, of course, be argued that in the period 1621-24 the furnaces must have been

75. The Jamestown glasshouse as reconstructed in 1957.

taken apart more than once, and consequently the fragments in the clay pit could just as well have come from a furnace built in 1621 and reconstructed in, say, 1623.

Evidence supporting the belief that the furnaces belong to the second factory is provided by the presence of bricks in the flooring of both the annealing oven and the siege pot kiln. Even though the first colonists included four bricklayers, it is unlikely that the glassmakers of 1608 would have brought bricks over with them aboard the Second Supply and even less probable that the colonists were making their own bricks at that early date. But by 1621 it is quite likely that bricks were in use for chimneys and foundations even though no actual brick buildings yet existed.

The appearance of the glass factory, be it first or second, is hard to determine. Archaeological evidence points to a working area measuring approximately thirty-seven by fifty feet, but gives no indication of the structure erected over it. No post holes were found nor were any pier bases or other traces of foundations; in short, there was not a

201

sign of the "goodly howse" built in 1608 or of the structure recorded as having blown down in 1621. There can be no doubting that the furnaces were covered by some kind of structure, and that most simple and obvious variety would have been supported on posts driven into the ground. But if that were so, it is strange that the working floor survived and that the holes in which the posts were seated did not. There is archaeological evidence that the site was robbed of some of its useful debris a few years after the factory closed down. Laid in the bottom of a kiln or furnace found in Jamestown itself were pieces of glazed stones similar to those used at the glasshouse, while a nearby refuse pit contained fragments of old glassmaking siege pots, one fragment of which joined to another actually recovered on the glasshouse site. Such evidence permits only one interpretation, and it can be used to suggest that anything worth salvaging from the glasshouse was carried off. But you cannot carry away a hole in the ground, and so we must assume that the glasshouse structure was erected on a frame laid on the surface of the land and not on posts driven into it.

In considering the slender evidence of the glass found in the vicinity of the factory, we must first recall that the two projects were manned by glassmakers of different nationalities with backgrounds of entirely different manufacturing traditions. The Poles or Germans manufactured a rough and ready green glass known as "waldglas" or forest glass. This metal (the term used to differentiate between the substance and the vessel) was suitable for making bottles (Fig. 76), beakers, simple ale glasses, urinals, linen smoothers, and window glass, but very little else. It was the type of glass that was made in England in the fifteenth and sixteenth centuries by emigrant Flemish and Lorraine workers, notably in the Weald of the counties of Surrey and Sussex. I have myself excavated quantities of rich green cullet from one of the later of these sites, Sidney Wood in Surrey, and a comparison with the cullet from Jamestown shows that they are visually almost identical. If the cullet found at the Jamestown factory was actually produced there, we can reasonably assume that the products were similar to those manufactured in the waldglas glasshouses of England.

If the Jamestown factory is believed to be that of the first and not of the second venture, the presence of the green cullet would be exactly what you would expect. But the second venture was manned

76. Small glass medicine bottles found in London, but of types that might have been attempted at the Jamestown glasshouse.

by Italians, presumably originally from Murano or emigrants from Antwerp, and these men were specialists in the manufacture of a clear crystal metal that could be worked into magnificent forms and ornamented in a wide variety of techniques. In addition, the Italians were masters in the making of multicolored beads, a craft which, though plied in various European countries, was traditionally Venetian. For such men to be content to turn out the coarse green forest glass would have been unthinkable. We may wonder, therefore, whether they found that the available ingredients would not make "cristallo," and that was why they were so unhappy in Virginia. If this is not the answer, then the presence of the green waste in the *second* factory is hard to explain.

It was to be hoped that a study of glass fragments found in early contexts at Jamestown might have provided clues to the nature of the local products. There might, for example, have been a group of glasses whose metal or style of manufacture would have been different from those of England, the Netherlands, or Venice, in which case they might have been the product of a colonial glassmaker working with materials and under conditions that were new to him. But as far as I can discover there is only one fragment that might belong in such a

203

category; it is a glass of reasonably good workmanship though made from a pale green metal. Unhappily, we cannot develop a thesis on the evidence of one fragment any more than you can build a castle with one brick.

The well-beloved and long-established belief that beads were made in great quantities at Jamestown vanished like a phantom at dawn as soon as Harrington's glasshouse excavations were completed. In the seventeenth century most beads were made by drawing out long tubes of glass some ten feet or so in length, breaking the tubes into manageable lengths of about a foot, and then chopping the resulting rods into bead lengths with a heavy axe-like knife held in the palm of the hand. The sharp-edged beads were then placed in a barrel with a quantity of sand and tumbled over and over until the sand ground away all the rough edges. According to Professor John M. Goggin of the University of Florida, America's foremost bead authority, the sand-eroded surfaces of the beads were then repolished by tumbling them in a drum of wheat husks. Had all these operations been conducted at the Jamestown glasshouse it would have been extremely unlikely that neither tubing fragments nor beads, rough or smooth, would have been left behind on the site. There is, of course, no denying that large quantities of beads have been found at Jamestown, most of them by visitors in the early part of the century who would pick them up on the rapidly eroding foreshore. But most of these were of complicated "millefiori" designs—made from rods of different colors fused together to create striped and zigzag patterns, techniques that were quite beyond the apparent capabilities of the Jamestown glass factory. Until evidence to the contrary is forthcoming, the beads from Jamestown must be dismissed as imports intended to ornament the colonists' wives and, more important, to be used in trading with the Indians.

The third glassmaking venture in Virginia would seem to have been undertaken on Governor Berkeley's plantation at Green Spring (see Chapter VI, p. 144), where the evidence is entirely archaeological. The recovery of a small glass-lined brick trough is the sole clue to an enterprise of great interest but uncertain purpose. As previously mentioned, two of the bricks are helpfully scored with the date "Aug. 6, 1666" (Fig. 50), which in itself is somewhat curious. Initials and dates were often scratched on bricks and tiles while drying in the sun before firing. But this was generally a one shot amusement and would not have been repeated over and over. Bricks are also found with similar inscriptions incised after firing, these often being the work of a brick-layer who left his name and date on a completed building. Here again, one marked brick would be enough. According to a report in the *Richmond Times-Dispatch* on May 16, 1948, a small glass furnace was found, each brick being intact and bearing the initials "H.A.L." as well as the date mentioned above. My own inquiries into the matter have come up with only two marked bricks, both part of the small brick trough which is currently in the safekeeping of National Park Service curator J. Paul Hudson, at Jamestown. The trough is not itself a fur-nace, although it might perhaps have been a permanently installed container for molten glass inside the furnace. Even this theory seems improbable as it appears unlikely that the bricks would have with-stood the intense heat for very long. Furthermore, minerals in the bricks would have been absorbed into the glass and would have had a somewhat unpredictable effect on its quality. Nevertheless, once-molten glass lies in the trough and its color is a rich bottle green.

Assuming that the date on the bricks is a valid clue to the period in which glass was being made at Green Spring, it is worth recalling that the simple tall-necked glass wine bottle had appeared on the English scene around 1650 (see Chapter X, p. 268) and had quickly achieved great popularity. There is evidence that such bottles were in use in Virginia as early as about 1651. In the early 1660's, Sir William Berkeley was in England and he doubtless talked with many people who were having their wines stored in bottles made to their own order. In 1663 Berkeley was making his own wine from grapes grown at Green Spring, and in that year he offered to send a friend "a Hogs-head of Virginia wine," adding that the previous year's grapes had yielded a wine "as good of my own planting as ever came out of Italy." Recalling the previous glassmaking ventures at Jamestown, it is quite possible that Berkeley tried to make bottles in which to put his wine. Such enterprise would be quite in character with a man who not only grew his own grapes but who also manufactured pottery and potash, experimented with making silk, raised crops of flax and rice (as well as tobacco) and whose orchards sported "Apricocks, Peaches, Melli-cotons, Quinces, Wardens, and such like fruits."

205

There were glasshouses in New Amsterdam, probably making bottles, in the 1660's, so why not in Virginia? Reasonable though the theory might be, it will remain without substance until the Green Spring "furnace" site is excavated and sufficient fragments are recovered to identify what, if anything, was made there. Almost exactly a century later another enterprising plantation owner and merchant, John Mercer, advertised in the *Virginia Gazette* of April 18, 1766, that if he met with sufficient encouragement he proposed the "fitting up of a glass house for making bottles, and to provide the proper vessels to deliver to such customers as favour me with their orders such liquors as they direct, at the several landings they desire . . ." The site of Mercer's home plantation at Marlborough in Stafford County was partially excavated in 1956 under the direction of Mr. Frank M. Setzler and Mr. C. Malcolm Watkins, of the Smithsonian Institution, but no sign of a glasshouse came to light. Perhaps the necessary encouragement was not forthcoming.

The story of Virginia's early manufacturing ventures ends most chapters on a note of lost enthusiasm. Time and again fine schemes would be thought up and even embarked upon, only to halt as soon as the main spring of initial optimism ran down. It may be that this is an unfair picture based simply on ignorance. Documentary sources in the seventeenth century are few and far between, and archaeological evidence is confined to a few principal sites such as Jamestown, Green Spring, and Kecoughtan. A small number of industrial sites are known, but have not been excavated, the most important being the early ironworks at Falling Creek.

In the eighteenth century, next to tobacco growing, ironworking was potentially Virginia's most successful commercial enterprise. Governor Spotswood, who was the official representative of both the king and the Lords of Trade and Plantations, was also one of the leading lights in the establishment of ironworking in Virginia—a project that would not have gladdened the hearts of either the king or the Lords of T and P, who automatically assumed that any such project would be injurious to the trade of Great Britain. Nevertheless, in 1714, forty German ironworkers were imported into the colony by the Governor and set up in business at a settlement specially built for them on the Rappahannock and appropriately named Germanna. He set up another furnace at Massaponax near Fredericksburg and a third thirty miles to the southwest at Fredericksville. This last was a major enterprise that employed up to a hundred slaves and used a twenty-six foot waterwheel to pump the bellows. Yet another, also near Fredericksburg, was in operation by 1726 at Accokeek Run on land owned by George Washington's father, Augustine.

As the eighteenth century progressed, the Board of Trade became conscious of the fact that England needed all the iron she could get. Consequently restrictions on the colonists were relaxed and in 1750 an act was passed to enable pig iron to be imported into England from the colonies free of duty. Virginians did not grasp the opportunity as boldly as they might, and it fell to the Germans in Pennsylvania to build up the iron industry that was destined to play such an important role in the years of the Revolution.

The Virginia iron furnaces were principally concerned with the production of pig iron for export; but they also produced a small quantity of cast items for the local market ranging from firebacks and nave boxes for carts, to fenders, pots, mortars, and "rollers for gardners." As none of the furnace sites have been excavated, we have no yardstick whereby to identify such objects, when they turn up elsewhere, as coming from Virginia foundries. Possible exceptions are provided by a couple of fragmentary iron firebacks in Colonial Williamsburg's archaeological collections. One of these bears the apparently helpful legend VIR[Gᴬ] 173 . . . [or 172 . . .], while the other, found near the President's House at the College of William and Mary, is elaborately molded with a scallop shell, dolphins, draperies, fleur-de-lis, and garlands, all providing a setting for a handsome female bust (Fig. 77). The latter motif has been described as "obviously in honor or memory of one of England's queens," but with her spiked radiate crown, flowing locks, and revealing drapery it is hard to imagine this bust doing much honor to any English queen since Boadicea. The bust is, however, very like the so-called "Indian Queen" crest of the Virginia colony. Thus, although the elaborate border is closely akin to a well-known class of firebacks found in England and the Netherlands, there is a good possibility that the Williamsburg example is a product of a Virginia ironworks.

Unfortunately, such helpfully and conveniently marked items, be they of iron or any other material, are almost as rare as feathers on a fish. An important addition to this select group of rarities was provided by the discovery of a pewter spoon handle (Fig. 78) found in the vicinity of one of Jamestown's lesser cottages, and stamped with the pewterer's mark of a heart surrounded by the legend IOSEPH COPELAND 1675 CHUCKATUCK. Chuckatuck was, and still is, a small settlement in Nansemond County from which Joseph Copeland moved to Jamestown to become caretaker of the fourth State House in the period 1688 to 1691. We do not know whether Copeland abandoned his trade as a pewterer when he moved to Jamestown or whether he continued it there, using his original touch (stamp); but in any case his spoon remains as the earliest example of American pewter so far discovered.

There were, of course, many manufacturing enterprises that were established to fill a specific need and then abandoned. Among these were such crafts as brickmaking and lime-burning which would be set up on the site where a building was to be constructed. But these do not really belong in the same category as such sustained crafts as pewtering, brass founding, ironworking, goldsmithing, cabinetmaking, or potting. The last of these was an art that could have been of major importance in colonial Virginia, and in the past five years evidence has slowly been building up to suggest that it may have been of greater significance than the skimpy records would have us believe.

There seems to be only one known reference to potting in early seventeenth century Virginia and that appears in Captain Nathaniel Butler's derogatory *The Unmasked face of our Colony in Virginia, as it was in the Winter of the yeare 1622*. In it he noted that ". . . the Iron Workes were utterly wasted and the men dead, the Furnaces for Glass and Potts at a stay and in a smale hope." In the following year the Virginia Company angrily published a rebuttal, replying to Butler's points one by one but omitting any comment on the "Furnaces for Glass and Pots." The Butler reference has since been misquoted to read "furnaces for glass and pottery are in decay," which may not mean the same thing at all; for it is conceivable that the word "pots" might refer to siege pots for melting glass and not to domestic wares. In 1620, two years before Butler passed through the colony, the Virginia Company had prepared a list of "The severall Tradesmen to be entertained" and shipped out, among whom were an unspec-

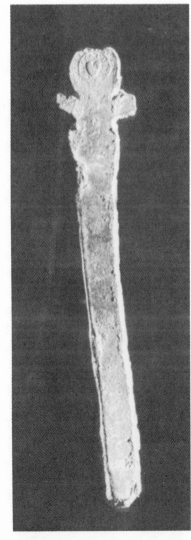

77. An iron fireback found at the President's House at the College of William and Mary, Williamsburg. Decorated with a bust resembling the "Indian Queen" crest of the Virginia Colony. Possibly a product of an 18th-century Virginia ironworks.

78. The earliest known example of American-made pewter, a spoon handle dated 1675, bearing the touch of Joseph Copeland of Chuckatuck.

ified number of potters. But unfortunately there is no knowing whether they were available or when, if ever, they arrived at Jamestown.

A generation later, in August 1677, we find another tantalizing reference, this time in the *Westmoreland County records* in which is tabled an article of agreement between Dennis Whit (or White) and Morgan Jones. It begins as follows:

"Know all men by these pnts y^t I Dennis Whit of Westmeland County & Morgan Jones have made a condicon or an aggreement for to be copartners for ye term of five yeares in making and selling of Earthen warre & ye said Dennis White is to finde three men dureing ye said terme to helpe[.] ye s^d Dennis White is to have one halfe of ye pduce what shall be made of the earthen ware . . ."

On the face of it, this seems a sound piece of evidence to show that the firm of White and Jones was in business in the late 1670's. But it really proves nothing. We have no proof that either man was a trained potter; it is possible that they were relying on finding the necessary skills in their three hired hands and that the partners were merely providing the land, the clay, and the money. Equally possible is the likelihood that the business never got off the paper. Consequently, until their kiln site is discovered and Messrs. White and Jones's industry is vindicated, we have an agreement, but nothing more.

Robert Beverley's *History and Present State of Virginia* published in 1705 repeatedly referred to the indigence of the colonists, yet stressed with enthusiasm the potential resources of the country. "There is likewise found great Variety of Earths," wrote Beverley, "for Physick, Cleansing, Scouring, and making all Sorts of Potters-Ware; such as Antimony, Talk, yellow red Oker, Fullers-Earth, Pipe-Clay, and other fat and fine Clays, Marle, &c. In a Word, there are all kinds of Earth fit for Use." Had there been potters at work in Virginia in 1705, it could be argued that Beverley would have taken pride in recording the fact. On the other hand, it is possible that he knew of such industry but said nothing about it for fear of arousing the wrath of the English Board of Trade. The emergence of a local potting industry might have been construed as a threat to the export trades of the potters of Bideford, Bristol, and Staffordshire. One fact, however, cannot be disputed—much of the local Tidewater Virginia clay was well suited for making "Potters-Ware," and it continues to be so today.

The first indication of the existence of a potter in Virginia in the seventeenth century was found in excavations at Jamestown where traces of three furnaces or kilns of uncertain purpose were found. In their vicinity was recovered a large quantity of broken roofing tiles, some of them bearing semi-circular marks where pots had stood on them in a kiln, and others with actual rim fragments of the vessels adhering to them. On this evidence it was assumed that at least two out of the three ovens had been used in the firing of earthenwares in the period 1625-50. There were, however, no piles of "wasters" (improperly fired pottery) nor, indeed, even a single true waster other than the two or three sherds stuck to the tiles. From such evidence we would have to believe that here was a paragon among potters, a man whose kiln never overfired or underfired, whose pots never split or fell over in the burning, and whose kiln roof never dripped into the vessels that it contained. It is a well-known fact that a wood-firing kiln rarely burns evenly and consequently there are always waste products. Their absence from the Jamestown "kilns" is extremely suspicious to say the very least. Indeed, it could perfectly well be argued that the tiles (with their red-herring clues attached) had been brought in from a kiln site outside the town and reused as paving materials. In support of this belief, we may point to the fact that one of the kilns contained a glazed stone identified as having come from the glasshouse site a mile or more from town.

Another supposed pottery kiln had been found at Jamestown in 1935 lying close to the river and it had first been identified as a flight of steps. In re-examining the earlier findings, John Cotter, in his report on Jamestown excavations, correctly identified the structure as a heating device. On the evidence of four glazed fragments of tile and part of a misshapen tobacco pipe, he went further and declared it to have been a pottery kiln. Although he admitted that there were no wasters in the vicinity of the kiln, he added that there was a "fair variety" of coarse earthenware in the general area, some of it of local manufacture. The greatest emphasis was placed on the fragments of brown clay pipe which at one point are labeled as "obviously a waster" and later on, with less certainty as a "probable clay pipe waster." There is little doubt that brown (as opposed to white) pipes were of local manu-

79. Earthenware storage jar of a type made in or near Jamestown in the mid-17th century.

facture, but it demands more than one warped example to identify that Jamestown locale as their place of manufacture. Nevertheless, there is documentary evidence to support the belief that tobacco pipe makers were among the early artisans to arrive at Jamestown. That fount of sometimes dubious information, Captain John Smith, complained in his *Advertisements: or The Path-way to Experience to erect a Plantation* that the aim of the financiers of the Virginia Company "was nothing but present profit, as most plainly appeared, by sending us so many Refiners, Gold-smiths, Iewellers, Lapidaries, Stone-cutters, Tobacco-pipe-makers, Imbroderers, Perfumers, Silke-men, with all their appurtenances but materialls . . ."

The local yellow Tidewater clay contains flecks of red ocher (iron) that remain in the body when it is fired at earthenware temperatures and can be seen as large and small grains of red, thus making this clay easily identifiable. It has been tempting, therefore, to identify any wares made from this clay as emanating from the kilns of Jamestown; indeed, such claims have appeared on the pages of distinguished journals and so created considerable confusion. There is no denying, however, that lead-glazed earthenwares were made in the colony in

212

the mid-seventeenth century (Fig. 79) and that there was more than one potter at work. The quality of the products runs the gamut from miserable to sheer delight, from hideous double-handled jars to jugs possessing all the elegant styling of the ancient world. But whether any of these vessels were actually made within the confines of "James Towne" still remains in doubt. Wasters have been found there but just to be difficult, as far as I can discover, none of them hail from the vicinity of the supposed kilns. The most obvious and dramatic of them was an overfired jar with a badly warped rim (Fig. 80) that was found in the upper filling of a well near the river. The well had been filled with refuse in the late seventeenth or early eighteenth century, thus making the waster considerably later than the supposed dates of operation of the Jamestown kilns. An examination of the many potsherds from the well's filling showed that they included numerous lead-glazed pan fragments made from the local clay. The waster jar, on the other hand, was so highly fired that it showed no tell-tale flecks of red ocher. Part of the rim was missing, as was most of the bottom, and it was not possible to determine whether both losses resulted from the pot's unhappy experience in the kiln. The more adventurous writers on Jamestown claimed this vessel as a product of one of the town's seventeenth century kilns, but John Cotter was more cautious, agreeing that it was an undoubted waster, but wisely resisting

80. A waster jar made by the Challis site potter. Found in the early 18th century filling of a well at Jamestown.

the temptation to claim it for Jamestown; although in all reasonableness, it could hardly be suggested that such a wretched pot could have been carried to Jamestown from a site elsewhere.

The jar sat mutely on its shelf for twenty years wearing a perpetually twisted grin, doubtless enjoying the fact that it was at once so obvious a clue and yet so deep a mystery. When, eventually, its origin was discovered, the answer was found not through brilliant Sherlock Holmesian deductions, but through a combination of improbable coincidences.

It so happened that in the summer of 1961, my wife and I gave up spending our hours of relaxation on a beach on the Surry shore of the James River and sought a quiet spot on the north bank where the fishing seemed better. The chosen beach lay beneath a somewhat dangerously eroding cliff approximately three miles up-river from Jamestown. One day while beaching the boat, my wife looked down and saw a fragment of an eighteenth century German stoneware tankard lying on the shore. As a result of this small discovery I began to amuse myself walking along the shore picking up any fragments of pottery that could be found. A close examination of the sherds showed that the majority were of local manufacture and a high proportion showed minor waster characteristics. On the strength of these finds a more serious examination of the shore line was made. Some skin diving in the river offshore at the points of the pottery's greatest concentration resulted in the recovery of further wasters and the location of bricks and tiles lying in the river mud. A concentration of twenty or so nine-inch square flooring tiles included one bearing an incised inscription that seemed to read "Amy Onimond 173–" or "Any Drumond 173–." Although the latter was certainly the most reasonable (particularly as the Drummond plantation extended to within half a mile of the point where the tile was found), the long-dead scribe was affectionately known to us as Amy Onimond. Consequently I experienced a sense of personal loss when my wife, while studying the lists of Governor Fauquier's effects disposed of after his death in 1768, came upon the following entry: "Sold Mrs. Amey Drummond 3 Blank Books 4s." Amey was such an unusual name in the eighteenth century that there was little doubt that it was she who had signed and dated the tile. As the three blanks books were Mrs. Drummond's only purchase, they seemed to us to be significant—but significant of what? Our only suggestion was that she ran a school, a possibility supported by the evidence of her educated handwriting as revealed by the tile. Some weeks later it was my turn to trip over Amey Drummond—when her name turned up again, this time among memoranda written by the merchant John Blair in a Virginia Almanac for 1751. It read: "Feb 25. James Burwell and Betty Blair entered with Mrs Drummond to learn to read today." There, for the time being, the trail ends, and one speculation has been replaced by another. It seemed at first that the tile had been scratched by a child, but now we find that Amey was already married—or perhaps about to be wed and trying out her new name in a moment of secret pleasure. But the most important remaining question is what, if anything, did Amey Drummond or her tile have to do with the waste products from a pottery kiln?

The quantity of wasters found on the shore and in the river left no doubt that a potter had been working in the vicinity and that one of his products was identical with the waster jar found in the well at Jamestown. With this much established, the next step was to try to find the site of the kiln by probing with steel rods along the top of the cliff in the vicinity of the greatest concentration of broken pottery. By remarkable good luck it required only five minutes searching before the potter's waster pile was discovered. Working outwards from that point a series of test holes subsequently revealed the extent of the potting area, although no kiln structure was found. At that point work stopped while a careful search of the documentary records was made. But as always happens in James City County, the destruction of the official court records in the Civil War quickly brought us to a halt. The only clue was provided by a survey map of the Governor's Land made in 1683 (see p. 116 and Fig. 49). It showed the site had then been rented by one Edward Challis who had come to the colony as an indentured servant in 1639 and who later acquired an acre of land at Jamestown. There was no evidence that Challis was a potter or that he owned a pottery. The only other clue that was forthcoming showed that the shoreline of the Governor's Land was rapidly eroding during the seventeenth century, a state of affairs that was still continuing in 1961. When, in the autumn, large sections of the cliff fell away, one fall revealed part of a refuse pit dug into the clay sixty yards east of the supposed kiln area. The contents of this pit were duly excavated and found to comprise other kiln refuse of a character quite different from that revealed by the main waster pile to the west. The uneven thickness of the walls and feeble rims of the pots strongly suggested that here was the work of an apprentice. The fact that his products were concentrated at some distance from the main waster piles, although a few of his sherds were present in these, seemed to build a picture of a student potter setting up his own kiln under the wing of the master craftsman.

In December 1961, both the main waster piles and the secondary site were excavated, but neither revealed any kiln foundations. From the first came vast quantities of waste pottery showing that the potter had been in business in no small way, producing large numbers of jars from eight and a half to thirteen inches in height, as well as large cream pans (Fig. 81), bowls of various sizes, pipkins, jugs, dishes, colanders, and cups. So great were the quantities of fragments that it was possible to determine from the ratio of overfired to underfired sherds which types of vessel had been fired in which parts of the kiln. In addition these same clues served to indicate the variations of temperature from the front to the back of the chamber and so suggested the approximate size of the structure. Slabs of sandstone were found in the debris bearing the marks of pots that had stood upside down on them, while many jar rims still had scraps of the sandstone glazed to them. From this it was deduced that the chamber had been lined with pieces of sandstone instead of the gravel that would have been more suitable had it been readily available. Like the clay used in making the pots, the sandstone was to be found exposed in the cliff face below the kiln site.

Although it was depressing to find that the kiln itself had almost certainly been eroded away, we were extremely fortunate in that we enjoyed the assistance of Mr. James E. Maloney, whose lifetime of experience as a potter enabled him to interpret the surviving clues for us. On the basis of these it was possible to produce the tentative impression of the kiln's size and appearance shown in Fig. 82. Maloney, in addition to being an experienced potter, had served his apprenticeship working a wood-fired kiln in the same area as the Challis site, using the same ocher-flecked clay. The kiln which he had worked continued in use until the mid-1930's, and part of it still survives, though now largely buried beneath a mountain of sawdust.

81. A small jar and 14-inch pan (restored) from the
Challis pottery site. Made between 1690 and 1730.

82. A tentative reconstruction of the type of kiln used
to fire the Challis pottery.

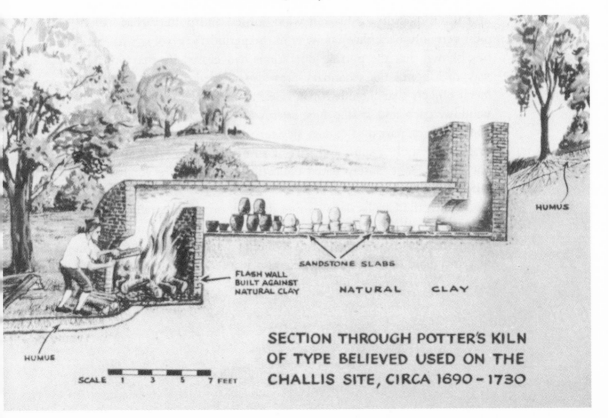

HUMUS

FLASH WALL
BUILT AGAINST
NATURAL CLAY

SANDSTONE SLABS

NATURAL   CLAY

HUMUS

SCALE 1 3 5 7 FEET

SECTION THROUGH POTTER'S KILN
OF TYPE BELIEVED USED ON THE
CHALLIS SITE, CIRCA 1690-1730

In moments of extreme frustration every archaeologist is prepared to barter his soul for an opportunity to talk to the people who once inhabited his site. The presence of Jim Maloney could have been the answer to just such a wish; for here was a man who had worked under almost exactly the same conditions as the Challis site potter and who had met with precisely the same difficulties. At the close of the project Maloney completed his contribution to our knowledge by reproducing examples of the Challis pots from the same clay—though in an up-to-date oil-burning kiln. The use of the modern kiln resulted in a more even firing and less smoke than would have been produced in a wood-burning kiln and as a result the pots baked a uniform reddish-brown. This would have been perfection in the eyes of the colonial potter, and he rarely achieved it: his vessels emerged with their lead-glazed surfaces ranging from pale yellow, through red, greens, browns and purplish-black, sometimes with three or four tones on a single pot.

Thanks to Jim Maloney and the great quantities of wasters, the Challis site excavation yielded much valuable information concerning the techniques and products of a colonial potter. The big question still remained: when was he working? No datable domestic trash was found amid the wasters and it seemed that the only clue would be the contents of the previously mentioned well at Jamestown. Our luck continued to hold. When the secondary area was cleared a large quantity of refuse was found overlying the apprentice potter's waste, and in it was a quantity of broken wine bottles, and pottery that had almost certainly been thrown away in the period 1725-30. It was therefore shown that the potting operations had ceased by that time. By way of a bonus the secondary area also yielded a pile of discarded metal objects that included iron hoes, a saddle bar from a casement window, curb and snaffle bits, stirrups, scissors, cutlery, locks, pot hooks, hinges, part of a cutlass, pewter spoons, a seventeenth century brass candlestick, a spur, and part of an ornamental brass tray. It was one of the finest closely dated collections of hardware yet found in Virginia.

When the Challis site was first located, one of the owners of the property recalled that some twenty-five years before, he had stumbled on the remains of a ruined brick building while squirrel shooting in that area close to the cliff edge. He also warned of the presence of an

218

83. An unglazed storage jar, 15 inches high, from the pottery kiln site at Green Spring. Made around 1680. The handle is typical of the Green Spring potter's work.

open well a few yards inland from the ruin; but although we searched for days through the woods, we failed to find any trace of either house or well. In the spring of 1962, some months after the completion of our excavations, I returned to the site and found that about six feet of the edge had fallen away to reveal the shaft of the well standing like a brick tower in the face of the cliff. Its site was not a dozen yards from where we had been digging, and it was immediately inland from the quantities of bricks and tiles that we had found in the river. As this page goes to the printer, only one small test hole has been cut into the side of the well, but it is large enough to show that the shaft was filled with clay and refuse in the eighteenth century. We have every hope that its eventual complete excavation will provide answers to some of the questions that have been posed here. In the meantime the brick shaft stands tantalizingly mute, safely protecting its treasures —treasures that may throw new light on the ceramic history of early Virginia or that may amount to nothing more than a legacy of mud.

The discovery of the Challis kiln site taught a number of valuable lessons, not the least of them being that the local clay could be used to make pots whose fired appearance varied widely in both body and

219

glaze color, and therefore color alone could not be used to identify the products of this or any other Virginia kiln. It also taught that if one kiln can be found by chance, a great many more may still be waiting to be discovered.

Mention has already been made of the earlier kiln at Green Spring, a site that lay about a mile and a half inland from the Challis property. The brick foundation of the former structure was located by Louis Caywood in the course of his 1954-55 Green Spring excavations and the artifacts from it are now stored in the National Park Service museum at Jamestown. They include large jars with heavy sausage-like handles (Fig. 83), massive brown-glazed dishes resembling the shape of English delftware "chargers" of the seventeenth century, and in complete contrast, part of a delicate candlestick whose shape seemed more reminiscent of the brass holders of the eighteenth than the seventeenth century. The quality of the candlestick was superior to that of anything from the Challis site. It is noteworthy that whereas the Challis potter often fired his vessels by standing them upside down on broken pots, the Green Spring potter stood his (also inverted) on flat roofing tiles—comparable to those that were found in the kiln areas at Jamestown. But before we read too much into such evidence, it must be noted that Caywood attributed the Green Spring kiln to the period 1660-80, while Cotter seems to infer that the Jamestown kilns were at least a decade earlier. The former was certainly in operation before the Challis potter started work, and it is tempting to suggest that if the Green Spring potter closed down when Governor Berkeley died, he may have moved across the road to the Challis site. Unfortunately the theory does not hold up, for the styles are entirely different, and an old potter does not learn new tricks every time he moves his kiln. We are therefore left wondering what became of both these men and their assistants when the factories went out of business. In all probability they went off into the woods elsewhere and started again, perhaps making the large quantities of local wares that turn up in Williamsburg and on every other eighteenth century site that is excavated.

Somewhere there lurks the kiln site of the "rolled rim potter" who is known to us only as the manufacturer of great quantities of large cream pans with characteristically rolled rims, most of them made in the second quarter of the eighteenth century. These vessels are frequently encountered in Williamsburg; they were found in one of the Tutter's Neck pits and were present in the topsoil of the Challis site, clearly indicating that that kiln had closed down before the "rolled rim potter" opened his business. For some years we fondly believed that he worked at Yorktown, a theory based on the same clay-footed deductions that had attributed all seventeenth century local earthenwares to kilns at Jamestown. The discovery of a potter working at Yorktown in the eighteenth century had simply resulted in his being given credit for all the local wares dating from that century.

The Yorktown potter is in many ways the most interesting because we are able to give him a face, or rather a name—Captain William Rogers, brewer, merchant, and man of quality. The first physical clues to Rogers's potting activities were encountered in early National Park Service excavations around the Swan Tavern at Yorktown where fragments of clay saggers (containers in which other pots were fired) and wasters of brown stoneware were found. These important clues remained unrecognized for some twenty years until a visiting English archaeologist noticed them in 1956. It was only then realized that there had been a potter working at Yorktown in the second quarter of the eighteenth century who manufactured tankards, bottles, and jugs quite as good as, and almost indistinguishable from, those made in England.

In 1957 Mr. Wilcomb Washburn, now Curator of Political History at the Smithsonian, but then living in the eighteenth century Digges House at Yorktown, drew my attention to numerous fragments of pottery that had been unearthed in front of his house in the course of repairing utility lines beside the road. An examination of one of the still open trenches showed that some eight inches to a foot below the present road surface lay a bed of broken pottery and sagger fragments. There was no doubt that this represented waste products from the Rogers kiln and that it included both good quality stonewares and coarse lead-glazed earthenwares. Here was the first indication that the potter manufactured both wares.

Having excavated on the site of a stoneware pottery on the Southwark Bankside at London, I was not particularly surpised to find Rogers's wasters being used as hard core to surface the roads of eighteenth century Yorktown. Similar refuse from the Bankside kiln had

221

84. Swan tavern mugs, a large jug neck, and a stoneware sagger with lid. Relics of William Rogers's 18th-century brown stoneware factory at Yorktown.

been used to line drainage channels and to make firm the muddy foreshore of the nearby River Thames. The date of operation for the London kiln was slightly earlier than that at Yorktown, but so similar are both the products and the sagger shapes that it is quite possible that the latter potter had learned his craft in London. Stretching conjecture a little further, it might be deduced that having seen the Bankside wasters being used as foreshore metaling, he suggested using his own debris for a similar purpose at Yorktown. An additional parallel to the London products was provided by the discovery of brown

222

stoneware tankards near the Swan Tavern that were ornamented with applied swans in high relief (Fig. 84). The same technique was displayed on a fragment of a tavern mug from Bankside decorated with the sign of a rampant unicorn.

The same type of brown stoneware was made first at the village of Fulham west of London and later at Bristol and other as yet unidentified factories. Most collectors and museums use the name "Fulham" for all these brown stonewares and thus it is safest to state only that the Yorktown potter must have been influenced by "Fulham" stoneware. It was just another coincidence that I should have been concerned with the Bankside site before coming to Virginia, but while we are stepping into the realm of chance, it is no more improbable that a potter than an archaeologist from Bankside should turn up at Yorktown.

Fortunately the story of the Yorktown potter is not confined to coincidences and idle speculation. Realizing the importance of the discovery, Mr. Malcolm Watkins embarked upon a spirited pursuit of documentary evidence with results that were remarkably successful. The letters of Governor Gooch to the English Board of Trade were found to contain passing derogatory references to the Yorktown potter, each promoting the belief that his work was hardly worthy of notice. In 1732 Gooch wrote that "The same poor potter's work is still continued at Yorktown without any great improvement or advantage to the owner or any injury to the trade of Great Britain." In 1739 Gooch added, "The poor Potter's Operation is unworthy of your Lordship's Notice." These statements did not seem to agree with the archaeological evidence that pointed to considerable potting activity and to a fairly high quality product.

85. Brown stoneware products from Rogers's Yorktown pottery. About 1730.

In searching through the York County Records, Mr. Watkins came upon the evidence that was needed to put both Gooch's statements and the archaeological data into their correct perspective and relationship. This all-important document was the will of William Rogers who had died in December 1739; among the many bequests and instructions was the statement that "no potters ware not burnt and fit for sale should be appraised." As no one but a potter would be in possession of unfired pottery, it went without saying that Rogers owned a kiln that undoubtedly produced the long list of ceramics that appear in his inventory, among them considerable quantities of quart mugs, milk pans, red saucepans, chamber pots, lamps (presumably cressets), cream pots large and small, porringers, redware and stoneware bottles as well as "crakt redware" and "crakt stone Dᵒ" to the value of two and five pounds respectively. In addition, the inventory listed a horse mill valued at eight pounds and forty bushels of salt worth four pounds. The mill was probably used to grind and mix the clay, while the salt was intended to be thrown into the kiln during firing as a necessary part of the manufacture of brown salt-glazed stoneware.

Not only did the will and inventory identify Rogers as the Yorktown potter but they also showed that he was a man of substance in the community, owning, for example, no fewer than twenty-nine Negro slaves and having fifty-two pictures hanging in his hall alone, as well as possessing a considerable quantity of elaborate and expensive furniture. Here was no "poor potter" whose pathetic efforts yielded him neither "improvement" nor "advantage." On the contrary, this man was a success and anyone who met him or visited his handsomely furnished house at Yorktown must have been enviously aware of the fact. We can only presume, therefore, that Governor Gooch gave tacit approval to Rogers's enterprise and deliberately suppressed the true facts when writing to the Board of Trade. As for the presence of Rogers's wares embedded in the streets of Yorktown, that too was explained by the documents. In 1734 William Rogers was appointed "Surveyor of the Landings, Streets, and Cosways in York Town." So here then was a poor potter who not only carried on a lucrative business in a colony where such enterprise was officially frowned upon but also managed to unload his waste products onto the city fathers of Yorktown.

Although Malcolm Watkins has completed his study of the documentary sources, the story of Yorktown's not so "poor potter" will not be ended until his kilns have been found and carefully excavated. While Rogers's properties in Yorktown are shown on a contemporary plan of the town, we still do not know whether his factory stood on one or more of them or whether it operated from his land elsewhere in York County. A careful watch is kept on any road work in Yorktown and many local house owners recover and report on any fragments of Rogers's pottery that turn up in their gardens. But instead of serving to show that the ware is concentrated in a specific area of the town, it merely proves that it is scattered everywhere.

Even if one cannot immediately pinpoint the location of a potter's kiln, the nature of his work ensures that clues to its existence are fairly liberally distributed. Such openhandedness in other manufacturing endeavors could quickly put their owners out of business and consequently the archaeologist is often hard put to find even the slightest traces of their activities. This, we assumed, would be the case when we were called upon to excavate around the Coke-Garrett House in Williamsburg, part of which had once been occupied by John Coke, a gold- and silversmith.

The site, well known to Williamsburg visitors, lies on rising ground east of the Public Gaol and north of the Capitol (Fig. 24). Much of the present building dates from the first half of the nineteenth century, but the west wing was originally a free-standing story-and-a-half building that was erected a hundred years earlier. Buried beneath the eastern end of the present Coke-Garrett House and passing under the adjacent brick office lies the remains of another colonial house which, like the present west wing, was once owned by John Coke. The purpose of the 1959 excavations was to try to find out as much as possible about the original appearances of both colonial buildings and to try to determine the uses to which Coke put them.

Although John Coke described himself as a goldsmith, he was also a tavern keeper, and quite a successful one at that. As a result most of our knowledge of the man centers around his hostelry; indeed, there was doubt in some quarters that he worked as a goldsmith at all while occupying this property. We first hear of him in 1739 when a Negro man was committed to the York County gaol for "breaking in and entering the shop house of John Coke, a silversmith," from which it might be construed that Coke had his shop on the same premises as his home; but whether or not this was the same site as the one he occupied during the latter part of his life is not clear. The first reference to his having acquired three lots behind the Capitol occurred in 1740. This parcel of land included the house whose foundations were explored beneath the later Coke-Garrett House, a property that had earlier belonged to another goldsmith, John Brodnax, who died in 1719.

It was hoped that the excavations would indicate the purpose to which John Coke put the eastern building, and that evidence was forthcoming in the shape of a number of broken crucibles (Fig. 86) found crushed under the relaid floor of the cellar. It was found that the building had burned in the early nineteenth century, the chimney falling inward and crushing quantities of burned crockery and bottles into the clay floor. It was not until a test hole was cut through this clay floor that we realized that late in the eighteenth century it had been relaid, sealing the crucibles underneath. But although the vessels were of a type generally associated with workers in fine metals, none of them had been used, thus leaving alive the possibility that Coke did not operate as a goldsmith on this site and so relegated his crucibles to the cellar.

Colonial Williamsburg's Research Department was able to show that John Coke acquired two additional lots to the west in 1755, one of them being the site of the single surviving eighteenth century house. In that year the bill of conveyance described Coke as a Tavern Keeper, but how long he had then pursued that trade is not known. Archaeological evidence around the western building pointed to such use of that structure as early as the 1740's, for large quantities of broken pottery tankards, punch bowls, porringers, glasses, and wine bottles were encountered in rubbish pits and in the ditch that marked the property boundary a few feet from the front door. The most important clues came from a massive rectangular hole to the rear of the house that seems to have been dug as the cellar hole for an outbuilding that was never erected. In the bottom of it were some well-preserved wine glasses (Fig. 111) and other artifacts that could be associated with a tavern, but further up, mixed with miscellaneous domestic trash, were found fragments of broken crucibles lined with the borax that goldsmiths used as a flux, and embedded in them were drops of both gold

226

86. Crucibles found in John Coke's cellar. The largest is 4 inches high.

and silver. The same deposit also yielded small strips of abrasive stone known as "India stones," which were used both to polish precious metals and to sharpen the tools of engravers. Also recovered was a bar of silver, not a very large one, being only an inch and a quarter in length—but a bar of silver just the same.

These finds left no doubt that John Coke was working as a gold- and silversmith on this property and operating his tavern there as well. Further information was found behind the present Coke-Garrett House where a delicately hinged gold earring was discovered in the silted north-south boundary ditch. More important was the discovery beneath the porch of a strip of copper, both sides of which had been used to try out engraved designs (Fig. 87). This was clearly an engraver's trial piece and the first archaeological evidence that Coke might have done his own engraving. Most silver experts considered it unlikely that he would have done so and further that he would not have had sufficient business to merit employing such a specialist. Yet the evidence of the trial piece coupled with that of the India stones certainly seems to point to one or the other of these explanations. In addition, there is a single piece of documentary evidence in a statement made in 1752 by one Ann Moody to the effect that the wealthy merchant John Custis had given her a pair of shoe buckles "made by John Coke engraved 'In Memory of John Custis.'"

By and large it would seem that Coke's business reflected the for-

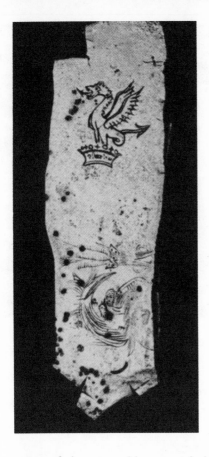

87. An engraver's copper trial piece with a wyvern crest and other devices. Three inches long.

tunes of the town, his tavern being busy during Public Times and his goldsmithing trade keeping him occupied during the slack periods. Yet unlike the goldsmiths of London or even the Northern colonies, that trade alone was not enough to sustain him—at least not in the manner to which he wished to be accustomed. We have very little indication of the extent of Coke's goldsmithing business, but it may be significant that his inventory made after his death included no items of silver, although an illegible number of silver spoons are among items listed in his will. Coke's inventory is in marked contrast to that of his goldsmithing predecessor, William Brodnax, whose possessions listed in 1719 included two silver porringers, a set of castors, an oil pot, vinegar pot, set of small salvers, various spoons, a silver snuffbox, a silver-hilted sword, silver-rimmed spectacles, shoe buckles, gold buttons and rings, as well as a collection of scrap bullion valued at more than a hundred and eighty pounds sterling.

We can only assume that John Coke worked to order and did not keep a stock of his products for sale to chance customers. In truth, there were not many such customers around. There is little doubt that most of his work would have come from people who wanted small pieces such as spoons or occasional cruets and they would supply their own bullion in the shape of old silver objects or in coin. While it is obvious that the possessors of silver would carefully preserve their pieces, it is doubtless a measure of the scarcity of precious metals in Williamsburg that the total unearthed, apart from the pieces found on the Coke site, amounts to four teaspoons, three Spanish coins, and the back of a watch. In addition, a gold coin of uncertain date and denomination is said to have been found in a garden to the west of the colonial Gaol though nobody knows what became of it—or even that it was gold at all. One learns through bitter experience that gilded memories and wishful thinking are powerful transmuters of baser metals. In preparing this book I have waded through many tales of treasures lost and found, most of them palpably legendary. One, however, did ring true and it duly found its way onto this page; it told of the discovery in the late nineteenth century of an English gold piece of George III found embedded in an old pine tree at Jamestown by a Negro servant. My informant could not remember what became of the coin, but he had no doubt that it was gold. Subsequently, another member of the family told me that the coin had since come to light again. It was only copper.

The total sum of the gold from Jamestown is therefore nil, while that of its silver is less than what has been found at Williamsburg. As far as I can discover, the excavated plantation sites have yielded nothing more than the previously mentioned coin and sleeve buttons from Rosewell and one silver spoon of 1660–70 that turned up in an Isle of Wight County field in 1962. Thus, when a visitor came into the Williamsburg archaeological laboratory in the fall of 1961 asking if the staff would care to see a collection of colonial salvers, tankards, and a cruet stand that he had dug up in a field near Bowers Hill in Nansemond County, a minor sensation resulted. It appeared that the hoard had been found while discing and that one of the mugs had come up attached to a blade of the machine. Subsequently the owner of the farm, Mr. Elwood Boyce, had obtained a mine detector and had quickly found the rest of the collection, along with a few iron nails, hidden between two pieces of roofing slate about a foot below the surface. All the items were engraved with the ciphered initials of their owner, J C G, and the marks of London silversmiths for the years 1768

229

and 1773 (Fig. 88). In the absence of evidence to the contrary, it must be presumed that the hoard represented the valued possessions of a landowner that were hastily hidden from the British during the Revolution and, for reasons unknown, were never retrieved. It is possible, but less likely, that the pieces were stolen property interred by a thief who intended to return for them once the heat was off.

The practice of burying loot, which modern treasure hunters can hope to recover, has given piracy a romance that it ill deserves. The number of bona fide pirate treasures that have been found either by accident or as a result of careful research is actually extremely small. The sad truth is that pirates did not go in for nearly as much treasure burying as we are led to believe, for the greater proportion of their plunder took the form of such valuables as tobacco, pepper, textiles, and indigo—commodities that do not lend themselves as readily as jewels or specie to interment in the ground. Nevertheless, pirates did acquire considerable quantities of plate and they did keep it in chests, as was attested at the examination at Jamestown in 1688 of three white men and a Negro who had been picked up by a British naval vessel while trying to sneak into the James River. The men at first denied that they were pirates, but had some difficulty in explaining away the contents of their small boat. It had contained one chest holding eight hundred pieces of eight and plate to the weight of a hundred and six pounds, another holding Spanish specie and plate weighing a hundred and forty-two pounds, three bags containing broken plate and basins weighing eighty-four pounds, and another bag holding "37 silver plates, two scollops, seaven dishes, silver lace, some cupps broken. Plate, weighing bagg string and all, 74-lb." Eventually, in 1692, after much litigation, the men were released and three quarters of their possessions returned to them, except for three hundred pounds which was deducted at the king's command "to be devoted to the building of a college in Virginia . . ."

We shall never know what the College of William and Mary's three benefactors were really trying to do with their treasure, but it is just possible that they intended to hide it somewhere on the banks of the James. There is a legend that Blackbeard (thirteen of whose crew ended their days on the gallows at Williamsburg) buried a treasure somewhere along the York River, and it is just possible that it was

88. A silver salver bearing the engraved cipher JCG and a cruet stand. Part of a hoard unearthed in 1961 in Nansemond County and comprising a collection of a London silver made between 1768 and 1773.

found shortly before the First World War. The late Colonel G. A. Greaves recalled that a luxury yacht from New York appeared in the river one day and anchored within sight of Rosewell close to the mouth of Carter's Creek. When the Deans family awoke the next morning the yacht had gone. But when they made their way down to the shore they found a hole dug in the bank and at the bottom the marks of a large rectangular object that had been banded with iron and whose rusted impressions were clearly visible.

It is a sad fact that most archaeologists go through their careers without ever discovering treasure in the popular sense of the word. As a rule, that pleasure falls to people who have no interest in archaeology: to plowmen, ditch diggers, and building contractors who come upon their treasures quite by accident. It is fortunate, therefore, that the archaeologist sees his "gems" as small scraps of information: broken siege pots on a glasshouse site, wasters near a potter's kiln, or a shattered crucible in the cellar of a goldsmith. To him these are treasures indeed—though it would be nice, just once, to find. . .

231

IX

Of Furnishing and Money-Making

FROM THE CRADLE to the grave the inhabitants of colonial Virginia needed furniture and they possessed it in varying quantities and qualities from the opulence of the "3 large mahog^y dining tables" and "1 large round walnut" dining table in the Ball Room of the Governor's Palace in Williamsburg, to the "1 Bed & furniture, 6 Dishes, 1 Iron Pot" that seemed to be the sole furnishings of James Shields's twenty-five slave "quarter" in York County. When the so-called "poor potter" of Yorktown died in 1739 (see p. 224), the inventory of his furnishings included a marble table, twelve chairs with walnut frames and cane bottoms, a "japand corner cupboard," and a "pcl Backgammon Tables" as well as many other pieces which, if they survived, would make a modern antique dealer ecstatic. But the sad truth is that the majority of Virginia's seventeenth and eighteenth century furniture is no longer with us and we are left to draw what conclusions we

232

may from the many contemporary inventories that dismiss each piece with a few inept words. The majority of this furniture never lived long enough to become antique—just as nine tenths of our twentieth century furnishings will have mercifully vanished into limbo long before the collectors of the future embarrass our ghosts by collecting them.

Because furniture was so necessary to life in the colony one might be tricked into believing that here would be an excellent field of study for the archaeologist. Indeed, I have been busily claiming throughout these pages that archaeology is ready to come to the rescue when the documentary sources let us down. But unfortunately I have to confess that in the study of furniture, archaeology is of pathetically little help. In the first place, furniture, being made of wood, generally ended up as fuel for the kitchens and fireplaces of the colony, and secondly, the few pieces that did find their way into the ground rotted away within a very few years, leaving behind nothing more than a dirty stain and a few pieces of hardware to mark their passing.

There is, of course, no shortage of surviving pieces of English seventeenth and eighteenth century furniture in the great museum collections, and we have little difficulty in envisaging the sort of English furniture that was used and favored in Jamestown, Williamsburg, or on the great and small plantations. But when we try to learn something about the furniture actually made in Virginia in the colonial period we immediately run into trouble.

As intimated earlier, the tobacco economy of Virginia did not encourage craftsmen of distinction. The great plantation owners shipped their tobacco to merchants in England in exchange for credit that was spent in England on English goods. Even the smaller landowners, who preferred to sell their tobacco at lower rates to planters and merchants with offices in Virginia, generally wound up buying English goods from local stores owned by these men. Just as the great planters were generally in debt to their factors in England, so the little men ran a charge account at the stores, to be paid when their tobacco crop was delivered. As a result a vicious circle was created—one that kept such people as goldsmiths and cabinetmakers firmly on the outside.

In the Northern industrial colonies with their cities and comparatively concentrated areas of population, specialist craftsmen could find

233

sufficient customers to keep them more or less constantly employed. It was not so in Virginia where the slaves made up more than thirty percent of the total eighteenth century population and where approximately one in ten of the white colonists was an indentured servant. It has been estimated that in the mid-eighteenth century the proportion of free population in the Northern and Middle colonies to those of the South was as high as four to one. In her book *The Cabinetmakers of America*, Ethel Hall Bjerkoe has tried to compile a listing of all the known cabinetmakers in the American colonies in the seventeenth and eighteenth centuries. Out of a total of 1,345, only ten are attributed to Virginia (all in Williamsburg) as against the two hundred and eighteen listed for Boston and the one hundred and nineteen for Salem, Massachusetts.

We know little or nothing about furniture-making in seventeenth-century Jamestown, but it must be assumed that many of the settlers, particularly those that came over as indentured servants, brought very little with them. There is, of course, a big difference between the products of a sophisticated cabinetmaker of the eighteenth century and the generally simple joinery of the early seventeenth. The English yeomen, Virginia's "common sort," were used to sitting on joint stools, eating from rough oak tables, and lying on simple frame or board beds. It is true that in England many of these items were given the distinction of turned legs; but this would not have been a particularly difficult embellishment for a Jamestown joiner once he had set up a lathe. It seems unlikely, however, that much, if any, furniture was produced in the first two or three years, as John Smith complained that in 1609 "we had but one Carpenter in the Countrey, and three others that could do little, but desired to be learners . . ." Nevertheless, we know from the pen of William Strachey who arrived in the colony in 1610, that the church in the fort was to be fitted with a communion table of black walnut, pews and pulpit of cedar, and a font "hewen hollow, like a canao . . ." Although these were items yet to be provided, it is obvious that the colonists thought they had craftsmen to hand sufficiently skilled to provide such items as church furniture. It naturally follows that if they could produce satisfactory pieces for so important a purpose, the making of simple domestic furniture would not have been beyond them. Mr. Paul Hudson, in his publication *Early Jamestown*

Commodities and Industries, has suggested that "most of the furniture used in Jamestown houses was made by colonial cabinetmakers." While this was probably true in the middle years of the Jamestown colony, it was perhaps less so of Virginia as a whole as the seventeenth century progressed and the pioneer spirit declined. An additional factor was injected by the restoration of the monarchy in 1660 and the arrival in London of Charles II armed with a hatful of new fashions in everything from women to walnut. The taste for elaborate turnings, Chinese lacquer and japanning, gesso, veneers, and marquetry combined to weed the men from the boys, or rather, the cabinetmakers from the country joiners. Thus anyone in Virginia who wished to keep pace with English fashion would have had to import his best furniture from England.

No wooden fragments of furniture have been found in Jamestown excavations or on any other seventeenth century sites for that matter. As pieces of styles common in the early years of the colony boasted no metal fittings other than occasional iron hinges, no hardware has been recovered that can be associated with specific types of furniture. From Jamestown come a few iron coffin or chest handles, but all are so simple as to be singularly uninformative. Although such brass items as keyhole escutcheons, handles, pulls from drawers and desk sliders, cabinet locks, and brass upholstery tacks have been found at Jamestown, the majority are of types that date from the eighteenth rather than the seventeenth century.

The documentary records of Williamsburg show that there were only six cabinetmakers there that stayed long enough to leave their mark on the furnishings of colonial Virginia; while one may have opened his business as early as 1732, all were working in the second half of the century. Their combined output was probably not large, and the number of definitely identified examples of their work can be counted on one hand—with fingers touching the thumb. Indeed, there are only three or four signed or labeled eighteenth century examples from the whole of Virginia. Of course, there are numerous other items with Virginia family traditions behind them, and in recent years there has been a tendency to see Virginia origins in many a piece that is unsophisticated yet characteristically English in style and built from Virginia timber. Being an archaeologist and not a student of American furniture, I do not propose to do more than dip my toe in these contro-versial waters. Nonetheless, the problem does have its archaeological connections for the simple reason that within the period 1957-61 Colo-nial Williamsburg's staff spent the best part of three years studying and exploring sites once occupied by four of the city's six principal cabinetmakers.

The earliest to start work was Peter Scott, who, in about 1732, rented a house owned by John Custis opposite Bruton Parish Church on Duke of Gloucester Street. Scott remained there as a tenant until his death in 1775; during his tenancy the house passed from John Cus-tis to his son Daniel Park Custis and after his death, to his widow Martha who had married George Washington in 1759. Little is known of Peter Scott's furniture, the most informative source being his adver-tisement in the *Virginia Gazette* for September 12, 1755, inserted when he thought he would leave Virginia and go to England. It read as follows:

To be SOLD

BEFORE Mr. Finnie's Door, on the 23rd Day of October next, Two Lots of Ground, situate on the Back Street [Francis Street]; near Col. *Custis's* in *Williamsburg;* on which there is a good Dwelling House, containing Six Rooms and Closets, a good dry Cellar, with all convenient Out-Houses, and a good Well: Twelve Months Credit will be allowed the Purchaser giving Bond and Security. At the same Time and Place will be sold, for Bills of Exchange or Ready Money, Two Negroes, bred to the business of a Cabinet-maker; likewise will be sold, at the subscriber's Shop near the Church, sundry Pieces of Cabinet Work; of Mahogany and Walnut, consisting of Desks, Book-Cases, Tables of various Sorts, Tools, and some Materials. Six Months Credit will be given to those that purchase above Value of Fifty Shillings, on their giving Bond and Security; and Five *per Cent.* will be allowed for ready Money.

And as I intend to go for *Great-Britain* the latter End of next Month, therefore I desire all Persons indebted to me, to make speedy Payment, otherwise they may expect Trouble without further Notice.   *Peter Scott.*

From this advertisement we can glean quite a variety of useful clues. Although Scott rented his shop (identified as being "near the Church") he owned two lots and a house on the Back Street; so one may suppose that he only continued to rent the shop because of its good position. We know also that his business was sufficiently large to make it worth the trouble of training two Negro slaves, and also that he made furniture without first receiving orders for it, in contrast to most cabinetwork which was undertaken to order. Finally, the notice suggests that Scott's business had been sufficiently lucrative for him to need to advertise for the payment of debts owed by more customers than he could find time to approach individually. All in all, therefore, it would seem that Peter Scott's business was reasonably successful. As it turned out, he did not go to England but continued to operate his shop on Duke of Gloucester Street for nearly another twenty years. When he died his executors disposed of "A GREAT variety of cabinet makers tools, Mohogany, Walnut, and Pine Plank, likewise new walnut book cases, desks, tables, &c." These items show that Scott had continued to make furniture for sale in his shop and to work to order as well.

Peter Scott died in the winter of 1775 and two months later the *Virginia Gazette* for January 26, 1776, announced that "Mr. Peter Scott's old house in this City, which he had rented and lived in for 43 years, was burned down last Sunday Night, by accident." Further details were provided by a letter of the same date from Edmund Randolph to George Washington relating that "About 5 Days since, Mr. Custis's tenement, where Scott lived, opposite to the Church, was burnt to the ground, by the Negligence of some of the Soldiers, who had been quartered there. The Wind, being due South, the out-house escaped Flames. The Difficulty of saving the Church became thereby very great. The Country are surely answerable for this Damage, as it accrued in their Service." Both statements refer to the building opposite the church as being the one in which Scott had lived; yet the advertisement of 1755 had shown that he owned a house on the Back Street and a shop near the church. In an attempt to discover whether Scott lived and had his shop in the same building, Colonial Williamsburg undertook two seasons of archaeological exploration in 1955 and 1958 and uncovered the brick-walled cellar of a building that had been destroyed by fire. The bricks were laid in English bond, the mortar was made from oystershell lime, and no one had the slightest doubt that this was the cellar of an eighteenth century building; but we needed more than that to definitely link it with Peter Scott. Fortunately the artifacts found in the debris were sufficient to establish each detail of both the *Gazette* notice and Randolph letter. The objects that achieved this were a coin, an iron tethering peg, a group of chicken bones, a heap of small panes of window glass, and two broken wine bottles.

The coin was a halfpenny minted in England in 1773 specifically for use in the Virginia Colony (Fig. 89); but, as Mr. Eric P. Newman has shown in *Coinage for Colonial Virginia*, such money was not issued until March 1775. This example was virtually in mint condition, and as it was found amid the destruction debris in the cellar, it could be construed that the coin had not been in circulation for very long before it was lost in the burning building. Thus, the disaster could not have occurred before March 1775 nor too long afterward; so the date of the burning of Scott's old house in January 1776 would fit very well. The next clues were provided by the iron tethering peg and chicken bones, the former resting on the clay floor of the cellar and the latter being pressed into the floor as though trampled under foot. The bones were mostly those of legs and wings and suggested that someone had been eating chickens in the cellar and that they were sufficiently untidy just to throw the bones on the floor and leave them there. Apprentices or slaves might have been the guilty ones, although their master would probably have taken a dim view of such slackness; but much more likely candidates would be found among the soldiers known to have been quartered in Scott's house in the winter of 1775-76. The tethering peg is believed to be an item of military equipment

89. Obverse and reverse of Virginia copper halfpenny of 1773 found in the Peter Scott cellar.

> all veſſels of American property, which obliged him to take a haſty leave of that port.
>
> Mr. Peter Scott's old houſe in this city, which he had rented and lived in for 43 years, was burnt down laſt Sunday night, by accident.
>
> A grenadier of the 14th regiment, completely armed (who ſaid he was a deſerter)

90. Extract from the *Virginia Gazette* for January 26, 1776, noting the burning of Peter Scott's house.

and so would support such a construction. The heap of window glass, misshapen and fused together by the fire, had clearly been a collection of small panes of the kind that a cabinetmaker would use to glaze the doors of bookcases, and we know from Scott's advertisement of 1755 and his executors' notice of 1775 that he did make bookcases. It could be construed, therefore, that when his effects were sold the glass was left behind in the cellar because nobody wanted it. All these clues fitted quite surprisingly well into the pattern of events surrounding the last days of "Mr. Peter Scott's old house," the only missing factor being evidence to show that the house was old when it burned. That corroboration was provided by the last of the clues, the two broken wine bottles which were found in a concavity in the cellar floor against the west wall and which had been filled with sand, presumably to level it up. The bottle fragments and sand overlaid a thin layer of brick dust that had been deposited while the building was being constructed, proving that the bottles must have been thrown away during the life of the building and could not, for example, have been lying in the bottom of a rubbish pit, the upper levels of which had been disturbed when the hole for the cellar was being dug. Both bottles were of a shape that was common in the first years of the eighteenth century and so it was likely that the building was in existence by about 1720, thus making it perfectly reasonable that Scott could have lived in it for forty-three years.

Although the history and the archaeology of the Peter Scott site fitted together as neatly as one of the cabinetmaker's own mortised joints, the basic problem of determining whether the residence and shop were in the same building remained unsolved. No trace of the outhouse mentioned in the Randolph letter was found, nor were any relics of Scott's trade—other than the pieces of fused window glass already mentioned. The absence of tools and furniture hardware was not particularly surprising when we realize that Scott's effects had been sold and moved out of the house before it burned. Regardless of this fact, we had hoped that some of Scott's rubbish pits would have been found to contain relics of his trade thrown away during his forty-three years of operation. The fact that not one such pit was discovered suggests either that Scott had his trash carried out of town or much more probably, that he buried it in the small valley to the rear of the lot that ran between it and his own property on the Back Street, an area that was not included in the excavations.

If Colonial Williamsburg's archaeologists were frustrated by the dearth of helpful trash on the Scott site, they were overwhelmed by the quantities unearthed on the second cabinetmaker's property. The lots in question straddled a ravine running north beyond Nicholson Street to the rear of Williamsburg's colonial printing office. They had been purchased by one Thomas Everard in 1745 for forty-five pounds sterling who sold them in 1756 to cabinetmaker Anthony Hay for two hundred pounds, from which we may deduce either that Everard was a remarkable businessman or that he increased the value of the property by building on it in the period 1745-56. Initial exploratory excavations in 1949 under the direction of archaeologist James M. Knight revealed the foundation remains of two buildings, one spanning a stream that flowed through the valley, and another on higher ground to the west. Documentary evidence showed that Hay owned two major buildings, a shop and a residence. The job of the archaeologists was to determine which was which.

Full-scale excavations began near the stream-spanning building in the winter of 1959-60 and it was soon apparent that we were dealing with a very complex relationship between the stream and the structures

91. Anthony Hay's cabinet shop during excavation in 1960.

(Fig. 91). It was found that the main building was rectangular in plan and had been built on a massive deposit of clay that had been dumped into the valley, thus diverting the stream bed to the west of it. At a later date an extension had been added to the building and this stood on brick piers spanning the new stream bed. There was no doubt that together the main building and its extension represented Anthony Hay's cabinet shop, for in the silt of the stream were found a large number of carpenters' or cabinetmakers' tools as well as actual fragments of wooden furniture that had been preserved in the wet sand. Also found in the silt were considerable quantities of domestic glass and ceramics which had been thrown down the slope from the building to the west, now clearly identified as the Hay residence. These artifacts were much more easily dated than either the tools or the pieces of wood, and they showed that the stream had silted up extremely rapidly in the years from about 1770 to 1780. The fact that colonial bricklayers generally scored the mortar joints around all the exterior bricks that showed above ground, made it a simple matter (by noting where the scoring stopped) to determine the colonial grade when the main shop structure was erected and also to see that the stream had silted up to a depth of some three feet shortly before the building was destroyed (Fig. 92). The destruction level created by the tearing down of the shop was readily discernible as a white shroudlike layer of plaster and mortar that stretched over the foundations and away from the building up the slopes to east and west. As no evidence of burning was found, it was assumed that the shop had been pulled down and that the spreading of the white plaster was occasioned by the hauling away of salvageable materials.

Potsherds in the form of creamware and occasional pieces of Rouen faïence (see Chapter X, p. 299), types used in Virginia in the Revolutionary period, were found directly beneath the white destruction stratum as also were a large number of musket flints and a few gun parts. It was deduced on this evidence that the shop was destroyed during or shortly after the Revolution and that in its last days it may have been used as a store for arms. The fact that the stream had been allowed to silt up and that it had returned to its natural course, flowing

92. Foundations of Hay's cabinet shop exposed to original grade after removal of silt deposited during the Revolution. The modern stream bed can be seen at a higher level in the background.

93. A conjectural reconstruction of Anthony Hay's cabinet shop and residence as they may have appeared about 1768.

through the foundations as soon as the shop was removed, suggested that the building was allowed to run down during its later years.

Whereas the archaeology of the Peter Scott site helpfully supported already existing documentary evidence, on the Hay site the archaeological evidence was garnered and interpreted before the documentation was discovered. The historical evidence subsequently turned up in the shape of Williamsburg Public Store Records for 1779 and 1780 that showed that a building was rented from Mrs. Hay (Anthony Hay having died in 1770) and used as a "PUBLICK ARMOURY . . . to repair & Clean the Public Arms by Mr Anderson's people." The excavated gun flints had been identified as French and it was therefore satisfying to note that many of the weapons placed in the safekeeping of Mr. Anderson were shown in the records to be French. In addition, the same Public Store Records included an expenditure of thirty-five shillings for "5 Quire paper @ 7/ to repare the windows of the House rented of *Mrs* Hay," confirming the belief that the building was in poor shape shortly before it was destroyed.

It is only rarely that the archaeologists' interpretation is so graphically and unequivocally confirmed by documentation that was not available when the excavations were in progress. As a rule the basic historical research precedes the archaeological work and consequently it is tempting for the excavator to try to progress backward by trying to see his artifacts as substantiation for a story that has already been told by the historians. Most archaeologists worth their salt try to avoid

243

this trap by giving the documentation little more than a cursory reading until the excavation is well advanced and until their initial deductions have been made on the basis of the archaeological data alone. This is usually a very satisfactory and, I think, a "no cheating" approach; but it does tend to give the historians a slightly tiresome air of superiority when they visit the excavation and find the archaeologist grubbing about in the dirt looking for answers that they have already provided in their historical research reports.

The Anthony Hay complex was in many respects an archaeologist's dream site, not only because of its corroborating documentation, but because the site of the shop had remained unoccupied since its destruction in the eighteenth century, and because it was built over a stream that preserved organic objects that would otherwise have vanished. In addition, the house and shop were on either side of the stream and the trash from each was thrown down opposite slopes and thus kept more or less separate.

Key archaeological dating for the construction of the two parts of the shop was provided by a quantity of broken wine bottles of the 1740's found in the original stream bed beneath the clay on which the shop was built, thus showing that the main structure was erected after that time—probably in the period 1745-56 when the value of the property increased fourfold. A clue to the building of the extension was provided by domestic trash of the 1760's from the Hay residence that was found sealed beneath the foundation piers of the addition.

Colonial Williamsburg archaeologists are extremely fortunate in being able to call on the assistance of a large and highly trained staff that includes specialists in most of the trades originally practiced in the city in the eighteenth century. Thus when John Coke's silversmithing relics were found at the Coke-Garrett House, a silversmith trained in the techniques of the eighteenth century trade was on hand to help identify and interpret the artifacts. Similarly, on the Anthony Hay site, a Colonial Williamsburg cabinetmaker was frequently seen watching the excavators at work and helping to identify the tools and pieces of wood as they were unearthed.

The collection of tools recovered included numerous jack plane irons, files, rasps, forming chisels, and one or two bits, but no hammers, molding plane irons, saws, pincers, or other tools of the cabinetmaking craft. This was thought somewhat surprising until the cabinet-maker explained what common sense should have revealed, that the objects found were those that saw the hardest use and were considered expendable—in contrast to the saws, hammers, and so forth that a cabinetmaker would continue to use throughout his working life.

While the presence of cabinetmaking tools was satisfying to the extent that their absence would have been disturbing, they did not add anything to our small store of information on colonial Virginia cabinet-making. The fragments of actual furniture, on the other hand, were received with considerable delight, for even if the majority did not reveal what was *manufactured* at the Hay cabinet shop, they did provide clues to the pieces that passed through it. I should add that this is no fine academic distinction, for the largest part of a cabinetmaker's work would have been devoted to repairing existing pieces rather than the building of new ones.

Before discussing the evidence of the furniture fragments, it is necessary to confuse the issue by briefly explaining the history of the Hay cabinet shop, for it involves three cabinetmakers and not just Mr. Hay alone. He bought the shop, as previously mentioned, in 1756 (although he may have rented it previously from Everard) and worked there for at least twelve years, during part of which time he appears to have employed one Edmund Dickinson as an apprentice. In 1767 Hay gave up the cabinetmaking trade and purchased the Raleigh Tavern, which he ran until his death from facial cancer in 1770. Although Hay retained his house adjacent to the shop, he leased the latter to another cabinetmaker, Benjamin Bucktrout, who worked there from 1767 until 1771. There is no knowing whether apprentice Dickinson stayed on with Bucktrout after Hay gave up, but we do know that when the premises were vacated in 1771, Edmund Dickinson rented them from the widow Hay, who still lived at the house next door. Dickinson worked there as a master cabinetmaker until he was commissioned as a captain in the 1st Virginia Regiment in 1776, promoted to major in the following year, and killed at the Battle of Monmouth on June 28, 1778. We can assume that he continued to rent the Hay cabinet shop during his years of army service, though being absent he was unable to keep the building in repair or prevent the stream from silting up around it. Thus, in a period of fifteen years or so we have three cabinetmakers at work in the shop and scattering their trash around it and into the stream. As they were all using the same sort of tools, making much the same sort of furniture, and embellishing it with similar hardware, it is well nigh impossible for the archaeologist to expect to distinguish between the relics of one occupancy and another. Nevertheless, on the evidence of their position in the strata of the stream silt, it is supposed that most of the furniture fragments and accessories date from the Bucktrout and Dickinson years between 1767 and 1776.

The most important item was an unfinished walnut table leg (Fig. 94) that had been thrown into the stream and was lying amid the decaying grasses at its edge shortly before the main silting began. The leg is in the rough-hewn state, but it is clear that it was intended for a straight-skirted table and had no knee in the manner of the more common cabriole leg. To this extent, therefore, the collectors' belief in the simplicity of colonial Virginia furniture is supported by the Williamsburg leg. Its foot, on the other hand, has every appearance of being in the first stages of being fashioned into a ball and claw, a feature that some authorities have described as "almost unknown on Virginia furniture." Being unfinished, this leg is hardly a thing of beauty or, indeed, a fair example of the skill of a Virginia cabinetmaker. Yet the very fact that it is unfinished and therefore indisputably the product of a Williamsburg craftsman makes it a pearl beyond price, a document as important to the history of American furniture as any of the famous labeled pieces from the Northern colonies.

In addition to the table leg, the stream silt yielded a much decayed crest rail from a chair of Chippendale form, two or three fragments that might have come from trunks or chests, part of a back leg from a side chair, plus another leg fragment burned at one end and having a fine brass caster at the other attached by three iron nails. This last item retains a sufficient amount of its shape to show that it came from a chair (probably an armchair) and not from a table. Two other wooden fragments are of interest, one seemingly a molding from the side of a church pew, the other part of a boxwood oboe with two brass stops (Fig. 95). The instrument, a most unexpected find, started one of those trails of research that always gladden the heart of the archaeological detective. From the pages of Carl Geiringer's book *Musical Instruments*, it was learned that in the first half of the eighteenth century

246

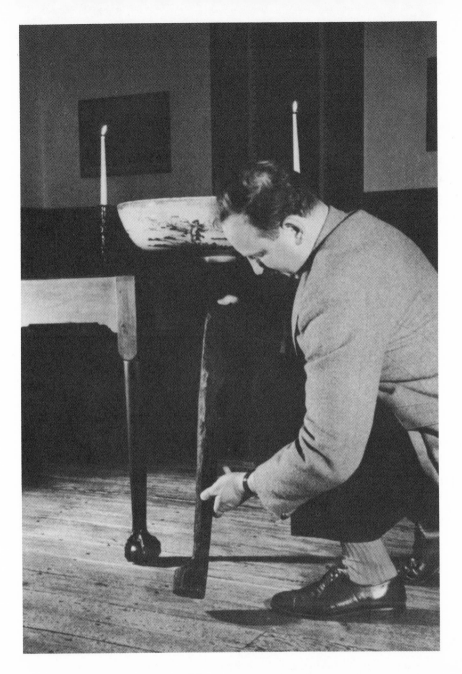

94. An unfinished wooden table leg from the Hay site is compared with that of a table in the Raleigh Tavern. The leg is a unique example of a colonial Virginia cabinetmaker's waste product.

95. Part of a boxwood oboe with two brass stops, found in the stream silt.

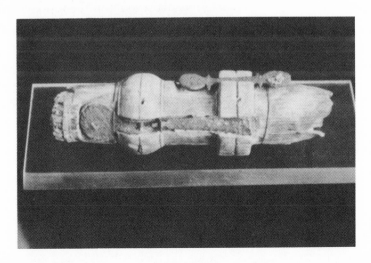

oboes possessed three stops, but that in the mid-century the fingering was changed and the stops were reduced to two. Thus it followed that the excavated oboe was made after about 1750 and, on the evidence of its position in the stream silt, before about 1776. A clue to help explain its presence in the shop of a cabinetmaker was provided by Benjamin Bucktrout's announcement in the *Virginia Gazette* of January 6, 1767, stating that:

> MR. ANTHONY HAY having lately removed to the RAWLEIGH tavern, the subscriber has taken his shop, where the business will be carried on in all its branches.
>
> He hopes that those Gentlemen who were Mr. *Hay's* customers will favour him with their orders, which shall be executed in the best and most expeditious manner. He likewise makes all sorts of Chinese and Gothick PALING for gardens and summer houses.
>
> N.B. SPINETS and HARPSICHORDS made and repaired.
>
> BENJAMIN BUCKTROUT.

From this advertisement it is clear that Bucktrout was not averse to turning his talents to other work besides the making of furniture, a fact supported by the accounts of Robert Carter of Nomini Plantation who employed him to set up and take down bedsteads, nail up palings, make a case for a harpsichord, and even repair an umbrella. Bucktrout's capitalized reference to musical instruments might very well have resulted in a customer bringing in an oboe to be renovated, although just why he threw it away, brass stops and all, remains a mystery.

The Virginia cabinetmaker's emphasis on the *repairing* of furniture as well as the manufacture of it, was given archaeological support by the discovery of numerous furniture handles and escutcheons of types common in the early years of the eighteenth century, but long since outmoded when Anthony Hay first set up in business. The only reasonable explanation for their presence is that they had been removed from old furniture brought into the shop to be renovated. Less readily explained was the high proportion of brass hardware intended for tall case clocks: hinges, keyhole escutcheons, and a brass capital from one of the orders decorating a clock's hood. None of the three cabinetmakers' advertisements or bills refers to work on clock cases;

248

nevertheless, there is archaeological evidence that such items did pass through the shop.

All save one of the brass hinges for clock doors were represented only by decorative brass terminals that had been trimmed off them, perhaps suggesting that the cabinetmakers had bought the hinges in quantity and had adapted them to other purposes. Most of the trimmings were found in a layer of wood ash immediately beyond the eastern end of the shop and sealed beneath the remains of the chimney that had been pulled down on top of it. A vitrified iron nail found in the ash was estimated by Colonial Williamsburg's blacksmith to have been in a fire whose temperature could not have been less than about 2000° F, a heat that would not be reached in a domestic fireplace. The accumulating evidence seemed to indicate that one of the cabinetmakers did a little metalworking as part of his business. In support of this theory, a roughly circular area of intense burning some two feet in diameter near the shop chimney suggested that a portable furnace might have stood there. Then, as the artifacts began to be washed and studied it was found that a few French musket flints were among the objects from the burned layer as well as scraps of brass from guns and part of the brass knuckle bow from a small sword. Because the majority of the objects were relics of cabinetmaking (more than six hundred brass upholstery tacks were found in the burned area), it was still supposed that the metalworking was associated with a cabinetmaker. When the Williamsburg Public Store Records came to light and confirmed the use of the shop as an armory during the Revolution, it became a near certainty that the traces of the furnace and the brass trimmings were relics of this operation. It is even possible that some of Dickinson's brass hardware was still in the shop when "Mʳ Andersons people" took it over and that they appropriated the brass for use in repairing the arms.

Just what the repairing and cleaning of the public arms entailed was not revealed by the archaeology. Two musket locks were found but both were much too decayed for them to be able to reveal why they were thrown away. Some of the flints were new, but others still had the lead grips stuck to them that originally helped to clamp them between the jaws of the cock, and it was therefore apparent, though certainly not surprising, that some of the weapons came into the armory with old flints in position and that these were removed in the course of repairing or cleaning. It is possible that a few of the tools used by the armorers had been acquired from the colonial magazine on Williamsburg's Market Square. After some of the heavily rusted files and rasps found in the excavations had been chemically cleaned, it was discovered that they were stamped with a crowned G R and were thus identified as British government property.

Throughout the coming and going of cabinetmakers, the decaying of the cabinet shop and the subsequent advent of the armorers, Mrs. Hay continued to live in her house beyond the stream and, not wishing to change the pattern of a lifetime, she continued to let her trash be thrown down the slope into the stream and around the piers of the shop's westerly extension. She did not die until 1787, nearly sixteen years after her husband, during which time the value of her property gradually decreased.

From an archaeological point of view, the fact that the widow Hay continued to live on the site so long after the death of her husband was extremely fortunate. As a rule the death of the householder results in a change of ownership even if it only amounts to the advent of a new generation. Thus the inventory made at the time of the man's death lists the possessions that he then owned and which were subsequently dispersed, ensuring that few, if any, of those objects would find their way into the ground of that property. But in the case of Anthony Hay, his widow remained there for sixteen years, continuing to use the same cutlery, glasses, Queen's china, chamber pots, tin tart molds, and whatnot that figured in her late husband's inventory. As these things wore out or were broken, out they went to join the treasure of garbage that littered the valley slope. There they remained for the archaeologists of the twentieth century to study and to try to associate with the right entries among the hundreds of items listed in Anthony Hay's inventory.

Inventories are, of course, the yardsticks whereby those whose job it is to furnish the reconstructed and restored buildings of Williamsburg must gauge their estimation of the appearance of the interior of each house. Without the evidence of archaeology the curators would be left to interpret as they liked such inventory entries as "16 china bowls . . . 18 wine glasses," or "15 bottles different sorts."

But in the case of Anthony Hay's inventory, more than forty different entries are supported by archaeological evidence, fragments which—even if we cannot *prove* that the excavated pieces are the very same as those that appear in the list—do provide excellent clues to their styles and quality.

Apart from the relics of a cabinetmaker's home and business, the Anthony Hay site yielded a few objects that were remarkable in their own right. Not the least of these was a carefully shaped iron plate with metal straps protruding from it that was found in the silt of the original stream bed and must therefore have found its way there before the cabinet shop was built. When the object was first discovered, it was thought to be part of an unusual suit of armor. The moisture of the silt coupled with the preservative powers of the decaying organic materials around it had protected the thin iron plate from all but the lightest surface rusting (Fig. 96). An examination of this rust showed that it contained impressions of threads, textile, and straw padding that had been attached to the iron; it was then clear that although the metal was fashioned to fit part of a human back and shoulder, it could not have been armor. There was only one reasonable alternative; it had to be part of a surgical corset, and that is exactly what it was. Photographs were sent to the Wellcome Historical Medical Museum in London where its director, Dr. E. Ashworth Underwood, confirmed this

96. Part of a child's iron orthopedic corset found in stream silt on the Hay cabinet shop site. Traces of straw padding and coarse textile still cling to the plate.

97. A conjectural sketch showing how the iron corset may have been worn.

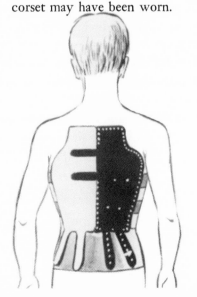

identification, adding that it was intended for the correction of spinal malformation in a child. He explained that the excavated section was for the right shoulder blade and that the two metal tongues would have been attached to a similar piece for the left shoulder. The two pierced metal straps at the lower edge would have been attached to a firm leather or metal belt worn round the waist (Fig. 97), while the holes around the edges of the plate were for stitching to a strong fabric or soft leather that would cover the straw padding. The object is certainly less than attractive, but it is important in that it is probably the only example of its type surviving from colonial America. Furthermore, it serves to remind us that life in the eighteenth century was not all silks, satins, and courtly elegance. For the child who wore this corset through a hot Virginia summer, it must have been something close to purgatory.

Another of the more unusual items from the Hay site was a short strip of lead onto which were stamped in reverse, letters reading FOUR C[ROWNS]. To Williamsburg archaeologists who had excavated at the site of the nearby printing office five years previously, this object was readily identified as a piece of type for the printing of paper money issued during the French and Indian War of the 1750's. Two other pieces had been found in the vicinity of the printing office; one of them had been used to print the coat of arms of colonial Virginia and the other provided the date 1758 within an ornamental border (Fig. 98). As as result of lengthy inquiries by Colonial Williamsburg's researchers, a bill printed from dies of this kind (Fig. 99) was discovered in the collection of the late Mr. F. C. C. Boyd of Ringoes, New Jersey.

The *Journal of the House of Burgesses* for September-October 1758, shows that William Hunter, then the printer of the *Virginia Gazette* and proprietor of the printing office, was also the printer of the paper money. Having done the work, Hunter submitted his bill for printing and binding two hundred and seventeen books of treasury notes "and all the Expense he was at in procuring necessary Plates, &c. for the Work," a bill that was considered so exorbitant that the colony agreed to pay only approximately half. Mr. Hunter's difficulties in getting his money from the government are no different from those suffered by the tradesmen of every century and as such they do not concern us. What is important is the reference to the printer's pro-

98. A border strip of 1758 used in printing paper currency.

curing the plates, showing that they were not supplied to him by the treasury and suggesting that he had to make his own arrangements regarding the cutting of dies and casting of the components.

Counterfeit coins circulated in eighteenth century England in large quantities, and there is every reason to suppose that they did so in Virginia. It is clear that in agreeing to print paper money to help pay for a war that could not be financed out of the colony's meager funds of gold and silver, the Assembly was very cognizant of the fact that if the notes could be easily counterfeited the economy of the whole colony might be jeopardized. Thus, in Governor Fauquier's "Act for the Defence of the Frontiers of this Colony, and for other Purposes therein mentioned" of October 12, 1758, it was specifically demanded that the ". . . several Notes [of various denominations] shall be prepared, printed and engraved in such Form, and after such Method as the said Treasurer shall judge will be the most safe from Counterfeits and Forgeries." Just to make sure that Hunter or his associates did not print themselves free samples or commit any other "fraudulent Practice used by the Printer, his Servants, or any Person concerned therein . . ." two trusted citizens were appointed to supervise the printing operation.

Probably because of a lack of suitably watermarked paper, the plates for the notes were made up from a series of specially cast components that would be more difficult to copy and assemble than would one simple plate. When the two used sections of a plate (the arms of the colony being carefully defaced before being thrown away) were found, it was supposed that the pieces would have been cast under the most careful guard and only the items actually required at any one time would be permitted to remain in the printing office. However, the discovery of the third piece on the Hay site seemed to disprove such a theory. The denomination strip was simply impressed into a piece of lead and had never been trimmed up for mounting on the plate. This would suggest that Hunter cast the components whenever he needed

253

99. A one-shilling bill of 1758.

them and that those which, for one reason or another, were not considered satisfactory were thrown away.

In the course of the printing office excavations, fragments of crucibles were found in which traces of lead remained, and in addition numerous scraps of waste lead were scattered about the site. Among these were pieces of sheet lead, one with circles cut out of it and another with a circle marked on it with the point of a pair of dividers (Fig. 100); all of these circles were about the size of an eighteenth century English copper halfpenny. This would not be particularly notable, for circles come in all sizes, were it not for the fact that the excavations also yielded two roughly cast lead copies of the copper halfpenny of George II (Fig. 101). One would hardly suppose that anyone, be he white, Indian, or Negro, would have been so naïve as to accept the "coins" as bona fide halfpennies and therefore we cannot class them as forgeries. Only two possible explanations come to mind, one that Hunter's apprentices were simply playing around—a dangerous game in an age when forgery could be a capital offense—or alterna-

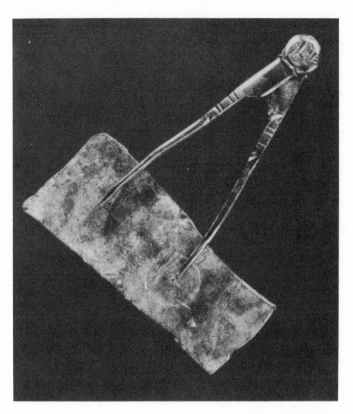

100. A pair of brass dividers
and a scored lead strip from
the printing office site.

101. Crude lead copies of
an English copper half-
penny (above) from the
printing office site.

tively that the printer had visions of becoming a temporary Virginia mint turning out both the inflationary treasury notes and a debased coinage to match it. Such a scheme is not as outrageous as it might at first seem, for pewter coinage had been common in the reigns of James II and William and Mary, and at least one piece had been made for circulation in the plantations, i.e. American colonies. The fact that the lead coins had been cast in a mold made from a halfpenny depicting the old head of George II and dated 1750 points to their being made during the French and Indian War and so perhaps in the same period that Hunter was printing the treasury notes.

The printing office itself was a brick building standing in the same valley as the Hay cabinet shop but one block to the south and fronting on Duke of Gloucester Street (Fig. 102). The street had been raised and the stream flowing across it had been confined within a vaulted brick channel, so it was hoped that a store of helpful artifacts would have been preserved in the silt on its floor. Unfortunately they proved to range from fragments of an eighteenth century delftware drug jar to cannon balls and shells of Civil War and World War I date and thus were too mixed up to be informative. This confusion of date was typical of a good deal of the site and such things as bicycle parts and coffin handles (the site had been occupied by a store in the early part of this century) were liberally scattered amid the eighteenth century's broken pottery, glass, and printers' type. This last and extremely important item was to be found strewn all around a secondary building to the rear of the printing office as well as in a tight concentration against the east wall of the office itself. Mr. James Knight, the archaeologist in charge of the excavation, suggested that this assemblage of type might have been thrown out of an upper window; so, when the building was reconstructed, a window was put back in such a position that it would be possible for the type to be thrown where it was found. Similar evidence was encountered at the Hay residence where plaster thrown out of an opening at the west end while the building was being dismantled pointed to the existence of a window or door in that section of the wall. It is only by the interpretation of such seemingly obscure clues as these that the archaeologist is ever able to help the reconstructing architects to envisage the above-ground positions of doors or windows.

256

102. The reconstructed printing office and the stream whose silt contained many important relics of the printing trade.

There were initial hopes that the printing office excavations would provide clues to some of the secondary activities carried on at the site, since the printer had operated a store selling such things as writing materials and mathematical instruments. The only possible relic of this activity was a single, though handsome, pair of brass dividers; but as these bore considerable signs of wear, they were certainly not new when thrown away. Other objects of brass which, like the dividers, were found in the stream silt near the printing office proved to be more informative (Fig. 103). These were stamps used

257

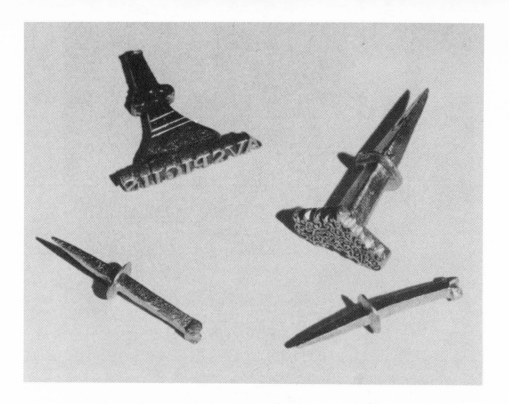

103. Brass bookbinder's stamps from the printing office. Average length 2 inches.

104. An ornamental brass bookbinder's stamp with a fox's head as part of the design. Found at Rosewell.

by bookbinders to impress gold-leaf ornaments and titles onto the leather, and among them were matrices for elaborate scroll corner ornaments, a fleur-de-lis and one bearing the word AVSPICIIS. Although no book using this Latin word in its title has been identified as having been printed on the site, there are surviving books that bear ornamentation similar to that created by the other stamps. Delicate and elaborate though some of the stamps are, they are unimpressive when compared with another (Fig. 104) picked up in a field near the plantation of Rosewell, an elaborate die combining a most intricate foliate scroll around the head of a fox. The style of manufacture, the way in which it had been seated in its wooden handle and the thickness of the shank and face were all similar to the Williamsburg examples, and it might be reasonable to suppose that a member of the Page family decided to take up bookbinding and purchased the necessary tools from the printing office in Williamsburg.

To visitors to Colonial Williamsburg's archaeological museum, the sight of the lead type and associated spacers from the printing office is often a gasp-evoking experience. For some reason, perhaps because the pieces are so small, they consider it remarkable that they should have been found. But when you come to think about it, the recovery of printer's type is no more unexpected than the finding of broken bottles on a tavern site. In point of fact, the type is not particularly informative, for examples of the work done in the printing office survive both as books and as copies of the *Virginia Gazette*. Even though type for printing the signs of the zodiac was among the items found, it still did not impress the research staff, which already knew that the printer produced almanacs. Had the type been found on a site that was not already known to have housed a printing office it would, of course, have enjoyed a more enthusiastic reception. This, I suppose, proves once more the old archaeological dictum that it's not *what* you find, but *where* you find it, that makes an artifact important.

Treasures
Without Price

It will have become apparent by now that in our sorties into the soil of colonial Virginia we have been guided along the way by the artifacts that the colonists left behind them. Without such clues the archaeologist could do no more than uncover old foundations and trust to luck that they belonged to the buildings that he hoped they did. When the plow slices, the bulldozer pushes, and the ground hog burrows into the ground, fragments of the past become scattered over the surface where they wait to be picked up and interpreted by anyone with the knowledge to do so. In this chapter I proposed to explore the evolution of the most common artifacts of the colonial centuries not only to show the kinds of things our ancestors used but also to indicate how an archaeologist can learn to date them and so use them as clues to the past.

The principal categories of excavated colonial objects are bottles, ceramics, tobacco pipes, and table glass in that order of frequency. In addition, we have a broad heading of "small finds" that embraces everything from builders' hardware to trouser buttons. To the archaeologist the most helpful of all these categories are those that comprise objects whose evolution of shape can be most readily dated. As a further refinement he needs items that would also have had a fairly short life, thus placing the date of manufacture close to the date of discard. It is not enough to know, say, that a plate was made in the factory of Josiah Wedgwood after 1765 if you have no idea when it was broken and thrown away, for it is the date of discard that marks its entry into the ground, thus transforming the sherds into an archaeological clue. If the home of a family that owns a set of early nineteenth century willow pattern dishes is destroyed in the present century and the dishes are the only things that survive for the archaeologists of the future to dig up, the excavators might deduce that the house burned in the 1820's instead of the 1960's.

Of all the European objects of the colonial period that survive in the ground, the tobacco pipe best fulfills the archaeological requirements of datable evolution and short life (Fig. 105). The pipe was, of course, an American device, having been introduced to the English, as early as 1565, by the Indians of Florida who smoked their dried herb "with a cane and an earthen cup in the end." The Indians of Virginia used a simple clay pipe that was merely a tapering pottery tube bent upward at the broad end, and it was from pipes of this kind that the European clay pipe developed.

Because of the scarcity and high price of tobacco, the first English pipes had extremely small bowls and stems that were no more than four or five inches in length. The earliest of these were probably made by hand, but by about 1590 or 1600 the majority were manufactured in molds; a wire was thrust down the solid casting while still in the mold to create the stem hole. At first the wires or metal rods were thick and the holes large, but as time went by the stems were made longer and so the wires needed to be small to avoid their bursting through the wall. Mr. J. C. Harrington discovered in the course of his work at Jamestown that it might be possible to date a fragment of pipe stem by measuring the size of its bore. By studying and measuring large quantities of pipe fragments from dated deposits in America and in England, Harrington was able to develop a chart whereby the per-

261

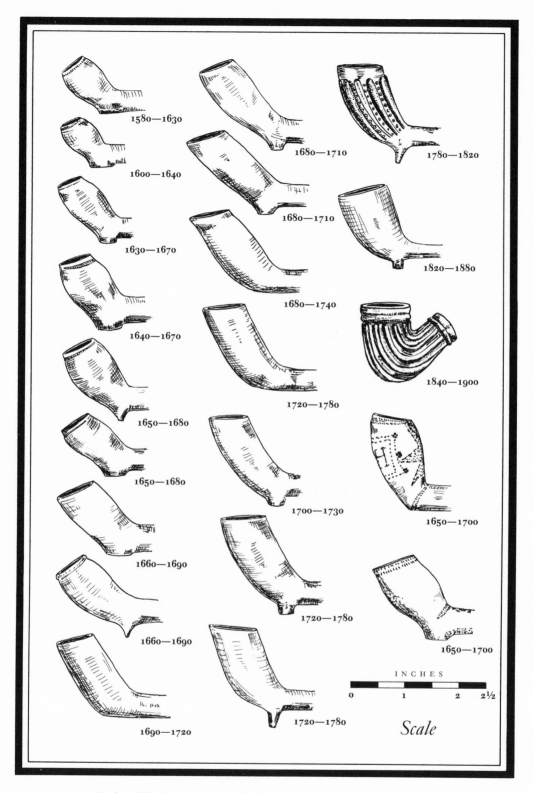

1580—1630

1600—1640

1630—1670

1640—1670

1650—1680

1650—1680

1660—1690

1660—1690

1690—1720

1680—1710

1680—1710

1680—1740

1720—1780

1700—1730

1720—1780

1720—1780

1780—1820

1820—1880

1840—1900

1650—1700

1650—1700

INCHES

0   1   2   2½

Scale

105. A simplified type-series of clay tobacco pipe bowls. The dates bracket the period in which the form was most common. All are English white-clay examples save for the last three which are of Virginia manufacture and are red-bodied (glazed), reddish brown, and yellow, respectively.

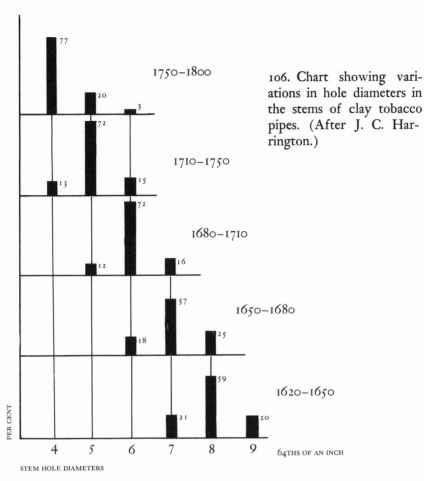

77

1750–1800

20

3

72

1710–1750

13

15

72

1680–1710

12

16

57

1650–1680

18

25

59

1620–1650

21

20

PER CENT

4   5   6   7   8   9   64THS OF AN INCH

STEM HOLE DIAMETERS

106. Chart showing variations in hole diameters in the stems of clay tobacco pipes. (After J. C. Harrington.)

centages of the various stem hole diameters in a deposit could be used to arrive at a twenty-year bracket for the date of deposition (Fig. 106). Although Harrington urges the greatest caution in using this chart, the fact remains that the chart has proved to be reasonably accurate, providing the group of pipe stems is large enough, preferably no fewer than seventy-five or a hundred. Experience has shown, however, that because there was considerable variation in stem lengths in the late eighteenth century with a general shortening trend predominating, the system ceases to work after about 1780. An important feature of Harrington's discovery is that it is extremely simple to use, requiring only a copy of his chart and a set of household drills (ranging from 4/64 inch up) that can be purchased for less than a dollar at any hardware store. Harrington first published his system in the *Quarterly Bulletin of the Archaeological Society of Virginia* in September 1954, at which time it met with considerable skepticism. But time has proved him right and now the system is used by all archaeologists working on sites of the seventeenth and eighteenth centuries. Recently Mr. Lewis R. Binford of the University of Chicago has taken the Harrington system a step further by evolving a mathematical formula that can be used to provide a mean date for any group of associated stem fragments, such as a collection of broken stems used as a necklace in an Indian grave, thus narrowing the twenty-year bracket provided by Harrington's chart. Here again the number of fragments must be considerable before the formula can be used with any hope of accuracy.

The shape of the pipe bowl went through a number of evolutionary changes during the colonial period as is shown in Fig. 105, and it is quite a simple matter to distinguish between pipes, say, of the mid-seventeenth century and those of the early eighteenth. Again, of course, it is not statistically possible to determine the date of a site on the evidence of only a small number of bowls, although individually they are safer guides than single stem fragments. Many bowls are marked on the heel or spur at the base of the bowl with the makers' initials. In the first half of the seventeenth century, London was the main center of manufacture, using clays brought in from the counties of Kent and Dorset. By mid-century, Bristol was gaining in importance and by the close of the seventeenth century such towns as Liverpool, Chester, Broseley, and Hull had sizeable outputs. But as far as Virginia was concerned, Bristol seems to have been the principal source of white clay pipes from about 1660 through to the end of the colonial period. Knowing that pipes were important items for use in trade with the Indians, many eighteenth century Bristol pipes were molded without heel or spur at the base of the bowl so as to resemble the traditional Indian pipe. Such pipes comprise as much as a third of all that are found in Williamsburg excavations and from this it is clear that this shape was perfectly acceptable to the colonists. It is noteworthy that the form is rarely found in England, indicating that it was reserved for the export trade. That they did find favor with the Indians is attested by a painting of the Indian chief Tishcohan by Gustavus Hesselius in 1735 (Collection of the Historical Society of Pennsylvania) which shows the chief with one of these pipes suspended in a little bag strung around his neck (Fig. 107).

The ornamenting of pipe bowls was not common in the seven-

107. The Indian chief Tishcohan shown with an English clay pipe suspended from his neck. Painted in 1735 by Gustavus Hesselius and owned by the Historical Society of Pennsylvania.

teenth century although a few are found decorated with impressed stamps, embossed with dots, or molded in the shape of human faces. In the eighteenth century, elaborately molded bowls are found decorated with the arms of Hanoverian England, Masonic emblems, or the three feathers crest of the Prince of Wales, all of which occur in the second quarter of the century. Some Bristol makers molded their names or initials in cartouches on the right side of the bowls, while Chester makers went in for elaborate stems bearing the arms of the city and

265

signs of local taverns. In the late eighteenth and nineteenth centuries all sorts of large decorative bowls were produced, most of the early American examples being heavily ribbed or gadrooned. These white pipes should not be confused with the many brown clay bowls molded in ribbed, Indian head, Turk's head, and other ornaments, that were attached to a reed instead of a clay stem, and which are characteristic of Virginia pipes in the nineteenth century.

Before leaving the clay pipe I should mention an important group that was common at Jamestown in the second half of the seventeenth century. These were fashioned from local clay and are usually red-brown or a dirty yellow in color, the bowls often decorated with pricked designs of stars, animals, or European initials. This last feature is somewhat disconcerting, as it has sometimes been suggested that these very crude pipes were made by the Indians. Closely allied to this series are others made in a dirty yellow clay that were shaped in molds in English forms. No examples of pipes of this colored clay have been found in England and it is believed that they were made in America. But regardless of where the red and yellow pipes were manufactured their presence on a site is a good indication that the area was occupied in the second half of the seventeenth century.

The English white clay pipe did most of its evolving in the seventeenth century with only a few changes occurring in the eighteenth; consequently, it is most valuable as a clue to archaeologists working on early sites. Glass wine bottles did not appear until about 1650 and they did most of their evolving in the eighteenth century (Fig. 108). Just as tobacco pipes were almost as expendable as cigarette butts so wine bottles were broken by the thousand and thrown away without any great loss to their owners. Broken bottles constitute more than sixty percent of all the artifacts dug up in Williamsburg, a proportion that is paralleled on most excavated sites of the eighteenth century. Actually the term "wine bottle" is something of a misnomer as precisely the same kinds of bottles were also used for cider, ale, spirits, or paint, and one that was fished out of the York River contained whale oil.

In the first half of the seventeenth century the only large glass bottles in common use were tall, four-sided vessels with short necks that were stored and transported in wooden or wicker containers called "cellars," which generally held a dozen. The same style of bot-

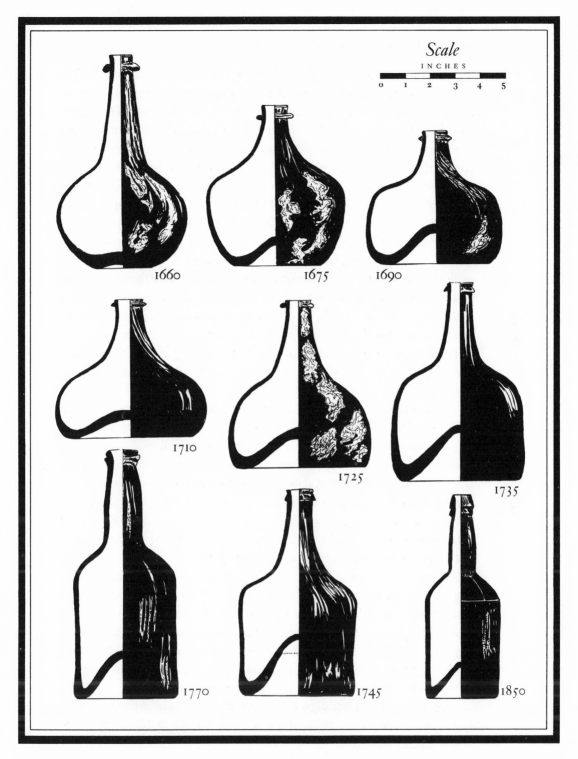

Scale
INCHES
0 1 2 3 4 5

1660

1675

1690

1710

1725

1735

1770

1745

1850

108. An evolutionary type-series of wine bottles showing their development through the colonial period, with a 19th century molded example for comparison. The drawn specimens are not all of the same capacity, and the given dates are approximately in the middle of their range.

tle, though tapering more toward the bottom to enable it to be lifted easily out of the mold and out of the wooden cellars, continued to be made through into the nineteenth century and collectors frequently call them Dutch gin bottles. They were in fact not all Dutch, being also made both in England and later in America, nor did they all contain gin. The early examples were a pale yellowish-green or amber in color and were extremely thin-walled, a fact that has ensured that very few have survived intact. The only unbroken example so far found in Virginia was discovered in the filling of a well at Jamestown attributed to a date in the second quarter of the seventeenth century.

The dark green glass wine bottle that we know today began its evolution in the mid-seventeenth century as a simple bubble on the end of a long neck, its only refinements being a slight pushing up of the bottom of the bubble to enable it to stand, plus a trail of glass wrapped around the neck and known as a string rim. Although string or pack thread had been replaced by brass wire before the close of the seventeenth century, the glass collar has continued to be known as the *string* rim.

The practice of marking bottles with a seal bearing the owners' crest or initials has already been mentioned and we have seen how helpful seals can be in identifying the owners of colonial sites. Occasionally the seals also bear a date which makes them even more valuable. Although the earliest dated specimen yet found in Virginia was the Richard Burbydge seal of 1701 from Tutter's Neck (Fig. 52), dated ones were being made almost half a century before. The earliest date so far authenticated is 1652 and it appears on a seal bearing a name with American overtones, that of John Jefferson. However, it was found in London and is in the London Museum. The Jefferson seal is attached to only a fragment of its bottle and therefore the honor of being the earliest dated bottle goes to one in the Northampton Museum in England which has on its seal the sign of a King's Head tavern, the initials R.M.P. and the date 1657. An even earlier bottle than either of these seals has been identified as a result of excavations at Jamestown—coupled with a remarkable coincidence.

In 1954, workmen digging on a bombed site in Aldermanbury, London, cut into the remains of a cellar that had probably been buried at the time of the Great Fire of 1666. In the cellar they found a quan-

109. A wine bottle with the initials of Ralph Wormeley, who died in 1651. Found in London.

tity of glass wine bottles which they proceeded to throw against a nearby brick wall. An antiquary acquaintance of mine happened to be passing, heard the crash of breaking glass and went to investigate. He gathered the fragments of two bottles and later gave them to me. Both bottles bore seals carrying the initials R W and at that time I had no hopes of identifying the owner (Fig. 109).

I should explain that in the seventeenth century—though never, as far as I know, in the eighteenth—people who could not afford or did not want the trouble of having special brass matrices made for their personal seals, could have their initials applied by the glassmaker from separate letter matrices that he kept for that purpose. Thus if John Doe wanted his initials on his bottles the glassmaker would take the two letters J and D and set them up together in a wooden handle to make the seal. Once the order was completed he would take the seal apart and it would be a thousand to one chance, even if the same John Doe later came back for a repeat order, against his ever setting the initials up again in precisely the same positions as before. The significance of this seeming irrelevant detail becomes apparent when I

269

explain that an *identical* R W seal was unearthed in excavations at Jamestown.

When I was given the R W bottles in London, I had no idea of ever coming to Virginia, but when I did so in 1957, I brought the bottles with me. Later while studying the Jamestown seals I found that the R W seals were the same in every detail. There was no doubt that all three were made for the same person and at the same time. The identity of the owner was revealed by the fact that the Jamestown seal was found on property that had belonged to Captain Ralph Wormeley, who had come to the colony in about 1635 and who sired a long line of distinguished Virginians whose later home was at Rosegill plantation in Middlesex County. Although there is some disagreement among historians as to the date of Ralph Wormeley I's death, it was probably in 1651 (his widow remarried in 1652), in which case the R W bottles can truly claim to be the oldest English wine bottles yet identified.

Figure 108 shows a series of wine bottles from various Virginia sites and illustrates their evolution as they progressed from the mid-seventeenth century through to the end of the eighteenth. Intact bottles are not common, for even if they were thrown whole into trash pits, they generally broke when they hit the bottom. A mid-eighteenth century cellar excavated on the site of the new Post Office being built in Williamsburg in 1961 had been used as a refuse pit and contained more than one thousand one hundred bottles; but although it was clear that many had been intact when thrown in, only one emerged undamaged. The majority of intact bottles are found in the wet silt of wells where they were cushioned as they landed. One such bottle dating from the first quarter of the eighteenth century was recovered from the well at Bassett Hall on the edge of the town. There, the wet silt had preserved its cork and wire, which in turn had kept the original wine contents sealed inside, but unhappily the wine had turned to vinegar and tasted disgusting.

It is only rarely that a bottle survives sufficiently intact for its entire profile to be seen and therefore we must base our dating on key features. The string rim is one of them, being broad, flat, and as much as half an inch below the mouth on bottles of the period *circa* 1650-75, becoming closer to the mouth, smaller, and V-shaped by the end of the century, and changing again in the latter part of the eighteenth century when it became secondary to a thickened mouth. The base shape also provides valuable dating clues. In the earliest forms the pushed up "kick" was very small, but as the bottles became broader and squatter, it became larger, resembling an inverted saucer. By the second quarter of the eighteenth century the body became taller and less broad, but the basal kick grew almost conical. As the bottles continued to increase in height, the bottom became steadily smaller and developed a slight sag or spread just above the base. Once bottles began to be made entirely in molds (a revolutionary change that began in the second decade of the nineteenth century) the sag at the base disappeared, the string rim became part of the molding of the neck, and mold marks appeared around and up the shoulders to the neck. As a general rule, any wine bottle bearing mold marks or with makers' and owners' names molded on them must be of post-colonial date.

It is probable that in the second half of the eighteenth century some Virginia wine bottles were of American manufacture, probably coming from glasshouses in Pennsylvania. While no one has yet been able to identify these with any degree of certainty, it is likely that some of the bodies were shaped in octagonal molds, like those made for John Greenhow of Williamsburg in 1769 and 1770. Similar body shapes were used for the short-necked bottles that were common in the latter years of the eighteenth century as containers for snuff and blacking, and many of these, too, may be of American manufacture.

Pharmaceutical bottles were already being manufactured in quantity in England when the first settlers arrived at Jamestown and they were just the sort of simple item that the Jamestown glasshouse might have produced. Some examples of typical early seventeenth century medicine bottles are shown in Fig. 76; they display a much greater variety of shape than we find in the later seventeenth century and through the rest of the colonial period. The earliest bottles ranged in color from a pale straw to a dark blue-green, but by about 1650 they had settled down to a consistent pale bluish-green that persisted into the early nineteenth century. The only difference between the bottles of the latter half of the seventeenth century and those of the eighteenth is that the former were more often weak-shouldered. By the second quarter of the eighteenth century we find bottles of the standard

271

shapes being made from a clear metal as well as the more usual blue-green, and the clear varieties seem to have become more common as the century progressed. A few of them were molded on the side with the name of the contents or the proudly displayed information that the elixir or whatever it was (usually an all-purpose laxative) was made under a royal patent.

Particularly popular in the American colonies was Turlington's Balsam of Life which was considered to be good for more or less anything and contained no fewer than twenty-seven miraculous ingredients. In 1754 Turlington put out a distinctively molded bottle which he claimed would put a stop to the villainous "Persons who buying up my empty Bottles, have basely and wickedly put therein a vile spurious Counterfeit-Sort." The new bottle, looking something like a cubist's pear, bore molded legends on practically every available surface informing the public that this was a container devised in "LONDON JANUY 26 1754" and "BY THE KINGS ROYALL PATENT GRANTED TO ROBᵗ TURLINGTON FOR HIS INVENTED BALSAM OF LIFE." So popular was Turlington's Balsam in America that it was widely imitated. But Robert Turlington had been quite right when he assumed that the counterfeiters would have marketing troubles without the new 1754 bottles. It says much for early American enterprise that it was able to overcome this problem by copying the bottles as well. Approximately the same bottle shape continued to be made in the United States well into the early nineteenth century complete with "LONDON, 1754 . . ." and all the rest. Figure 110 shows two examples found in Williamsburg, one probably an original from the site of the *Virginia Gazette* Printing Office, and the other a copy from a nineteenth century filling of a well at the house once owned by George Wythe. The copies were generally poorly molded and the lettering consequently indistinct. But I doubt whether any of the customers were particularly concerned with these details; after all, Turlington's Balsam was Turlington's Balsam regardless of whether it was made in London or Philadelphia. We may reasonably suppose that such problems had not weighed too heavily on the mind of the Indian in whose grave one of these counterfeit bottles was found in South Dakota. Had he been a glass collector, however, he might very easily have suffered a fatal stroke on discovering that his bottle was not made in 1754. I recall that a few years ago I nearly

110. Glass bottles made for Turlington's patent, Balsam of Life. Left, English third quarter of 18th century. Right, American copy, early 19th century.

walked into this trap myself when a Virginia antique dealer offered me just such a bottle at a price that would have been steep if it had dated from 1654 let alone 1754. So collectors beware—Mr. Turlington is not always what he seems.

The majority of medicine bottles of the eighteenth century were not identified by molded inscriptions, the principal exceptions, besides Turlington's Balsam, being the green phials that contained Daffy's Elixir and Dalby's Carminative, both of which are shown in the records to have been used in quantity in colonial Virginia. Dalby's Carminative was put out in a conical green phial with the words embossed down opposite sides. This bottle too was copied in America although the early flat mouth was replaced by a short and stubby neck.

Today, regardless of the horrifying potion-pushing powers of television, we tend to look back at the last century as the great era of the patent medicine. But in truth there have been customers for quack cures as long as there have been sickness, old age, and falling hair. In the seventeenth century, as far as the world of medicine was concerned,

273

the average Englishman was still being awed by the smoke of alchemy and the brimstone of witchcraft; but by the eighteenth, though better educated and more sophisticated, he paradoxically had become a sitting duck for the promoters of pharmaceutical trash. A great many cures were sold in perfectly good faith and some of them contained ingredients that did have a curative effect. An indication of the range of a Virginia apothecary's stock in the eighteenth century, and also of his bottles, is provided by a notice in the *Virginia Gazette* for April 4, 1766, announcing the arrival from England of a

> *Large and genuine assortment of* DRUGS *and* MEDICINES, *among which are fine Peruvian bark, ipecacuanha, India and Russia rhubarb, jalap, Glauber and Epsom salts, camphire, saffron, antimony, saltpeter, borax, calomel, red precipitate, quicksilver, crucus of antimony, Venice treacle and turpentine, gentian, orange peal, juniper berries, camomile flowers, sarsaparilla, China root, aloes, Spanich flies, balsam capivi, lucatelli, Peru, tolu, sulphur, &c . . . Florence and palm oil, mercurial and other ointments, plaisters, Bateman's drops, Anderson's pills, British oil, Squire's and Daffy's elixir, Godfrey's cordial, Stoughtone's bitters, Turlington's balsam of life . . .*

In addition to the many imports there were doubtless numerous remedies that were made up in the colonies from local ingredients, most of which would have been dispensed in plain cylindrical green or clear glass phials bearing only a paper label. Until evidence to the contrary is forthcoming, it must be supposed that the majority of all such phials are of English origin.

Although, quantitatively, drinking glasses are not nearly as archaeologically significant as bottles, it seems reasonable to say a word or two about them while we are thinking in terms of glass. They were certainly a great deal more attractive than laxative or even wine bottles, but while they pleased the eye of the colonists, they come back to us as pathetic shadows of their former selves. They were not considered expendable, were never thrown away whole, and when a building burned or tumbled about their bowls, they invariably broke into a multitude of very small pieces. In short, not one wine glass of either seventeenth or eighteenth century date has yet been found intact in

274

any Virginia excavation. The best that we can offer is the group of three shown in Fig. 111 that date from the period *circa* 1725-40 and were found in the cellar hole to the rear of John Coke's tavern in Williamsburg. Although they were in their day cheap, run-of-the-mill pieces, they exhibit lines and proportions that are rarely rivaled in modern glass. Such typically English pieces are in marked contrast to the elaborate European forms that were copied and imported by the English in the early seventeenth century, and that Captain Norton hoped his Venetians would make at Jamestown in 1621.

In the course of the sixteenth century, Venetian glassmakers from the island factories of Murano spread their influence up through Europe to Antwerp and thence to London where the first glasshouse making drinking glasses "en façon de Venise" was set up near the Tower of London in 1570. Very few examples of the products of this factory have been positively identified and none has been found in Virginia. The basic goblet forms, however, with their elaborately molded stems which *could* have been made there, as well as in the Netherlands and in Venice itself, have been found in early contexts at Jamestown. Typical among them are glasses of a thin gray to straw-colored metal with stems shaped into lion masks or vertically ribbed (ladder stems) or more commonly with plain slender inverted bal-

111. Wine glasses from John Coke's tavern in Williamsburg. Second quarter of 18th century.

112. Drinking glasses of the third quarter of the
17th century from Jamestown. In the style of the
Greene designs of 1667-73.

usters (cigar stems) with collars at top and bottom. The very thin
feet of these glasses were invariably folded over at the edge to give
them greater strength.

As the seventeenth century progressed, England continued to
look to Venice for its designs and some glass sellers even preferred
to import Venetian-made glasses rather than market the products of
their own factories. Between the years 1667 and 1673 the London firm
of Measey and Greene conducted a voluminous correspondence with
their Venetian manufacturer which included numerous sheets of designs. Fortunately these documents are preserved in the British Museum and from them we can obtain the best possible evidence of the
types of table glass that found favor in the England of Charles II. A
large number of such glasses with their characteristic small-knopped
stems have been found at Jamestown (Fig. 112).

The alkali used in the making of Venice style glasses was known
as *barilla* and was derived from burning marine plants, a commodity
that was imported into England by the glassmakers, as also were Venetian pebbles to provide the silica. In the early 1670's the London Glass-
Sellers' Company was busily promoting research that would make the
English industry free of these foreign imports, and the man they chose

276

to head the research team was one George Ravenscroft. His experiments were directed not only at making an improved metal from English components but also at making one that was stronger than the Venetian. The new ingredients were ground English flints to make the silica, and potash and lead oxide for the alkali, the result being known as flint or lead glass. In 1676 Ravenscroft's new glass seemed to have overcome its initial tendencies to craze or "crissel," and the delighted Glass-Sellers' Company authorized that all the new glasses should be marked with a small seal bearing the head of a raven— George Ravenscroft's rebus. Fewer than thirty examples of Ravenscroft's sealed products are known to survive, and in London, where you might expect them to have been the most common, only two or three have been found in archaeological excavations. It is surprising, therefore, to find that the Jamestown collections possess at least one Ravenscroft seal, as well as four others, all except one either too decayed or too crudely shaped to be identified (Fig. 113). The exception is marked with the clearly defined relief impression of a bell, and it is possible that this might be the rebus of John Bellingham who managed the Duke of Buckingham's mirror plate glasshouse at Vauxhall from 1671 to 1674 and who previously had been in charge of a factory making drinking glasses and French mirror plate at Haarlem in the Netherlands. But regardless of whether or not the identification of the bell rebus is correct, the presence of the five seals at Jamestown assures Virginia of its niche in the history of English glass.

In the winter of 1962 the removal of a tree stump at Clay Bank on the York River in Gloucester County revealed the sand-filled cellar of a house destroyed around 1700. In the filling, mixed with a motley collection of iron tools and unimportant refuse, lay a magnificent example of the English glassmakers' craft in the late seventeenth century. Only the stem and part of the foot survives, and so we cannot be sure whether it was made as a large drinking glass or perhaps as a candlestick. In either case, as far as I can discover, it is without parallel. The stem (Fig. 114) stands five inches in height, is of lead crystal, and even after two hundred and fifty years in the ground, the metal still sparkles like a sun-kissed icicle. So fine and large an object is it that before its discovery I, for one, would have refused to believe that such a piece would have found its way to Virginia. After all, seventy-five years

277

later, the remarkably astute Josiah Wedgwood considered continental America so unripe for expensive wares that he would only send over his cheaper products. Yet here on a Virginia site that exhibited no other surviving signs of opulence was as handsome a piece of glass as ever graced the home of a seventeenth century English nobleman.

If the object were the stem of a glass it would, most probably, have been part of a covered goblet, a rare item even in England. Nonetheless, a few weeks after finding the stem I learned that in 1732 Colonel Thomas Jones (whose casement windows have been discussed earlier) made a settlement on his wife in case of his death; among the items listed were ". . . flower bottles, 6 glass decanters, 6 glasses with covers . . ." Because such glasses were even less common in the eighteenth than the late seventeenth century, we may be forgiven for wondering whether the Colonel's legacy might not refer to examples in the same class as the stem from Clay Bank. Thus, an archaeological discovery from one site can serve to breathe life into the flat and faded words of documentary history from another.

Eighteenth century Williamsburg was, as we have seen, a city of taverns and it is not surprising that large quantities of table glass have been found. While each piece, if it were intact, would today be hailed as a choice collector's item, few were then anything more than average serviceable tableware. Nearly all are of English lead glass and follow the general evolution of form that started in the 1690's with extremely heavy baluster stems, which became lighter and better proportioned in the early eighteenth century (Fig. 111). These gave way in the mid-century to straight stems, often attractively ornamented with patterns of internal hollow tubes (air twists) and opaque white threads, the air twists appearing about fifteen years earlier than the opaque. I hasten to add that such generalizations are extremely dangerous and readily open to criticism. Nevertheless, the above summary represents the basic evolution of the English wine glass in the eighteenth century as seen through excavated examples from Virginia.

As a general rule, stems and feet that bear mold marks are not of colonial date, although, just to confuse matters, there was a group of glasses with molded pedestal stems produced between about 1715 and 1765 which were used largely for champagne and sweetmeats. But with these, as in all other English glasses of the eighteenth century,

278

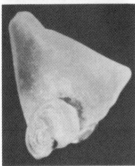

113. Fragments of sealed wine glasses from Jamestown. Top, perhaps the bell rebus of John Bellingham. Bottom, the raven's head of George Ravenscroft. About 1670-80.

114. Stem and base of massive lead-glass goblet or candlestick found at Clay Bank. English, late 17th century.

115. Rare opaque white glass tankard found in Williamsburg. Possibly made in Bristol, about 1750.

the feet and bowls were shaped by hand. It is not my purpose here to embark on a history of English glass, but merely to mention some of the more interesting examples that have been found in Virginia excavations.

In the Williamsburg archaeological collections two items are outstanding, the first being an opaque white tankard of great rarity (Fig. 115) found on the site of the Anthony Hay cabinet shop in 1960; it may well have been the property of Hay when he was owner and host of the Raleigh Tavern. Opaque white glass was first produced in England in the late seventeenth century in imitation of the Chinese porcelains that were then rapidly gaining in popularity. There has been a popular tendency to attribute all English eighteenth century white glass to Bristol, although it was undoubtedly manufactured in numerous centers. Most of the pieces in the great museum collections are decorated with enamels and many are quite thin and translucent. The Hay tankard was never decorated and its body is extremely dense. It would seem to be a glassmaker's attempt to compete with the tavern tankard market that was held so firmly by the white salt-glazed stoneware potters of the mid-eighteenth century, for this vessel is an extremely close copy of the salt-glaze form, with the addition of a wonderfully plastic handle that could only be created in glass. Mr. R. J. Charleston of the Victoria and Albert Museum feels that it dates from the mid-eighteenth century, while its archaeological context suggests a "throw away" date some fifteen years later. Although opaque white glass was made in numerous English factories, I think it likely that this handsome vessel is a product of Bristol on the grounds that so large a part of Virginia's trade was with that city. Furthermore, we know that a certain Jacob Little ran a "White Flint Glasshouse" there in 1752, and that his successors employed the enameler Michael Edkins whose ledgers include references to his decorating pint "Canns," which a 1749 dictionary describes as "Pot[s] to drink out of."

Williamsburg's second important glass object had actually resided in the archaeological collections for a number of years before it was identified. It had been found in two pieces, a cone-shaped bottle and terminal in the form of a human head wearing a wig and tricorn hat. This last fragment had been supposed to have been part of the stem of an elaborate wine glass and so had been separated from the bottle.

They were actually two pieces of an extremely rare type of glass bird feeder (Fig. 116). I had had the good fortune to have seen one of these things that had been found years ago in London and which is now in that city's Guildhall Museum. Consequently, when I saw the little glass head in a drawer with the wine glasses, I was able to recognize it. A search through the other glass fragments that had been unearthed from the same cellar in which the top had been found, soon yielded the bottom of the bottle and the two were then reunited. Shortly afterward, in searching through some tavern inventories, we found that in 1746 in Burdett's Ordinary on Duke of Gloucester Street there were "16 bird bottles" valued at three shillings. Just how these bottles were used was not entirely clear until we found a 1799 Rowlandson etching of the "The Tax Gatherer"; in the corner of it was a bird cage with one of the tricorn-hatted feeders attached to the outside. Shortly after this small piece of research had been completed, the Duke of Richmond found an intact specimen walled up in an old doorway at his home at Chichester in Sussex, England. He sent a picture of it to the magazine *Country Life* asking what it might be, and Colonial Williamsburg's archaeological section was able to pass its newly acquired information on to him. I mention this simply to show that the results of historical and archaeological research in America often have unexpected uses.

A rather similar trail was created when a Williamsburg archaeologist, who had been studying the pottery of Rouen in the Revolutionary period, met a fellow excavator from Kenya in the Victoria and Albert Museum in London. The latter had brought with him a quantity of sherds dug up at Fort Jesus near Mombasa and among them was a fragment of the Rouen faïence that had been the subject of study in Williamsburg. The dating and identification of the sherd proved to be an important factor in the chronology of the Fort Jesus site. Even if this little academic coincidence is not particularly breath-catching, it is a way of getting us away from glass into the realm of ceramics—which is the object of the exercise.

It would be quite impossible, and certainly out of place here, to try to embark on a history of ceramics in colonial Virginia. The subject is unquestionably fascinating and of major importance to collectors and archaeologists alike, but it would take an entire book of this

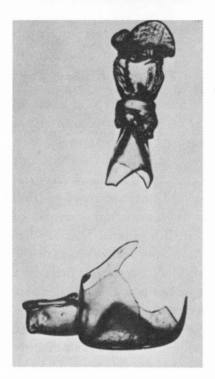

116. Glass bird feeders with anthropomorphic finials.
Left, from Williamsburg. Right, found in London,
18th century.

size, or maybe two, to do the subject anything like the justice it deserves. Between the excavated collections at Jamestown and Williamsburg plus the material from the few plantation sites that have been explored, we have representative examples of nearly all the wares that were in use in England in the seventeenth and eighteenth centuries as well as most of those of the early nineteenth century.

In the available space I can do no more than touch on the basic pottery evolution and pick out a few of the most interesting and important pieces. In the early days of the Virginia colony the settlers' pottery was drawn from any quarter that catered to their needs, be it England, the Netherlands, Spain, Portugal, France, or Italy. Later, when Virginia had become a Crown Colony and the Board of Trade had a say in what Virginians should or should not make, sell, or purchase, the sources were limited to those wares that were either manufactured in the mother country or carried through her ports in English ships.

The basic wares can be not too neatly boxed into the following categories: (a) *coarse earthenwares* fired at low temperature that com-

282

prised simple utilitarian items and the traditional country potters' or-namental slipwares; (b) the tin-glazed earthenwares that are loosely known at *delftwares* in England and the Netherlands, *faïence* in France, and *maiolica* in Italy, Spain, and Portugal, and that included table, ornamental, and pharmaceutical wares; (c) *refined earthenwares* like those produced by the famous English potters of the eighteenth century for table and ornamental uses; (d) *stonewares* that were made first in the Rhineland and then in England for general household du-ties; (e) *porcelains*, first from China and later from English factories; and finally (f) the inferior earthenwares made by the Indians for sale to the colonists or their slaves, which, for want of a better name, have been termed *Colono-Indian* wares.

Apart from the coarse earthenwares manufactured in Virginia, which were discussed in Chapter VIII, the majority of crude kitchen wares were shipped to the colony from the ports of Bideford, Bristol, and Liverpool, the Bideford and Bristol trade predominating in the seventeenth century and Liverpool coming on strongly in the eight-eenth. Bideford and its neighboring North Devonshire port town of Barnstaple both traded briskly with the colony in the seventeenth century and it was doubtless from these harbors that large quantities of North Devon earthenwares were shipped to Virginia. The principal characteristic of these wares is the very rough appearance of the un-glazed surfaces which is produced by a grit or gravel temper (Fig. 117). Although the Devonshire potters made such elaborate items as baking ovens, chafing dishes, and pipkins, their most common export, particularly in the eighteenth century, was a simple wide cream pan with a brown to green glaze on the inside. Next in importance was the North Wales potting industry generally attributed to the vicinity of the town of Buckley, whose wares were shipped to the American col-onies from Liverpool. The principal characteristics of these Buckley wares are a thick purplish-black glaze and a body made from a mixture of red and yellow firing clays that were mixed together and created a veined agate effect when seen in section. The North Wales potters were just about as conservative as their Devonshire competitors and confined their exports largely to wide-mouthed pans and bowls (Fig. 117) and to tall, somewhat ribbed storage jars.

Both the North Devon and the Buckley potters ornamented their better quality wares with clays of different colors, and the numerous varieties of the technique were collectively known as slipwares. The Buckley potters did not produce slipwares of styles clearly their own and consequently their products have not been identified, even if they have been found, in Virginia excavations. The West of England slipwares have characteristics that are quite unforgettable and many examples have been found in late seventeenth century contexts at Jamestown (Fig. 118). The potters coated their red-bodied earthenware with a white slip, which turned yellow under a lead glaze, and proceeded to scratch their floral and geometric decoration through it, exposing the dark clay beneath—a technique called *sgraffito*. Although the bowls, dishes, jugs, and cups made in this way were simple and rustic in their style, they were among the most attractive wares ever used in colonial America. West of England potters at Bideford and elsewhere continued to employ the same decorative techniques well into the nineteenth century, and it is therefore strange that such delightful pieces should have been imported into the colony only in the latter years of the seventeenth century. Only one sherd of it has ever been found in Williamsburg excavations, strongly suggesting that importation had ceased by the beginning of the eighteenth century. The principal sites where North Devon sgraffito pottery has been found and recorded are at Kecoughtan, Green Spring, Yorktown, and John Washington's home site in Westmoreland County, all seventeenth century sites, but none of them produced anything like the quantities that were unearthed at Jamestown.

The famed slipwares of seventeenth century Staffordshire are noticeably absent from Virginia, a fact that can be explained in part by the colony's relatively small trade with Liverpool as well as by the prevalence of earthenware exports out of the West of England. In the eighteenth century the picture changed and great quantities of Staffordshire yellow and black combed-ware dishes, cups, and posset pots arrived in Virginia (Fig. 119). Until recently all these yellow wares with their black dots below the rims and combed black lines around the bodies were accepted as hailing from the many kilns of Staffordshire. In 1961 Mr. Kenneth Barton of Bristol City Museum cast doubts on the origins of many of these vessels, suggesting that quantities of "yellow ware" were manufactured at Bristol. The truth

284

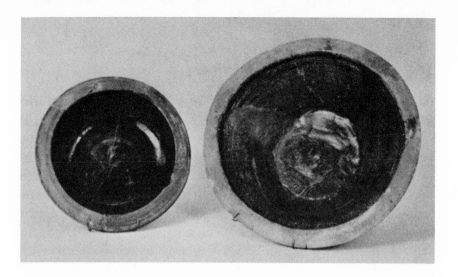

117. Eighteenth-century kitchen bowls from Williamsburg. Left, black-glazed Buckley ware from North Wales. Right, green-glazed gravel-tempered earthenware from the West of England.

of this theory is to be found in the historical records where, for example, in a letter from the merchant Thomas Beekman to Thomas Gilbert in Philadelphia in 1750, we find the former asserting: "You must [be] mistake[n] about Liverpool ware being 21 shillings sterling. Otherwise it must not be such yellow sort as comes from Bristol. I am sensible it cost 8/6 in Bristol, but the same sort of yellow ware with small black dashes on it comes also from Liverpool at 2/– sterling a crate less than they cost at Bristol and the crates are larger." While it is useful to have such clear documentation for Mr. Barton's theory, we are left with the problem of how to tell the difference between the "yellow ware" of Bristol and that from Liverpool, presumably made in Staffordshire. If the merchants of the eighteenth century had difficulty in telling one from the other, the student of ceramics in the twentieth century cannot expect to fare much better.

Apart from the main groups of North Devon, Staffordshire, and Bristol slipwares, a few pieces from other sources are notable, if only in that they indicate that colonists were not entirely dependent on a few potters and English agents as the arbiters of ceramic taste. From Jamestown have come occasional examples of elaborately decorated bowls from Wanfried in the Rhineland, exhibiting a sophisticated use of trailed white slips and sgraffito ornament that was popular in England in the first thirty years or so of the seventeenth century. A later and more rustic version of the same basic style has been found

285

on a bowl from Green Spring (Fig. 120), which is closely paralleled by bowls found in Dutch Limburg.

The citizens of London in the seventeenth century enjoyed the brown and white-clay-decorated slipwares made in Essex and known to collectors as Metropolitan slipware. These potters specialized in jugs and chamber pots ornamented with pious mottoes such as "Praise God and Honour the King," special gift items marked "The Gift is Small Good Will is All," and sometimes chamber pots urgently inscribed "Be Quick and Piff." Two fragments of this ware have been found at Jamestown, one of them a jug handle, the other the base of a chafing dish, and neither of them, unhappily, bearing any traces of a slipped inscription.

Among other oddities that have come to light is a single mid-eighteenth century fragment of a sgraffito-ornamented dish probably made near the village of Donyat in Somerset and found at the Coke-Garrett House in Williamsburg. The Williamsburg collections also include numerous examples of some rather unimpressive bowls that may have been made either in Pennsylvania or in New England. It is worth noting, incidentally, that the famous Pennsylvania German sgraffito slipwares as well as the generally similar products of Winston-Salem are absent from Williamsburg and, as far as I can discover, from every other carefully excavated Virginia site of the eighteenth century.

By firing your clay at a higher temperature—always providing that the clay will stand it—coarse earthenwares develop into the extremely strong and acid-resistant body known as stoneware. By throwing salt into the kiln during firing, potters commonly gave stoneware a salt glaze that was actually part of the body and that would not flake off as did the lead glaze from simple earthenwares. The manufacture of salt-glaze stoneware developed in the Rhineland in the late fifteenth century, and by the end of the sixteenth it had become a major export item, reaching England in vast quantities. The most common form was that of a mottled brown, handled bottle ornamented on the body with decorative medallions and on the neck with a bearded human face. Such vessels have come to be known as *Bellarmines* in the mistaken belief that the face was intended to be a Protestant caricature of the hated Cardinal Roberto Bellarmino. But as one of the bottles bears a medallion dated 1550 when Bellarmine was only eight years

118. One of many West of England sgraffito slipware dishes found in late 17th-century contexts at Jamestown.

119. Yellow-glazed slipware decorated in brown, made in Staffordshire or Bristol. Early to mid-18th century.

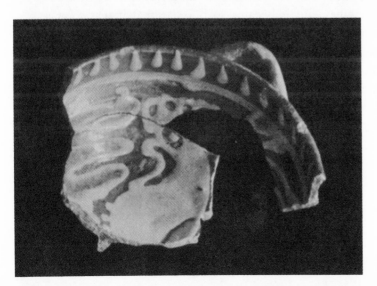

120. Fragments of Rhenish late Wanfried slipware bowl, probably mid-17th century. Found at Green Spring Plantation.

old, it is obvious that the Bellarmine association came along later, as also did the term "d'alva bottle" given to them when the Spanish Duke of Alva was being unpleasant in the Netherlands in the 1670's. Literally hundreds of different molds were used to impress the medallions on the bodies of Bellarmines and it is only rarely that one encounters more than one example from each. Figure 12 illustrates one of the exceptions; it shows a pair dating from about 1640 and found in Virginia, the one on the left coming from Kecoughtan and that on the right from a rubbish-filled well at Jamestown, covered over before 1650. While both can be roughly dated on the evidence of their shape, more accurate data is provided by the sealed context of the Jamestown specimen—information that was not forthcoming at Kecoughtan. Thus, as so often happens, the careful study of artifacts from one site helps to throw light on the history of another.

Bellarmines come in all sizes from pint to five-gallon capacities and bear dates from 1550 to 1699. The pint and quart sizes were by far the most common and many examples have been found at Jamestown. It is to Jamestown that we must go to see the only dated example found in Virginia, an extremely handsome specimen with three medallions each dated 1661. The bottle was found in the remains of a Jamestown house, perhaps destroyed in Bacon's Rebellion of 1676, and the vessel itself had suffered badly in the flames. (See Fig. 19.) A simple guide to the dating of these commonly found bottles is that in the late sixteenth and early seventeenth centuries the bodies were attractively and comfortably globular and had necks ornamented with extremely lifelike bearded masks; whereas those of the later seventeenth century had become pear-shaped, ill-proportioned, and were adorned with grotesque masks that might have been designed to scare a drinker half to death.

At first the Bellarmine was generally a mere container for the export of Rhenish wines, but it became so popular that it was soon a saleable item in its own right. It remained the Englishman's most common form of bottle until the advent of the glass bottle in the mid-seventeenth century. Thereafter it gradually lost popularity, a decline that is mirrored by the evidence of Virginia archaeology wherein we find numerous examples of smaller bottles at Jamestown but not one at Williamsburg. One would expect that the larger examples would

288

have had a longer life than the small and this too is supported by excavations that have revealed fragments of at least four from Williamsburg excavations, most of them in contexts of the 1760's, about a century after they were made. This, however, is by no means a record for Bellarmine longevity, an honor that probably belongs to the example that was found in the 1950's among the ceremonial possessions of an aboriginal chief living in the interior of the Dutch colony of Surinam.

The Rhenish stoneware potters of the seventeenth century did not confine themselves to the manufacture of bottles, although certain centers, notably Cologne and Frechen, were particularly known for them. Others such as Raeren and Grenzhausen, specialized in gray stoneware pitchers, mugs, and jugs, often elaborately molded and colored in blue and purple. A distressingly small number of fragments of a magnificent jug found at Jamestown shows that the vessel was decorated with carefully molded panels depicting the Biblical story of Judith and Holofernes (Fig. 121). Mr. F. S. Thomas of London has an identical jug in his collection and he is of the opinion that it was made in the Westerwald district of the Rhineland about 1610-20 (Fig. 20). The presence of such a jug at Jamestown clearly indicates that some of the settlers possessed ceramic pieces of excellent quality.

When the bottom fell out of the Bellarmine market, the potters of Westerwald stepped up their exports of blue and gray wares; the most common were chamber pots, tavern mugs, and jugs—in that order. These products were specifically aimed at the English market and were decorated with the portraits and ciphers of William III, Queen Anne, and most commonly with the G R cipher of England's George I and George II. (See Fig. 55.) The only items that were not so ornamented were the chamber pots, which were decorated with rosettes and crowned lions. Later, in the 1760's and 1770's, English potters imitated the German wares and perhaps overstepped the bounds of patriotism by decorating mugs, jugs, and chamber pots with ciphers or portraits of George III.

The English makers of brown stonewares, whose products have been mentioned in connection with William Rogers's factory at Yorktown (Chapter VIII, p. 221), produced quantities of tavern mugs and bottles but did not try to compete with the Rhineland in the chamber

121. Fragments of rare Rhenish Westerwald gray and blue stoneware jug decorated with an applied frieze telling the story of Judith and Holofernes. Found at Jamestown. About 1610.

pot business. The English brown stoneware potters specialized in tankards made for the use of specific taverns, many of them ornamented with appropriate tavern signs molded in high relief. They seem to have been made throughout most of the eighteenth century, and many were inscribed with dates and the names of their owners. It is extremely rare for the potter to sign any of his pieces, but in excavations at the Anthony Hay site in Williamsburg in 1960, the base of a large jug was found bearing the incised inscription "Evans [Ann]o Domini 1740." It is possible that this was a product of the John Evans who was working at Westbury-on-Trym outside Bristol in the mid-eighteenth century.

Bristol was a major center for the manufacture of English delftware, a soft-bodied earthenware coated with a lead glaze containing tin oxide that gave it the appearance of porcelain. The ware had been developed in Spain and Italy and had reached England by way of Antwerp in the reign of Elizabeth I; the first potters set up a business at Norwich and quickly moved to London in 1570. It would be more correct to refer to this early English tin-enameled pottery as maiolica; for although huge quantities of it were being made in the Netherlands at the same time, Antwerp was the principal center and it was not until the mid-seventeenth century that the town of Delft switched from brewing to potting as its principal industry. Nevertheless, the maiolicas of England and the Netherlands are generally known as delftwares.

In seventeenth century Virginia the delftware of Holland and the maiolica of Portugal was well in evidence, but by the end of the century the English delft trade had cornered the market. Consequently, it is extremely unusual for any tin-enameled earthenwares other than

290

those from England to be found on eighteenth century Virginia sites. By and large the early English products from Jamestown are typical of their period, being confined largely to pharmaceutical drug pots and jars, porringers, and chamber pots. But just as the Judith and Holofernes jug lifted the Jamestown German stoneware collection out of the pedestrian, and the Ravenscroft and other sealed glasses embellished its glass collection, so a few sherds of a delftware bottle provided an unexpected sparkle to an otherwise unimpressive delft collection. The bottle is represented by only four or five fragments of the base and side decorated in blue with birds and flowers in the Chinese manner. Such bottles are very rare, but at least two of the known examples are dated 1628 and are attributed to the factory of the potter Christian Wilhelm that stood on the south bank of the river Thames at London in the Borough of Southwark.

Among the more interesting and attractive products of the delftware potters' trade were the large dishes or *chargers* as they are popularly termed, which were elaborately decorated and used as wall ornaments. The earliest English example is dated 1602 and is adorned with a charming though none too accurate picture of London. As the seventeenth century progressed similar chargers were adorned with Biblical scenes—the Adam and Eve debacle being the most common—and later with the portraits of royalty and other popular figures of the day. The latest of the portrait chargers are those that bear the figure of George II, and as these are not common, it is reasonable to suppose that such wall ornaments had gone out of fashion by the mid-eighteenth century. We do know, however, that the Dutch in Albany continued the practice as late as 1744, for in that year Dr. Alexander Hamilton of Maryland wrote in his *Itinerarium* that "Their kitchens are likewise very clean, and there they hang earthen or delft plates and dishes all round the walls in manner of pictures, having a hole drilled through the edge of the plate or dish and a loop of ribbon put into it to hang it by." It may be significant that no fragments of such decorative chargers have been found in Williamsburg excavations and that as far as I can determine pieces of only one have been unearthed at Jamestown, suggesting that the ornamental use of delftware dishes was never very popular in Virginia. Yet, it can very easily be argued that we are dealing only with negative evidence, and it can equally well be claimed that as the chargers were used as pictures they would rarely have been broken and thrown away.

The Jamestown charger was not a pictorial example (none of those have been found) but was decorated with vine leaves and bunches of grapes and was probably made at Southwark in about 1640-60. The only other charger so far recorded was found in a context of about 1710 at Tutter's Neck, and its decoration was a simple geometric type that could have emanated from a factory in what is now Bermondsey, the next borough to Southwark on the south bank of the Thames. It would be foolish to assume that all large decorative dishes, twelve to sixteen inches in diameter, were used simply for wall decoration. We have only to examine a few seventeenth century Dutch still-life paintings to see that they were frequently used for fruit and even as fish dishes. No doubt the Green Spring potter had such a prosaic purpose in mind when he made a large lead-glazed dish almost identical in size and shape to many of the delftware chargers.

In the first half of the eighteenth century the manufacture of delftware had spread from London and the vicinity of Bristol north to Liverpool and later to Dublin, but the wares of Bristol and London seem to be most commonly represented among the fragments unearthed in Virginia. The most popular forms for eighteenth century delftware in the colony would appear to have been drug pots, dinner plates, and punch bowls, with chamber pots, wash basins, mugs, and porringers bringing up the rear, in that order.

The majority of delft plates found in Williamsburg have been so fragmentary that out of thousands of sherds unearthed less than a dozen examples have been pieced together. In 1961 the luck improved when the contents of a well at the site of the new United States Post Office on South Henry Street yielded four excellent plates dating from the first thirty years of the eighteenth century. Two were a pair decorated in green, blue, and red in an elaborate floral (mimosa) pattern, a style rare in Virginia (Fig. 122); the others bore floral motifs less striking in character. One of the latter, however, was found to be a smaller version of another that had been found two years previously at the Coke-Garrett House. Yet another plate, rather later in date, found in a cellar on the Post Office site had a border of moths around a Chinese landscape, and this was exactly paralleled by another fragment

122. English delftware plate decorated in blue and red within a green border, found in Williamsburg. About 1720-30.

found many years ago at the Norton-Cole House on Williamsburg's Market Square.

To an archaeologist the distribution of plates of similar style can be a valuable clue to the similarities of possessions and perhaps of taste among different colonial families. Taste is, of course, one of the most difficult commodities in the world to evaluate, largely because our yardstick is marked with the measures of our own likes and dislikes. Nevertheless, it is possible to use archaeological evidence like that of the delft plates to suggest patterns of fashion and popularity even if we cannot fairly arbitrate on their colonial owners' good or bad taste.

The floral-ornamented plate from the Coke-Garrett House that I mentioned above was just one item in a large group of ceramic and other objects found in a refuse dump west of the house and east of the Public Gaol. From the same deposit came another delftware plate (Fig. 123) decorated in blue with the figure of an acrobat balancing on a thin rod stretched between two braces. Although broken, it was quite a simple matter to restore this plate to its original amusing appearance and having done so we set about trying to find a parallel for it —without any success. I later took a photograph of it to England and showed it to a dealer friend who specialized in delftwares, and although he had never seen anything like it himself, he mentioned that

293

a customer of his had once told him that many of these peasant designs had originally been copied from the ornaments on Dutch tiles. I thought no more about it until I was driving through the east end of London a week later and saw a junk shop with a number of Dutch tiles in its window. As you may have guessed, I would not be recounting this story if one of those tiles had not proved to be decorated with the acrobat design. Here was another of those million to one coincidences that seem to be much more common than the law of averages would lead us to believe.

Although delftware plates were still being made in England at the end of the colonial period, they had started to lose favor in the second quarter of the eighteenth century when the makers of white saltglaze (Chapter VI, p. 138) began to produce mold-impressed plates and hollow wares in large quantities. The earliest form of this hard white-surfaced stoneware was actually made in Staffordshire from two clays, a drab-colored local clay and a fine white, transported there from Devonshire. The cost of hauling the white clay over long distances required its sparing use, and it was for that reason that it was at first applied only as a slip covering a body of the local drab clay. This was probably the "dipped white" stoneware that Josiah Wedgwood mentioned as being made at Burslem in Staffordshire in the period 1710-15. The trouble with this dipped stoneware was that when it was fired the white slip tended to fall away from rims and spouts, leaving the drab body-clay coyly exposed. In a not always successful attempt to overcome this problem, the potters added a band of iron oxide around the offending areas before firing so that the dark clay would not show when the white fell away. Figure 46 shows that the pleasantly proportioned little pitcher from the ruins of Corotoman is decorated in this way. Once the fine white clay became more cheaply and readily available, the potters abandoned the drab core and made the entire vessels from the refined ware. Consequently, the discovery of this very distinctive pottery can point to an early date in the eighteenth century for the site on which it is found. But just to make sure that this criterion is not followed too slavishly, I must recall the discovery of an undamaged and miraculously preserved, dipped stoneware mug that was recovered by divers from one of the York River wrecks claimed to have been sunk during the siege of 1781. It is strange, to say the very

295

123. Above, an apparently unique London delftware plate decorated in blue, found in Williamsburg. About 1710-20. Below, a Dutch delftware tile that may have inspired the English design. Late 17th century.

least, that so vulnerable an item should have continued in use through the century, been lost in a sunken wreck and then been recovered by divers, all without suffering so much as a chip. One might be forgiven for wondering, as intimated earlier, whether the divers did not stumble on a much earlier wreck while searching for relics of the Revolution.

Some white saltglaze vessels are helpfully ornamented with names and dates, the earliest of which would seem to be a posset bowl marked 1720 now in the Nelson-Atkins Gallery of Art in Kansas City. We know from newspaper advertisements that white stoneware of one sort or another was being sold in the colonies (Boston) as early as 1724, but it does not seem to have become generally popular until the 1730's. Thereafter, until the 1760's, white saltglaze successfully rivaled delftware as the best selling general purpose tableware (Fig. 124). Some of the pieces were ornamented with incised decoration, the lines carefully filled with cobalt blue, a fabric popularly known as "scratch-blue" stoneware. Other pieces were molded in relief, generally after about 1740; some were adorned with enameled decoration, and yet another group was embellished with transfer prints of royal arms, Aesop's fables, and pastoral scenes.

As the eighteenth century progressed a number of potters were experimenting with production of a refined lead-glazed earthenware that would be stronger than delft and less coarse than white saltglaze. The best known of these pioneers were Thomas Whieldon and Josiah Wedgwood, who were in partnership until 1759 and who developed a pale yellow body that became known as creamware. In its early forms the ware was often decorated with oxides of many colors, but when Wedgwood set up on his own, he refined the ware to the point where it was pleasing enough in itself to find public favor without the embellishment of green, blue, purple, and orange "clouded" glazes. While the plain creamware became increasingly popular in England after it obtained the patronage of Queen Charlotte in 1765, creamware or "Queen's China," as it was then frequently called, did not seem to have been common in Virginia until about 1769. In 1770, Mann Page II, late of Rosewell and then of Fredericksburg, wrote to England for a long list of merchandise that included "1 Dozn. Tea Cups, 1 Dozn. Saucers, 1 Dozn. Coffee Cups & 1 Dozn. Saucers, 1 Slop Bowl of Queen China." In the same year in Williamsburg, Anthony Hay

124. English white saltglaze ware in the Governor's Palace at Williamsburg paralleling examples found in the excavations.

the cabinetmaker and tavern keeper expired, leaving behind an inventory that listed 9 "Queen's china" coffee cups, 10 saucers, 139 plates, 4 butter boats, 2 "turin and dishes," 2 fish strainers, 5 sauce boats and dishes with two spoons, 8 egg cups, 2 fruit baskets, 5 fruit dishes, 34 dishes, and 6 corner dishes to the value of £7.1.3d, no small sum in those days.

By the time the guns of the Revolution began to rattle the dishes on colonial kitchen dressers, most of them were of creamware; this new lead-glazed earthenware had bested the white saltglaze just as the latter had superseded delftware. I do not intend to suggest that both saltglaze and delft had vanished from every home, far from it. But it is clear that

297

125. English creamware sherds bearing the black transfer-printed cipher of Dr. Phillip and Anne Barraud, who were married in 1783. Found in Williamsburg.

126. Fragments from a Rouen faïence dish decorated in pale blue and black, of the type imported during the Revolution. Found in Williamsburg.

when it came to buying new tableware, creamware was the most favored. Examples decorated with black Liverpool transfer prints were found in excavations at the Governor's Palace in Williamsburg, and at the home of Dr. Phillip Barraud which still stands on Francis Street. The good doctor married Anne Hansford in 1783 and soon after must have ordered creamwares specially made for him in England (Fig. 125), for fragments of plates bearing the black printed cipher P.A.B. (Phillip and Anne Barraud) were found in the garden, as well as on a site on the opposite side of the street—suggesting, perhaps, that he was not too particular where his trash was thrown.

By the mid 1770's Wedgwood was busily trying to improve on his creamware, for it was by then being produced in a number of other factories, notably at Leeds. Wedgwood proceeded to refine the cream glaze, creating an almost white ware that he called "Pearl" and which was used by most Staffordshire earthenware potters from about 1785 through the first quarter of the nineteenth century. The pearlware is most easily recognized by the way that the glaze appears blue in corners and around the feet of the vessels. The earliest forms were decorated with blue, green, and occasionally red shell-edging; later the ware was decorated with all sorts of hand-painted devices as well as for early underglaze transfer printing of the well-known "willow" and other patterns. Although Wedgwood illustrated a blue shell-edged ware in his pattern book of 1774, it has never yet been found in Virginia in contexts prior to about 1785, and consequently its presence invariably points to a site occupied after the end of the colonial era.

A similar clue is provided by the presence of a red-bodied faïence from Rouen (Fig. 126) characterized by a brown lead glaze on the backs of dishes and white tin-glazing on the front, which is generally ornamented with a central motif of a basket of flowers in pale blue or a deep purple. In the same class were bowls, pipkins, and other kitchen items glazed brown on the outside and plain white inside. The discovery of this coarse faïence in numerous deposits of the Revolutionary period prompted Colonial Williamsburg archaeologists to try to find out where it came from and at what date. The first clue was found in Diderot's encyclopaedia where he stated that French faïence may sometimes be "of two colors, that is to say, brown outside and white inside, the latter [as opposed to other colors previously mentioned] meant to be near the fire." From this scrap of information it was deduced that the pottery was largely intended for kitchen use and that it probably came from France. Next, the baskets of flowers ornamenting the dishes were somewhat reminiscent of the magnificently ornamented dishes of Rouen in the earlier part of the eighteenth century. Unfortunately this was none too conclusive a parallel as many factories had copied the Rouen designs. A search through American newspaper advertisements of the Revolutionary period provided the necessary confirmation, for between 1778 and 1784 china shops in Baltimore and Philadelphia were advertising ". . . a variety of China, Glass, & Roen ware," and "Delph and Roan wares, Dishes, plates, tureens, bowls, fruit baskets, etc." all offered "on the most reasonable terms." It was not hard to see "Roen," and "Roan" and even "Rhoan" as misspelling resulting from the poor pronunciation of Rouen, a hypothesis that was later born out by the discovery of a dish similar to those found in excavations, in the collection of the Victoria and Albert Museum in London and bearing the impressed mark DELAMETTAIRIE ROUEN. It seems that during and immediately after the Revolution the French potters of Rouen thought that they could capture the American ceramic market, which they expected would be surrendered by the Brtisih along with their colonies. But the English have a tradition of snatching victories out of defeat, and instead of losing their ceramic export trade, they enlarged it by producing vast quantities of tablewares specifically for the American market, often decorating them with transfer-printed portraits of American heroes, ships, and eagles. The Rouen potters never had a chance, and their industry which was already in decline continued on its downward path, dwindling from eighteen faïence factories in 1786 to six in 1802.

The very fact that the importation of Rouen faïence was short-lived and never very popular has made it a useful archaeological clue in the hands of the historic archaeologist. The presence of this distinctive ware tells us at a glance that the place where it was found was occupied during the Revolutionary period.

Many ceramic wares are extremely difficult to date with sufficient accuracy for them to be useful to the archaeologist, and none is harder than the common Chinese export porcelain that was so prized in the English home and that turns up in prodigious quantities on eighteenth

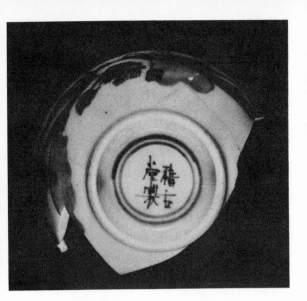

127. Base and side view of a small Chinese porcelain bowl decorated in underglaze blue and made for a Chinese civil servant about 1630-40. Found in Williamsburg.

century Virginia sites. The majority is decorated in underglaze blue in patterns of bamboos, willow trees, and variations of the lakeland scene that inspired the English design known the world over as the "willow pattern." This design was actually developed at Thomas Turner's Caughley factory, probably by Thomas Minton, as a transfer print. It was subsequently shipped to Canton to be copied in freehand painting on Chinese porcelain, and the first products arrived in England in about 1792. Thus the true willow pattern will not be found on colonial Virginia sites.

The blue and white porcelain of the great production center of Ching-tê Chên was shipped to Europe in considerable quantities in the early seventeenth century and numerous fragments have been found at Jamestown, but the proportion of porcelain to European wares was still small, at least in comparison to those of eighteenth century Williamsburg. But while it is possible to see obvious differences of painting skill between the Chinese export porcelains of the colonial period and the so-called "blue Canton" of the early nineteenth century, there are no such obvious yardsticks with which to distinguish between the run-of-the-mill products of the seventeenth and eighteenth centuries. Very few pieces are marked, and those that are, rarely bear anything more informative than the symbols for wealth, happiness, or fertility. One small bowl, found near the Chiswell-Bucktrout House in Williamsburg, did conceal some rather remarkable information in the Chinese characters painted on its bottom (Fig. 127). But when Mr. John A. Pope, assistant director of the Freer Gallery of Art in Washington, translated the inscription for us, more questions were posed than solved.

It was the practice for educated Chinese to devote their leisure hours to some mind-improving hobby and to give its name to their "hall," a room that paralleled our study or den. This hall name then became the owner's mark and it would appear on his possessions just as western gentlemen used their crests or shields-of-arms. The hall mark on the Chiswell-Bucktrout bowl proved to be that of Kao Ch'eng-yen a native of Chia-hsing, midway between Shanghai and Hangchow, who was a senior civil servant in the reign of Ch'ung Chêng (1628-43). The translation of his hall mark reads *Investigate Antiquity Hall*, indicating that Kao Ch'eng-yen was an antiquary, probably a collector of old books, but perhaps even an archaeologist. This intriguing possibility still leaves all sorts of unanswered questions. Regardless of whether or not Kao Ch'eng-yen was an archaeologist, the problem remaining is why a bowl specially made for a wealthy Chinese official in the second quarter of the seventeenth century should find its way into the export trade and wind up in Williamsburg in the eighteenth century.

Much more easy to explain and no less intriguing are the fragments of handsome Chinese export porcelain plates and dishes that have been found in various parts of Williamsburg, all bearing a carefully executed shield-of-arms painted in black, red, and gold. The arms are those of Lord Dunmore, Virginia's last royal governor, who arrived in the colony in 1771 and left it in unseemly haste in June 1775. Packing a few bags of necessities and his most precious possessions, the Governor and his family fled to a British warship lying in the York and later departed for England without returning for the bulk of his effects left behind in the Palace at Williamsburg. After the dust of revolution had settled, Dunmore prepared a schedule of his losses to obtain compensation from the British government, and among the entries was "A large quantity of very valuable China, Glass and Household Utensils of every kind."

One dinner plate and one soup plate with the Dunmore arms were found in the Palace excavations (Fig. 128); but fragments of three

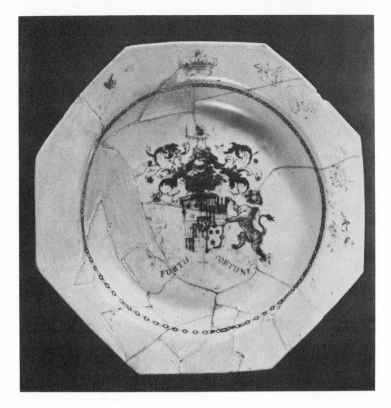

128. Chinese export porcelain plate decorated in overglaze enamels with the arms of Lord Dunmore and found on the site of the Governor's Palace in Williamsburg. About 1770.

other Dunmore plates, one a large serving dish, have been found on widely scattered sites in Williamsburg, and we can only speculate how they came to be there. None of the owners of the lots in question had any close associations with the Governor that would have prompted him to break up his expensive dinner service and present pieces to them, and so we must seek another explanation for their distribution. A study of the documentary evidence shows that the Palace was broken into by a group of Williamsburg citizens while the Governor was still at Yorktown, but all that was taken was Dunmore's fine collection of muskets and other weapons. It appears that someone had made an inventory of the Palace's contents, for in February 1776, three men were ordered to check the inventory to see whether anything was missing. In June of that year, Dunmore's slaves and personal estate were put up for public auction and it is possible that his armorial porcelain was sold off at that time, being purchased piece by piece by the citizens of Williamsburg as souvenirs of their last royal Governor. A week before the auction a resolution was passed authorizing the use of the Palace as a hospital, and it might seem logical that anything useful to such a project would be withdrawn from the sale. An inventory of the Palace made in 1779 referred to "11 Red & White china Dishes" and "28 Red & White china Plates." Were these, we may wonder, the remains of the Dunmore service?

The Governor's armorial porcelain was painted on top of the glaze, and unfortunately the colors used in this technique do not stand up very well when buried for any length of time in wet ground. Greens are more tenacious than most colors, although they generally turn a dirty brown, but black, red, and gold frequently disappear altogether, leaving the porcelain apparently undecorated. It is not until the fragments are tilted under a bright light that traces of the design can be seen lightly etched into the surface of the glaze. A fragment of one of Lord Dunmore's plates found on Anthony Hay's house site was only identifiable in this way, having lost every trace of its colors. In some cases Chinese export porcelains were decorated with overglaze enamels as well as underglaze blue, the two combining to create a single elaborate design. Frequently all the enameling has disappeared, leaving only the underglaze blue intact and a design of which half the lines appear at first glance never to have been completed.

Just as most excavated Chinese porcelain from Virginia is confined to simple blue and white varieties (the famous *famille rose* so prized by collectors is rarely found), so it is with English porcelain. This appears from the 1760's onward and is generally restricted to cups and saucers, small bowls, sauce boats, and mugs, predominantly from factories at Bow and Worcester, with decreasing quantities of Liverpool, Caughley, and Lowestoft bringing up the rear. Williamsburg excavations have yielded a few pieces of blue and white porcelain plates attributed to Tournay, but these are the only examples of Continental European porcelain that have so far been found.

Swinging back from the most delicate of eighteenth century ceramics to the heaviest and crudest to be found in a colonial Virginia household, I cannot end these brief comments on ceramics without saying a word or two about a series of massive jars that were common in about 1750-80. They stand thirty-two inches in height, have thick rolled rims, two vestigial moon-shaped handles on the sides, and are thinly glazed on the inside. In the arcs of the handles we sometimes

129. Detail of a 1757 painting by Samuel Scott of London's Custom House Quay with a large storage jar in the foreground.

find initials painted in white slip, or molded medallions bearing initials or crudely executed shields-of-arms. The giant vessels are popularly known as "Spanish oil jars," but Professor John M. Goggin of the University of Florida is certain that they are not Spanish. Instead, he notes that the jars are frequently found on British colonial sites in the Caribbean as well as in continental America, and he therefore feels that they should be English.

They are certainly encountered in England and we can point to a 1757 painting of London's Custom House Quay in which one such jar is being inspected on the dock (Fig. 129). I have found fragments of the same jars lying in the mud of the Thames foreshore at low tide. So we have pictorial and archaeological evidence that these vessels reached London. But even so it does not necessarily follow that they were made in England. On the contrary, the shape of the jars is not in the least English and furthermore some of the relief-molded medallions bear Catholic symbols, a feature that would be unusual if not down-right improbable on pottery manufactured in Protestant England. At a guess, one might suggest that they came from Portugal or Italy. The former was an odds on favorite until a new piece of evidence turned up in an English popular magazine *Today*, whose cover was adorned with a titillating picture of an Italian movie starlet. But the most intriguing objects in the picture were the two large pottery jars against which she was leaning and which closely resembled our disputed "Spanish" vessels. The picture had presumably been taken in Italy. I immediately wrote to the magazine and requested a copy of the picture shorn of the caption material that partially obscured the jars, and asked where it was taken. In due course the print arrived. It was a different picture and the girl was now perched uncomfortably on top of the jars, but both showed to advantage. Here, at last, was the evidence we needed. The agency that distributed the picture had attached a lengthy caption to the back giving me complete details and measurements—of the girl, but not a word about the jars, except for a line at the end, which stated that the movie had a Sicilian setting but that the photograph was taken on the M.G.M. lot at Boreham Wood, England. If there is any moral to be drawn from this experience it must be that, in archaeological research, magazine covers should not always be taken at their face value.

Even if we cannot be sure where the large jars were made, there is no doubting their popularity in Virginia in the second half of the eighteenth century. Two examples from the York River are in the National Park Service Visitor Center at Yorktown (Fig. 70); another new restored specimen was found in excavations on Francis Street in Williamsburg, while small fragments from more than a hundred and twenty jars have been recovered from other sites in the town. An undamaged example reputed to have been in a Williamsburg house since the eighteenth century was presented to Colonial Williamsburg early in 1962. In addition, sherds have been found at Rosewell, in whose hall another intact jar stood into the late nineteenth century, as is helpfully attested by a photograph of that date. So large, strong, and heavy were these vessels that once installed in a house it is unlikely that any one would be anxious to move them around. Thus they would stand a better chance of survival than the smaller utilitarian ceramic items that were more readily handled—and dropped.

An inventory of the contents of Mount Vernon after the death of George Washington listed "8 Soap Jars" valued at twenty-five dollars. Family tradition has it that these soap jars were the same as the so-called "Spanish oil jars," and in 1943 a descendant of Martha Washington presented one such jar to the Mount Vernon Ladies Association, the organization that administers Mount Vernon today. Mr. Charles C. Wall, resident director at Mount Vernon, has stated that a second jar, slightly smaller and darker in color, is owned by another descendant of Martha Washington, thus, perhaps, accounting for two of the "8 Soap Jars" owned by the General.

There can be no denying the romantic appeal that George Washington's soap jar may have for many American visitors to Mount Vernon, or, for that matter, the comparable impact that Lord Dunmore's porcelain may have on English visitors to Williamsburg. But I would hate to think that all the research and all the digging has no more lasting merit than the enhancing of tourist attractions. Nevertheless, there *are* people who hold such views, who look upon historical research as no more useful than teaching Greek to a football major, and who think that treating the relics of colonial Virginia archaeologically is sheer pretension.

Even if we admit, for the sake of argument, that history is bunk and that it is only today, tomorrow, and the years ahead that matter, we are still forced to measure progress on the yardstick of our experience. If we are to appreciate our own place in history, our past must be studied and preserved; and if its fragments, lying buried in the ground, can tell something that the future needs to know—then archaeologists must dig for them with all the care and all the skill at their command. If the methods that are used were pioneered in Egypt or perfected on the sites of ancient Rome—so much the better; we know that they are worthy of Virginia. We know also, that to the history of America, a few potsherds at Jamestown, a table leg from Williamsburg, or a brace of bottles found by divers in the York River are potentially more eloquent than the Rosetta Stone and more precious than a dozen pharaohs' gold.

We must guard them well.

The Art of Ending:
An Afterword

Great is the art of beginning,
but greater the art is of ending.
H. W. LONGFELLOW

IN MY NEW PREFACE I admitted to a shortcoming that anthropologists rarely forgive, namely my failure to be schooled in their discipline. In the 1950s that was not as damning as it has since become, for what we now call historical archaeology was still in its infancy, and most of the work had been directed by people trained as architects, landscape architects, or architectural draftsmen. Such was the case when I first came to Williamsburg as a consultant in 1956. While on the one hand that was reassuring to this new immigrant, on the other I knew that critics could scoff that I lacked even architectural training. I had, however, learned the principles of fieldwork as assistant to the pioneer of historical (post-medieval) archaeology in England, Adrian Oswald, and for six years had been responsible for archaeological salvage during postwar rebuilding in the City of London. I could play the music, by which I mean that I knew enough about seventeenth- and eighteenth-century artifact dating—the notes—and how to read them on the musical page—the ground stratigraphy. And in those halcyon precomputer days that was enough to do the job, and arguably to do it better than it had hitherto been done. But convincing others of that—others who knew nothing about achaeological procedures—was not to be easy. *Here Lies Virginia* was an attempt—albeit a very gentle attempt—to do so.

In its first incarnation the manuscript had focused only on Williamsburg and was prosaically titled "Williamsburg's Buried Treasure," and was to be published by Colonial Williamsburg—which meant that each line first required everyone's approval. Dissatisfied with the result, I shelved the book. A year later, however, Alfred Knopf, who was then on the board of the Institute of Early American History and Culture, asked to see it. He suggested broadening its scope to include discoveries in what was then called "historic sites archeology" made elsewhere in Virginia.

In the five years that preceded the book's publication I discovered that I was fighting my educational battle on two fronts. I was daring to tell anthropologists whose archaeological experience was limited to prehistory that unless they knew the differences between, say, creamware and pearlware, they had no business digging on late eighteenth-century sites. At the same time I was trying to get my own employers at Colonial Williamsburg—archaeology then being an adjunct of the Department of Architecture—to recognize that focusing on foundations and saving builders' hardware were missing most of the point. Archaeology, I insisted—and it is a thread that runs like barbed wire through the book—is less about buildings than it is about the people who lived and worked in them. In short, historical archaeology is about history. It turned out that this seeming simply notion was even less well received by historians than by architects. Said an eminent scholar, "Real historians aren't interested in pots-and-pans history." Others told me that unlike documents, archaeological evidence was always subject to interpretation and therefore always suspect. Furthermore, anthropologists talked and wrote in a language as obscure as Dr. Zamenhof's and as relevant as his doctorate. The doctor, in case you forget, was a Polish oculist who invented Esperanto—which I laboriously studied at school before learning that nobody spoke it.

In all my writing I have tried to portray archaeology, not as a profession tied to any one discipline, but as a tool, a mechanical process to be used by anyone asking a question that the ground and associated artifacts could answer. Thus, in 1962, to excavate John Frederick Amelung's eighteenth-century glass factory in Maryland, Colonial Williamsburg excavators joined with glass scholars from the Corning Museum of Glass and cultural history curators from the Smithsonian Institution. It was an ideal team, but it would have been quite the wrong one to excavate, say, an iron foundry site or the remains of a boatyard. Regardless of such demonstrations, there was no rush by social historians and curators to learn the craft of archaeological digging and interpretation. Instead, as interest in historical archaeology grew through the 1960s and 1970s, anthropologists stepped forward to don the mantle as though by intellectual birthright and soon began to insist that nobody should be allowed to excavate an historical site unless he and she were schooled in anthropology.

Recognizing that a successful excavator's principal attribute is a disciplined and inquiring mind, and that with diligence the artifactual evidence of any period can be read and understood, it followed that anthropologists could learn as quickly and as well as might any other reasonably sensible individual. But that they should be the *only* practitioners was something else again. On the contrary, because students were learning their archaeology in anthropology classrooms, the questions they were being taught to ask were anthropological: having to do with "the science of human beings, especially in relation to distribution, origin, classification, and relationship of races, physical character, environmental and social relations, and culture." These were cosmic considerations, far removed from determining whether the Raleigh Tavern had leaded rather than sash windows or whether Anthony Hay's wife wore an orthopedic corset.

It was this kind of finely focused question to which archaeology could and did contribute. But far too few sites had been dug, and more importantly *well* dug, for larger questions to be addressed or societal conclusions to be drawn. One cannot build a ziggurat from three bricks, but with thirty a foundation can be begun. I insisted, therefore, that our role was that of brickmakers, and that if the bricks proved sound, historians and anthropologists could safely build on them. But if they turned out to be more straw than clay, whatever they supported would one day collapse.

In Chapter III I briefly mentioned the early ironworking site at Falling Creek that fell victim to the Indian attack of March 22, 1622. "There has been talk in recent years," I wrote, "of undertaking extensive archaeological work on the ironworks site, but as yet nothing has come of it." Eventually it did—providing a classic example of the straw-rich brick. When the site was threatened by development, volunteers from the Archeological Society of Virginia went to the rescue and found considerable quantities of telltale iron slag, as well as a few artifacts that included a sherd of English brown stoneware and a tobacco pipe fragment, both dating from the eighteenth rather than the early seventeenth century. When I gave the project director that unwelcome news, he replied that he could confidently dismiss them as later intrusions. The ironworks excavation was duly published, and samples of the iron were sent to several museums that might contemplate ferrous research for which 1622 iron could be an important diagnostic building brick. Several years later, while reading John Ferdinand Dalziel Smyth's *Tour in the United States of America* I discovered that it described a 1773 visit to William Byrd's iron foundry on Falling Creek. The weight of evidence therefore pointed to the excavated samples dating from the 1770s rather than from 1622, yet they doubtless remain in the host collections as a virus to confound any research that makes use of them.

One of the "advantages" of archaeology over many another academic or scientific discipline is that once a site has been dug, the matrix invariably has been disturbed or destroyed, thus making it extremely difficult for us to be proved wrong. Rarely, if ever, does a fully dug site get reexcavated. For that reason, when working in Williamsburg I argued that representative parts of any site should be left untouched to enable future archaeologists with better techniques and fresh insights to reassess my conclusions. That unfortunately looks better on paper than in practice. On the one hand, allowing part of a site to remain undug can leave crucial information undiscovered and result in wrong interpretations, and on the other (as I would find to my dismay in Martin's Hundred), sites set aside for the future are liable to be forgotten and destroyed.

How many of my conclusions have been wrong and gone unde-
tected, I have no idea; but one boldly illustrated in this book has always
haunted me. On page 29 you will find a handsome brass finial from a
fireplace andiron that had been found near the Elizabethan "Lost Colony" site on Roanoke Island, and in the text I unhesitatingly declared
it "easily attributable to the period." Archaeologist Pinky Harrington
believed me and in his report wrote that "it could well date from the
16th century." But it didn't. It was made in New York around 1800.
More humiliating still was the discovery of it in a 1921 photograph
that showed it in use as a theatrical prop in a "Lost Colony" film being
made by the Atlas Film Corporation!

That was one of my first checkable mistakes, and by a quirk of
fate I was to make another just like it on the same site in what was to
be my last archaeological project. A heavily rust-obscured iron object
that I thought would turn out to be a pommel from an Elizabethan
dagger—and still looked like it when X-rayed—turned out to be an
automobile spark plug!

When, in 1957, I accepted Colonial Williamsburg's invitation to
take charge of its archaeological office—an offer that had more to do
with my experience as an exhibit designer and theatrical director than
with a perceived need to upgrade its archaeology—I needed a dramatic venue to demonstrate that there was more to archaeology than
uncovering foundations. But in Williamsburg no such opportunity immediately presented itself. Remembering my previous year's visit to
the ruined Page family mansion in Gloucester County (Chapter VI)
where deep in the surrounding woods a groundhog's digging had led
me to the site of a large eighteenth-century trash pit, I decided that
this should be it.

Over the next two years and through innumerable weekends, my
wife Audrey and an intrepid team of volunteers had braved poison ivy
and dog-sized mosquitoes to excavate the Rosewell pit. It proved as
rewarding as I had hoped. Thanks to the generosity of Edwin Kendrew, Colonial Williamsburg's senior vice president, we were allowed
to use his basement at the James Anderson House as a laboratory—
foretelling, perhaps, the day when the house would be mine to convert
into an archaeological exhibit.

From the outset of my tenure I had thought it essential that Colonial Williamsburg's archaeological responsibilities should be confined to its own property, for once it became officially involved in or responsible for any outside archaeological project, its energies would quickly be dissipated and its competence compromised. It was for this reason that the Rosewell material was not conserved and studied in our own archaeological laboratory, nor was it accessioned into our collections. Instead, the artifacts went to the Smithsonian Institution where the report was published in its 1963 *Bulletin 225*. This was, to my knowledge, the first time that an American historical site had been interpreted on the basis of a tightly dated archaeological unit in tandem with related documentary sources. Other Rosewell-like extramural projects at Tutter's Neck (1960–61) in James City County (Chapter VI) and at Clay Bank (1962–63) in Gloucester County (Chapter X) were to be published in the Smithsonian Institution's *Bulletin 249* in 1968, and both played their part as candles lighting the way toward a broader understanding of archaeology's use as an historical resource.

The work at Rosewell had been my first American excavation and among its many recovered artifacts was a lump of copper ore (pp. 127–28) illustrative of Mann Page's known interest in minerals and mining. Thirty-three years were to elapse before I would find another lump of copper ore, a discovery having omenlike qualities that convinced me that the place should the scene of my last excavation.

The site was Pinky Harrington's Fort Raleigh, and the copper ore was one of many artifacts proving that the ground had supported a 1585–86 research center used by Sir Walter Ralegh's scientific leader Thomas Hariot and "minerall man" Joachim Gans. These and other related discoveries proved that the reconstructed earthwork (p. 19) presented as Ralph Lane's "New Fort in Virginia" was not his, and instead the accumulating evidence pointed to its construction in the eighteenth century, either during King George's War or the French and Indian War. That devastating and reluctantly reached reassessment was not the product of the advanced remote-sensing technology that would be brought to bear on the "Lane's Fort" enigma in 1982 but only of the interdisciplinary principles espoused in the pages of this book, a demonstration that old and simple need not be synonyms with obsolete and simplistic, any more than new is necessarily necessary.

For the methods used at Fort Raleigh I can claim very little credit. They were and remain Jeffersonian in concept, coupled with the kind of area excavation and concern for stratigraphy taught by such Old World masters as Sir Mortimer Wheeler and Kathleen Kenyon and used by them at sites as diverse as the British Iron Age earthwork of Maiden Castle and Bronze Age Jericho in Israel. If I contributed anything at all, it may have been the process now widely known as cross-mending whereby ceramic and glass fragments from an entire site are divided by ware, form, and detail, in the hope that joining sherds may identify contemporary features and strata. In Williamsburg where stratigraphic evidence had hitherto been ignored and at James-town where artifact placement had been recorded by measured depth rather than by soil layer, repairing pots had been an exercise in curatorial conservation. Adoption of the cross-mending procedure changed it into a function of archaeological interpretation.

In 1955 an address by Pinky Harrington to the American Anthropological Society titled "Archeology as an Auxiliary Science to American History" was published in the *American Anthropologist*. It remains the most important paper ever written on the subject, stressing as it did the need for analysis, synthesis, and the publication of "the evidence that archeologists clamor for—detailed descriptions of all artifact material." No modern student of archaeology should leave the classroom without having read Harrington's paper, and no professor should be excused the responsibility of speaking to each of its points.

Harrington had told his audience—along with much else—that "we cannot expect a single individual to be qualified to excavate and interpret cultural remains so varied and so complex as those represented in this country any more than we should consider an Egyptologist qualified to excavate in the Roman Forum. Yet," Harrington went on, "we send out an archeologist to investigate a seventeenth-century English plantation site, a Civil War fort site, or a Hudson's Bay post, naïvely assuming he can do the job because he has successfully excavated prehistoric Indian sites." That was not what anthropologists wanted to hear, and few were moved by it.

Fifteen years later I again followed in Harrington's footsteps, by participating in the American Anthropological Society's annual meeting in New Orleans. However, I was not there to make a speech but

315

to introduce *Doorway to the Past*, a new Colonial Williamsburg film designed to show how archaeology could help reconstruct eighteenth-century colonial life. As the film's writer-director I well knew for whom it was intended and so opposed the idea that it should be premiered in New Orleans. I was right. Some in the audience booed it. Nevertheless, the scholarly jeers not withstanding, the film went on to win awards and, more than twenty years later, is still used in schools and occasionally turns up on television.

Harrington had correctly pinpointed the need for historical sites to be excavated only be people with the necessary historical knowledge, but he had not said where these people were to be found or whether or not they had to be anthropologists. He also had discussed the new discipline's name, admitting that the term "historic sites archeology" that he had proposed in 1952 had not caught on. A 1966 Smithsonian Institution symposium chaired by historian Wilcomb E. Washburn had addressed the questions of Who's to do it? and What's it to be called? Although no conclusions were reached, the debate led indirectly to the founding of a society for the people (whoever they were) to do whatever they'd call it.

The first meeting was held in Dallas in 1967 with an unelected roster of founders that included Harrington and myself. Agreement was reached that all sites of the postaboriginal (i.e., historical) period are not of historic significance, and so the discipline was defined as historical archaeology—with the extra *a*. I had argued for that on the grounds that American colonial history was rooted in the Old World and because Old World archaeological techniques were best suited for the job. Probably because it was getting late and the clink of glasses could be heard without, my fellow founders ceded me the point. And thus was born the American Society for Historical Archaeology. A similarly named Australian society was established in the same year.

Because most archaeological practitioners were already anthropologists, it naturally followed that most of the people who joined the new society were coming from the ranks of prehistorians. Having thus determined who would dig—there being no rush of historians to grasp shovels and no real need among prehistorians to advance their own researches by digging on historical sites—the next question was, Why? followed almost instantly by, Who will pay for it?

The customers remained where they had always been: among the architectural restorationists, the garden club recreationists, and state and national park administrators with historic sites to exhibit. But their needs were both limited and finite. The Park Service needed, say, to find the gate postholes for one of its forts; a local garden club wanted to restore the maze at the town's oldest mansion, and an incorporated restoration needed another tavern reconstruction. It mattered little to the customers how well the archaeology was done, but only that it provided the desired answers—preferably quickly and cheaply.

Discovering and measuring fort postholes, plotting maze planting trenches, or digging out tavern foundations carried no requirement that the archaeologists spend time studying hitherto unidentified potsherds or the evolution of horseshoes and bayonets, even though all three might be found in their excavations. Furthermore, there was no call for prolonged and expensive postexcavation research and report writing. The gate was up, the maze planted, and the tavern open. Those were the desired end products, and so a short report "just for the record" was quite sufficient and, with no one clamoring to read it, not worth publishing. Only the archaeologist's conscience cried for more—providing he knew enough to recognize that more was indeed possible.

There were notable and laudable exceptions such as Harrington's reports on Fort Raleigh and Fort Necessity and John Cotter's seminal study of past archaeology at Jamestown—all National Park Service publications. The Colonial Williamsburg restoration, as Harrington had pointed out in 1955, had been in progress for more than a quarter century without publishing a single archaeological report. They existed, but containing no information of use to others, they remained as manuscripts in the architectural library where, predictably, nobody read them.

The same policy persisted throughout my own quarter-century tenure as head of Colonial Williamsburg's archaeological program. Although in the early 1960s the office was elevated to department status, it continued always to serve the needs of architecture rather than pursuing research interests of its own. With fieldwork geared to architecturally driven schedules, there rarely was time to do more than to conserve, number, and box the artifacts before the next excavation began.

Consequently, there was no time to write reports that included detailed descriptions of artifacts or to address their cultural significance. The department was a factory turning out parts ordered by others and assembled elsewhere.

Knowing that even in the most benevolent of institutions, publishing reports for which there was no cost-returning market was carrying "nonprofit" to extremes, I placated my archaeological conscience by developing a series of booklets that contained the kind of information colleagues might use but were dressed up as souvenirs. I called them "thumbers' booklets": they had enough illustrations printed to the page edges that when thumbed through they looked as though they were worth a dollar. The first was published in 1969 and the tenth in 1983, and all but one are still in print—alas, no longer at a dollar.

The booklets' success enabled me to propose publishing occasional volumes of artifact research. The first contained five sturdy papers ranging from the contents of a 1720s well to an analysis, both historical and archaeological, of the widespread use of casement and leaded windows in eighteenth-century Williamsburg. The book reached the publications warehouse in 1973, and there most of the copies remained. I had hoped that the window paper would shame my architectural colleagues into replacing at least a token number of Williamsburg's sashed dormers with leaded casements, but there was no sale there either.

The assumption that having found a means of getting archaeological information into print, one has assured its future application is at best naive. Chapter VII dealt at some length with the excavation of the Revolutionary War cemetery discovered in 1930 in the garden of the Governor's Palace, paying special attention to skeleton no. 151 and allowing half a page to illustrate its trepanned skull. In the days before social sensibilities were pandered to by the dogma of correctness, I exhibited the skull in Williamsburg's Courthouse Museum along with tools and illustrations showing how trepanning was performed, and it became one of our most familiar artifacts. In 1992, with the skull embarrassingly mislaid after the museum was closed and *Here Lies Virginia's* testimony notwithstanding, Colonial Williamsburg's archaeological spokesman told the *Virginia Gazette* that it had been found "near the Wren Building" at the College of William and Mary. The skull, he explained, "was excavated at a time when digs were not done by archaeologists, but by people who were looking for building remains and foundations. The people who dug didn't keep records on whether it was from a graveyard, but," he added sagely, "I think it's highly unlikely." In truth, the Palace cemetery graves had been studied and reported on by the most eminent physical anthropologist of his day, the Smithsonian's Dr. Arles Hrdlicka.

I find it strange that a profession dedicated to studying and separating one time frame from another has such difficulty recognizing and being charitable toward the phases of its own evolution. What was good archaeology in the last century can be unacceptable today, but to condemn its practitioners for not being as smart as we think we are is not only misleading, it implies that we lack the single attribute that all good archaeologists must possess: the knowledge and wisdom to put ourselves in the other fellow's historical place.

The restoration and reconstruction of Williamsburg began as an architectural endeavor, but in 1928 so little was known about the process that the Governor's Office referred to the supervising architects as archaeologists—and by some dictionary definitions they could have been. But they knew that they were not, and so endeavored to secure the services of someone who was. They chose Prentice Duell, an architectural draftsman en route to join the University of Chicago's Oriental Institute's expedition at Sakkara in Egypt. His Old World commitments quickly called him away, however, and he subsequently did a masterly job of recording the wall paintings in the Sixth Dynasty mastaba of courtier Mereruka. As Dr. Veronica Seton Williams, an eminent Egyptologist, told me, "He drew what he saw, but he did not, could not interpret. He was not an archaeologist." His place at Williamsburg was taken by a Richmond-based architectural surveyor, Herbert Ragland, whose meticulously kept records reveal a keen and analytical mind that asked questions that undeniably were archaeological and thus made him the archaeologist that Duell was not.

If the problem of defining who should or should not be called an archaeologist seems confusing and contradictory, it is. But does it matter? The answer to that is, Yes, it does—when professionals claim that those who do not possess higher degrees in anthropology are unacceptable as archaeologists, and that if their sponsors expect a return for their investment (as frequently happens in underwater archaeology), all involved risk being condemned as treasure hunters and barred from presenting their findings—no matter how useful and well researched—at professional archaeological meetings.

Because I consider archaeological excavating and interpretation a tool to be used by any trained-in-the-field person having a question to ask that digging can answer, I argue that archaeology is no more a profession than a chisel is a carpenter. It is a technique to be used by anthropologists, classicists, Egyptologists, historians, curators. . . . As for myself, I have always skirted the issue and in biographies am listed as an antiquary—not an antiquarian but an old-fashioned antiquary. It was a title first conferred on William Camden by Henry VIII after the dissolution of the monasteries and defined as an official recorder and custodian of antiquities. The *Oxford English Dictionary* notes that the term is "now tending to be restricted to one who investigates the monuments and relics of the more recent past"—what I have been doing for the past forty and more years.

Although Thomas Jefferson has been hailed as Virginia's—even America's—first excavator-analyst and therefore the first acceptable, albeit amateur, archaeologist, some credit belongs to George Sandys who, before coming to Virginia as the colony's secretary in 1621, had visited Egypt where he was the first Englishman to measure and describe the interior of the Great Pyramid at Giza. Whether Sandys continued his antiquarian interests in Virginia is unknown, but like Hariot and others of this time, he probably saw in the Native Americans living parallels to European prehistoric peoples.

Such thinking invariably was the product of men blessed with the education, the leisure, and the wisdom to wonder—about the universe, about Mankind, about the past. Those who had the learning but not the leisure sought the patronage of men who had the interest but not the knowledge, and thereby became antiquarian professionals. In rare instances, such as England's retired general Pitt Rivers, money, education, and leisure came together with majestic results, but more often archaeological digging was the pastime of amateurs—such as the first excavators at Jamestown.

I, who never intended to become a professional antiquary, had been interested in archaeology from childhood, and had I the money

I would gladly have done for nothing what I have been paid most of my working life to do. Few of us are that lucky! Nevertheless, I suspect that if nailed to the wall, most of today's paid diggers also would admit that they are driven less by a consuming desire to get a better grasp on the advance or frailties of Personkind than by the pleasure of finding things, a satisfaction second only to finding out.

That amateurs properly led can make major contributions has been demonstrated at Rosewell (Chapter VI) where Gloucester County residents, dismayed at the continuing decay and vandalous destruction of their most historic ruin, created the nonprofit Rosewell Foundation to clean up the overgrown site and to hire professional archaeologists to work with local volunteers to better understand the mansion's environs. Digging began in 1989, and over the next three years they discovered that many of the buried foundations were associated, not with the ca. 1726 mansion, but with a series of buildings of an earlier date and superseded by it. This was to be one of the most significant archaeological discoveries of the post–*Here Lies Virginia* decades.

In Chapter VIII I discussed and illustrated a broken cast-iron fireback found in excavations at the President's House at the College of William and Mary and speculated that it might prove to be the product of a Virginia ironworks. I also suggested that the crowned female depicted on it might be the "Indian Queen" crest of the Virginia colony. I failed to note that it also resembled the crowned "maiden's head" emblem of the Mercers Company of London. However, in 1970 while digging at the Chiswell House site on Williamsburg's Francis Street, we found a bronze harness boss bearing the same device that seemed to give renewed credence to the Indian Queen interpretation. There was to be no further doubt about the Virginia origin of the College fireback. Another example cast from the same master matrix, but this time intact, would be found in 1984 on the site of the Orange County "Enchanted Castle" home of Governor Spotswood, the owner of the Germanna iron foundry.

The same chapter discussed preliminary discoveries of waste products associated with the early eighteenth-century stoneware factory operated by William Rogers at Yorktown. That site was fully excavated in the 1970s and reported on by archaeologists from the College of William and Mary under the direction of Dr. Norman Barka who thereby made a major contribution to our knowledge of American ceramic production in the colonial period. On page 210 I drew attention to a 1677 agreement between Dennis Whit and Morgan Jones for the making and selling of "Earthen warre" in Westmoreland County. I speculated that their project might never have progressed beyond the contract, and that "until their kiln site is discovered," one would have to keep an open mind. But no longer. The kiln was found in 1973 and later excavated by Dr. William Kelso and Edward Chappell who thereby provided the best-preserved groundplan of a seventeenth-century Virginia potter's kiln as well as a highly informative range of Morgan Jones's products.

To discuss every major discovery made in the three decades since *Here Lies Virginia* was first published would be to embark on another book. But a few cannot pass unnoticed: Under the auspices of the Virginia Research Center for Archaeology, Governor Spotswood's extraordinary mansion site in Orange County was partially excavated in the 1980s; the Bacon's Castle gardens in Surry County were uncovered by Nicholas Luccketti in 1984; and also in the 1980s a major seventeenth-century site at Jordan's Point in Prince George County was explored by Daniel Mouer. Near Jamestown the early seventeenth-century Governor's Land site was excavated by Alain Outlaw in 1976, and in 1984 Carter Hudgins explored Robert "King" Carter's mansion site at Corotoman (Chapter VI), a project that added greatly to our knowledge of building practices in the early eighteenth century. Over several years in the same period, also on behalf of the Commonwealth of Virginia and with substantial federal funding, John D. Broadwater excavated a scuttled Revolutionary War shipwreck at Yorktown. Alas, it proved to be an almost prohibitively costly undertaking that made more headlines through its failure to make itself visible to tourists than by the historical value of its discoveries.

It was only fitting that the archaeological pioneer Thomas Jefferson's homes at Shadwell, Poplar Forest, and Monticello should be the subjects of archaeological investigation. All three projects were carried out in the period 1979–93 by Dr. Kelso on behalf of the Thomas Jefferson Memorial Foundation, the work at Monticello providing unparalleled information about the lives of Jefferson's slaves. On the

Eastern Shore the John Custis family home at Arlington was partly excavated by the James River Institute for Archaeology in 1988, and between 1976 and 1983 the Colonial Williamsburg Foundation dug in Martin's Hundred and in 1987 excavated a seventeenth-century site on the campus of Hampton University. However, the Foundation's most attention-catching foray turned back the archaeological clock to 1938.

The Shakespeare/Bacon theories that had first brought Marie Bauer to Williamsburg's Bruton Parish Church (Chapter VII) led her disciples there again in 1991. In a blaze of carefully engendered publicity, New Age prophets claimed that even more planet-improving revelations lay buried in what one newspaper dubbed the "now infamous Bruton Parish vault." Through more than half a century Mrs. Marie Bauer Hall (I had inadvertently called her Maria) believed that she had been stopped in 1938 at the very moment she was about to uncover the Baconian vault. It mattered little that what she claimed to have found sounded suspiciously like the corner of a coffin.

The New Agers made several nocturnal raids on the churchyard and dug themselves an impressive hole before being barred by court order. However, they were not about to go away, and although there was strong sentiment for locking them up, the church preferred to prove them wrong. It therefore contracted with Colonial Williamsburg (which had wisely kept its distance in 1938) to undertake new excavations to determine once and for all whether the vault existed. Attempting to restore a modicum of professionalism to what had become a media circus, Colonial Williamsburg agreed to undertake an excavation designed to "produce a much better understanding of the architectural character of the First Bruton Parish Brick Church." But after reexcavating Marie Bauer's big hole and finding the coffin, the Foundation declared victory and went home. Not so the New Agers, who continued to claim that the vault was there—somewhere, and if not there, somewhere else. When last heard from they were heading for Nova Scotia.

It can at least be said of the Bruton dig that it generated very few artifacts, for the preservation of what is found has become so time consuming and costly that many a project director is relieved when his supervisors find none. Through the first thirty years of Williamsburg's restoration, archaeological conservation was limited to the simple (yet lastingly effective) treatment of such metal artifacts as were "not in too bad a shape." Although through my tenure we kept everything that could reach the lab—and by the mid-1970s that included even dirty marks in the ground—the conservation process began each afternoon when the day's bagged artifacts arrived. I had learned from my London experience that nine-tenths of all excavated artifacts needed relatively simple treatment, and that only the last tenth required the attention of fully trained chemists who would soon rebel if called upon to preserve a daily stream of rusty nails and horseshoes. It made more sense, therefore, to train someone "good with his/her hands" and to risk losing a more tricky object if a professional conservation expert could not be found in time.

Eventually, however, as historical archaeology became more formalized and doing anything without a computer printout to document it became taboo, archaeological conservation elevated itself from a trade or craft to a profession with its practitioners the possessors of certificates and degrees. In consequence an impressive stream of paper accompanied every artifact's progress through the lab. Where once treatment had begun within hours of an object's changed environment—a change that began its accelerated process of decay—now it could wait for days, even weeks, while its paperwork was processed and "signed off on" by those responsible for its future, though not necessarily by the archaeologist who gave it one. As the record-keeping expanded, the number of artifacts treated contracted to a point where many died before the admission procedures were complete.

The advent of the computer and the recognition that anything that came out of it had to be infinitely more scholarly than work reliant on experience and the human brain had a profound impact on historical archaeology. For a while it became fashionable for every excavating student to have a laptop computer perched on a nearby bucket so that everything could be instantly processed. Some steam went out of this need when it became apparent, even to the most devout, that when recording a site's buried garbage, if one could not instantly identify it, the resulting printout would itself be garbage.

In 1969 I had published what I hoped would be a helpful *Guide to Artifacts of Colonial America*, which in broad and simplistic terms identified the basic types and outlined their stylistic or technical evolution. To my horror those time brackets was seized upon by a mathematically adept anthropologist who devised a numerical method whereby it would be possible to arrive at a mean date for a site's occupation. Using it, anyone capable of telling delftware from salt glaze could count the sherds and apply the formula, thus becoming an instant archaeological interpreter. It mattered little that arriving at the mean for a twice-occupied site could provide a date when no one was there!

The next inevitable step would be to use these barn-door artifact-dating brackets as the basis for computer-recorded cataloguing systems, and that, too, came to pass. Where once museum curators would apply their lifelong experience to each new accession, they began to be replaced by managers adept in creating and applying computer programs that could tell at the press of a button where an object was stored, how long it was, and how heavy, and where there were seven more like it. But gone was the person who could explain how one object differed from another or expound on its aesthetic qualities or its technical shortcomings. World-famous museums retired their curators of metalwork, ceramics, glass, sculpture, even ships' ordnance. Unhappily, this loss of people of long experience comes at a time when they are most needed to ensure that what goes into the basic computer programs is not garbage but the sum of their knowledge.

In the archaeological world the advances of the late 1960s that had seen senior archaeologists accepting the notion that they needed to be down in the dirt identifying the artifacts before they were moved from the earth lost ground in the 1970s and 1980s—no doubt to the relief of many an archaeological bureaucrat. Like the great Egyptologists, Assyriologists, and classical archaeologists of earlier generations, he could leave it to the fellaheen to shift the dirt and rely on junior supervisors to keep the record. Unwashed and unseen, the excavated fragments began to be whisked away to computer-equipped artifact-processing centers where they would be studied and interpreted by specialists unfamiliar with the ground whence they came. Not only did it cease to be necessary for the archaeologists to have immediate and continuing access to what they were finding, but in the end the reports on the artifacts were written entirely by collections specialists. Thus, for example, a 1993 "Archeological Collections Management" report on an historically important site designed, so it said, "to make the collections information more accessible" contained not a single artifact photograph or drawing and no index. To compensate, it provided a twenty-nine-page computer-generated "Artifact Inventory" that counted the sherds and provided their collective weight by type (e.g., "Redware, plain") as well as its percentages in relation to both the total artifact count and their total weight. Small wonder is it, therefore, that historians and the public at large find archaeology ever more baffling and esoteric. And in the long run, what one does not understand, one does not use or support.

The separation of artifact studies from archaeological site interpretation means, of course, that when the director has to write the final report, he or she can do no more than repeat—be it right or wrong—what the project assistants have first written. In such a system the artifacts play no significant role in the site's interpretation and appear in the report—if at all—as mere decoration. This has the advantage of avoiding the once long and costly task of drawing all the significant objects. Ironically, however, one of the computer age's great boons to archaeology has been the ability to render artifact drawings quickly and accurately through digital imagery.

There is no denying that by themselves, potsherds—whether drawn or computer generated—are hard and often impossible to interpret correctly. Consequently, each needs to be rendered as part of a complete object, or at least to be accompanied by a photograph of an intact specimen. A 1993 report on a major Virginia site took that notion and moved it sideways, ignoring the fragments entirely in favor of photographs of museum-quality objects allegedly like the found pieces! These look-alike objects were then provided with computer-style date brackets of the kind originally culled from my sorely misused *Guide to Artifacts*. Thus, in the report, a delftware plate of about 1740 would stand for all delftware sherds found on the site and be given time brackets of 1570–1770—which made no sense within the history either of delftware or of the site.

I noted earlier that because archaeological excavation is a destructive process, it is one of the few academic disciplines wherein its

326

practitioners' work cannot be checked or corrected. Thanks to the growing acceptance of artifact studies that either illustrate no artifacts or substitute alleged look-alikes, they, too, can hide interpretive errors. But worse, such publications cannot be used to provide what Harrington pleaded for in 1954: "the evidence that archeologists clamor for—detailed descriptions of all artifact material."

No drawings, photographs, or written descriptions can adequately substitute for examining the artifacts themselves. Unfortunately few of us can do that, in part because we lack the time and money to track them down, and no less because, having done so, they may no longer be accessible. Thus, for example, the artifacts from Rosewell, Tutter's Neck, and Clay Bank that illustrate these chapters were parts of collections for which there was no Virginia home. Instead, to ensue their survival (and publication) they were donated to the Smithsonian Institution where, as is inevitable over time, they have been relegated ever deeper into storage. When writing this book in 1962, therefore, one of my premier concerns was the lack of a central repository for all artifacts excavated from historical sites in Virginia.

The National Park Service's conscientious curator at Jamestown, J. Paul Hudson, looked after material found there both by its own archaeologists and by the amateur excavators who preceded them on behalf of the Association for the Preservation of Virginia Antiquities, as well as artifacts from Yorktown and Green Spring (pp. 175–80, 219–20). The Virginia Historical Society also owned and exhibited artifacts from Jamestown (p. 54). Colonial Williamsburg carefully housed large, if highly selective, collections of unstratified artifacts and exhibited some of them in the Courthouse of 1770 on Duke of Gloucester Street. At Newport News the Mariners Museum retained and displayed bottles and other objects salvaged from Revolutionary War wrecks at Yorktown (pp. 180–85). All these repositories were limited to housing artifacts found on their own properties or that were recovered under their aegis. Anything found elsewhere by amateurs or by accident went homeless.

What was needed was a state-supported institution to conduct excavations under professional leadership, to train volunteer labor, to process, to store and to exhibit the resulting collections and, no less important, one possessing a lecture hall wherein ideas could be ex-

327

pressed and knowledge shared at both popular and professional levels. I had hoped that following the publication of *Here Lies Virginia* support might be forthcoming from the academic community; instead it came from James E. Maloney, owner of the fledgling Williamsburg Pottery, his brother Andrew, and motel-owner John Yancey who offered the land if the state would build a Virginia Institute for Historical Archaeology. Governor Mills E. Godwin appointed an advisory committee, plans were drawn, and the College of William and Mary in the person of Dean Melville Jones endorsed the proposal and offered land for a building adjacent to the Founders Theater site. It all seemed too good to be true. And of course it was.

One member of the Governor's Committee speaking on behalf of the Archeological Society of Virginia wanted to know why the institute should be limited to historical archaeology and not to Virginia's past both historical and prehistoric. As the committee's vice chairman I tried to argue that historical archaeology was a quasi-separate discipline with conservation, storage, and research problems and opportunities very different from the more limited needs of prehistory. But eventually the College, on the advice of its Department of Anthropology, withdrew its support, and the Virginia Institute for Historical Archaeology died on the drawing board. However, the impetus created on its behalf eventually led to the creation of an organization that did what the prehistorians wanted. The Virginia Research Center for Archaeology came into being as an adjunct of the Virginia Historic Landmarks Commission and was housed on the William and Mary campus, not in fine, newly erected quarters but in a cramped basement of the Wren Building. In 1982 it moved to a bigger and better basement in the newly built Victory Center at Yorktown where it remained until evicted as an alleged fire hazard in 1986, when it shifted to yet another basement, this time at its parent agency's headquarters in Richmond. Dreams of a state museum to house and display the products of historical archaeology across the state had long since faded.

In 1970 Colonial Williamsburg's president, Carlisle Humelsine, agreed to hire consultants to explore the advantages of creating "A Museum of Archaeology for Colonial Williamsburg," and shortly thereafter when the Foundation was planning to reconstruct the Public Hospital on Francis Street, he offered me its interior as an archaeological museum. But I concluded that the building was too small and its traffic pattern too cramped to serve as a stand-alone museum. Nevertheless, Carl Humelsine's encouragement kept the archaeological museum idea alive, and when in 1982 the hospital building became the entrance to the largely underground DeWitt Wallace Decorative Arts Gallery, I proposed constructing a tunnel-linked archaeological museum on the other side of Nassau Street. At the heart of the scheme was a basement where "the museum's responsibility to archaeologists, both amateur and professional, . . . seeking documentation for the material cultures of the 17th, 18th, and even later centuries" would be fulfilled. It was a grandiose proposal with a matching price tag in excess of $8 million, and none too surprisingly, it was rejected.

Five years later, following a successful nine-month exhibition of artifacts from seventeenth-century Martin's Hundred at the National Geographic Society's headquarters in Washington, D.C., planning began for an archaeological museum at Carter's Grove. It was my fourth attempt to build such a museum there, and like its predecessors it was to include basement storage and research areas. By the nature of the site, its scope would be limited to the seventeenth century, providing both popular exhibits and a focus and clearinghouse for early colonial archaeology across the state.

Between the planning committee's creation in 1987 and the day the doors of the Winthrop Rockefeller Archaeology Museum opened in June 1991 (I had lost my battle for "Archaeological" rather than "Archaeology"), the cost had escalated and the space shrunk. Gone were the basement-housed collections and the study and conference rooms, gone the conservation laboratory and photo studio, and gone, too, the professional staff to give the museum its intellectual life. What remained was not a museum but a successful frozen-in-time-and-place exhibit. Though a far cry from the state research center that had seemed such a real possibility twenty-eight years earlier, at least it ensured that one Colonial Williamsburg archaeological site shared its story with the public. But at a price. The James Anderson House on Duke of Gloucester Street, whose archaeological exhibit had for more than a decade provided an overview of the Foundation's eighteenth-century archaeology in Williamsburg itself, was soon closed on the grounds that one archaeological museum (albeit seven miles from town and confined to the seventeenth century) was enough.

Although politics of various stripes have played a major role in shaping the future of historical archaeology as it matured through the decades since *Here Lies Virginia* was first published, much has been accomplished. Following the College of William and Mary's lead, several universities have successfully built their own programs in historical archaeology. Laudable though this is, it sometimes can pose as grave a danger to the future of Virginia's still undisturbed historical sites as do the greedy eyes of land developers. The notion that rather than being sources of knowledge, archaeological sites are classrooms whose resources can be expended to teach students how to dig developed in the 1970s and 1980s as universities became increasingly involved in archaeological fieldwork.

In tandem with the ever increasing cost of technologically enriched state-of-the-art archaeology, the sources of funding were shrinking as more and more universities and restoration projects vied for a share of the grant-supplied monetary pie. Because the size of the grants was also getting smaller, the field school solution became ever more popular. What, proponents argued, could be more advantageous than letting students young and old pay the project to do the work that hitherto it would have hired field crews to do? As some of those digging jobs had previously gone to untrained laborers, substituting untrained paying students could be no worse, and probably much better. Right?

Well, yes and no. Hired hands for whom one had no educational commitment—beyond teaching them to do the job—could be expected to arrive on the site ready to work at eight in the morning and would keep doing it until five in the afternoon. And on that basis a director could get a pretty good idea of how much could be accomplished in a season and what it would cost. Field school students, on the other hand, are there to learn, to question, to debate, to be lectured to, and to a degree to be cosseted, entertained, transported, and even fed. Thus are the tables turned, the director and his staff becoming, at least in some measure, the employees of the students. Consequently the work proceeds at their intellectual and physical pace, even if in the end much of it doesn't get done.

In 1972 I devised and directed Colonial Williamsburg's first archaeological field school, not to secure project funding (we paid the students to participate!), but to provide Virginia social studies teachers with an opportunity to add an archaeological dimension to their teaching of history. The chosen site was the 1773 Public Hospital for the Insane that had burned in 1885, and although the students spent more of their time than anticipated digging through unyielding brick rubble, their curriculum included working in the processing lab and daily lectures from in-house and imported speakers. In sum, therefore, we gave far more to the students than they did to us, and it was clear even at the planning stage that if the purpose of a field school is to teach—rather than being a perhaps cynical device to secure paying labor—then student education takes precedence over the director's research goals.

The Public Hospital excavations were research driven, at least in the long run (meaning *after* the students departed), for the recovered information was needed to enable the building to be reconstructed. The operative word here is *needed*, for it was necessity that inspired the project, and that is very different from unnecessarily putting an important site in harm's way by submitting it to the mercies of untrained students. There can be a real temptation, however, to let curiosity rather than an established need to know (coupled with an enduring end product) dictate where to dig. Undeniably, an important site gets the program more attention and more paying students than does digging at the home of an unimportant person from an uninteresting period. Yet expendable sites can provide all the field conditions a student needs to experience, while at the same time ensuring that posterity suffers no great loss if mistakes are made and the school goes home before the site has yielded its last secrets.

Be that as it may, university-based and prehistorically trained anthropologists have expanded their skills and outlook to successfully excavate historic sites, and today they call the shots in the planning and execution of most of the work—much of it of fine quality. Then, too, beginning with builder L. B. Weber at Denbigh in 1963 and later with

331

philanthropist David Harrison's splendid commitment to three centuries of buried history at Flowerdew Hundred, developers and landowners have learned by example that when planning for the future the past has its place.

How prominent that place should or will be depends on our ability to make the public care. If through the alienating use of bureaucratic and anthropological jargon ("verbalizing" when others speak, "visualizing" and not seeing, or "ground truthing" when we mean digging) and by failing to publish readable accounts or to exhibit what is found in an entertaining way we are unable to justify our existence, then we cannot expect to be either favored or funded. And if we believe that by substituting paper shuffling for dirt shoveling we are thereby preserving Virginia's archaeological sites for some future, richer generation, we are, I submit, deluding ourselves. Overpopulation, environmental rapine, and the resulting breakdown of civilized society as we enjoy it are not phantom bugaboos under somebody else's bed. They are real; they are the future. As later generations fracture into tribal units ever more desperately battling each other for turf and survival, our successors' contribution to archaeology will only be as specimens to be puzzled over by antenna-scratching visitors from another planet.

Principal Sources

FROM WHICH QUOTATIONS AND INFORMATION
HAVE BEEN OBTAINED

CHAPTER I

Thomas Jefferson: *Notes on the State of Virginia*, 1784.
Sir Mortimer Wheeler: *Archaeology from the Earth*, Oxford, 1954.
Howard Carter and A. C. Mace: *The Tomb of Tut·Ankh·Amen*, New
York, 1923.

CHAPTER II

Charles W. Porter: *Fort Raleigh*, National Park Service Historical Hand-
book Series, No. 16, Washington, 1956.
David Beers Quinn: *The Roanoke Voyages 1584-1590*, Vols. I & II,
Hakluyt Society, London, 1955.
A. L. Rowse: "Of Raleigh and the First Plantation," *American Heritage*,
Vol. X, No. 4, New York, June 1959.
Francis C. Rosenberger: (editor) *Virginia Reader*, New York, 1948.
J. C. Harrington: *Search for the Cittie of Ralegh*, National Park Service
Archeological Research Series Number Six, Washington, 1962.
J. C. Harrington: "Evidence of Manual Reckoning in the Cittie of Ralegh,"
The North Carolina Historical Review, Vol. XXXIII, No. 1,
Raleigh, N.C., January 1956.

333

Principal Sources

J. C. Harrington: "Archeological Explorations at Fort Raleigh National Historic Site," *The North Carolina Historical Review*, Vol. XXVI, No. 2, Raleigh, N.C., April 1949.

CHAPTER III

Rosenberger: *Virginia Reader*, op. cit. (Chapter II).

Lyon Gardner Tyler (editor): *Narratives of Early Virginia 1606-1625*, New York, 1907.

Robert Johnson: *The New Life in Virginia*, 1612, London edition of 1835.

Mary Newton Stanard: *The Story of Virginia's First Century*, Philadelphia, 1928.

Charles E. Hatch, Jr.: *Jamestown, Virginia*, U.S. National Park Service Historical Handbook Series, No.2, Washington, 1955.

John Smith: *The General Historie of Virginia, New England & The Summer Isles*, 1624, Glasgow, 1907.

Charles E. Hatch, Jr.: *America's Oldest Legislative Assembly*, National Park Service Interpretive Series, History No. 2, Washington, 1956.

Edward M. Riley and Charles E. Hatch (editors): *James Towne in the Words of Contemporaries*, National Park Service Source Book Series No. 5, Washington, 1955.

John L. Cotter: *Archeological Excavations at Jamestown Virginia*, National Park Service Research Series No. 4, Washington, 1958.

John L. Cotter and J. Paul Hudson: *New Discoveries at Jamestown*, National Park Service, Washington, 1957.

Harold L. Peterson: *Arms and Armor in Colonial America 1526-1783*, Harrisburg, Penn., 1956.

T. M. Hamilton (editor): "Indian Trade Guns," *The Missouri Archaeologist*, Vol. 22, Columbia, 1960.

J. F. Hayward: *European Firearms*, London, 1955.

Charles Ffoulkes: *Arms & Armament*, London, 1945.

Joseph B. Brittingham and Alvin W. Brittingham, Sr.: *The First Trading Post at Kicotan (Kecoughtan) Hampton, Virginia*, Hampton, 1947.

Floyd Painter: "The Helmet Site," *Quarterly Bulletin*, Archaeological Society of Virginia, Vol. 10, No. 3, Richmond, March 1956.

Martha Perrine Munger: "James Towne, 1607-1698," *The Antiquarian*, New York, March 1926.

Hugh Jones: *The Present State of Virginia*, 1724, ed. Richard L. Morton, Chapel Hill, 1956.

"A French Traveller in the Colonies, 1765," *The American Historical Review*, Vol. XXVI, No. 4, July 1921.

Samuel H. Yonge: *The Site of Old "James Towne" 1607-1698*, Richmond, 1903; Fifth Edition, 1936.

CHAPTER IV

Rutherfoord Goodwin: *A Brief and True Report Concerning Williamsburg in Virginia*, Williamsburg, 1940.

Marcus Whiffen: *The Public Buildings of Williamsburg*, Williamsburg, 1958.

Ben C. McCary: *Indians in Seventeenth-Century Virginia*, Jamestown 350th Anniversary Historical Booklet, Number 18, Williamsburg, 1957.

I. Noël Hume: *The Buried Treasure of Williamsburg*, Colonial Williamsburg, Ms., 1959.

Rutherfoord Goodwin: *The Williamsburg Restoration, Its Conception*, Colonial Williamsburg Ms. (no date).

Colonial Williamsburg Official Guidebook, Williamsburg, 1955 (no author).

Carlisle H. Humelsine: *Colonial Williamsburg: The President's Report 1960*, Williamsburg, 1961.

Jones: *The Present State of Virginia*, 1724, op. cit. (Chapter III).

Andrew Burnaby: *Travels through the Middle Settlements in North-America in the years 1759 and 1760*, London, 1775; Second Edition, Cornell University, Ithaca, N.Y., 1960.

Arthur Pierce Middleton: *Tobacco Coast*, Newport News, 1953.

J. C. Harrington: "Archeology as an Auxiliary Science to American History," *American Anthropologist*, Vol. 57, No. 6, Washington, December 1955.

CHAPTER V

Harold R. Shurtleff: *Research Report on the Governor's Palace*, Colonial Williamsburg Ms. research report, 1930.

Prentice Duell: *Archaeology Report on Excavations for Summer Season 1930, June 30 to September 5*, Colonial Williamsburg Ms. archaeological report, 1930.

Jones: *The Present State of Virginia*, op. cit. (Chapter III).

Goodwin: *Williamsburg in Virginia*, op. cit. (Chapter IV).

Principal Sources

Noël Hume: *The Buried Treasure of Williamsburg*, op. cit. (Chapter IV).
Whiffen: *The Public Buildings of Williamsburg*, op. cit. (Chapter IV).

CHAPTER VI

Burnaby: *Travels*, op. cit. (Chapter IV).
Louis B. Wright: *The Cultural Life of the American Colonies*, New York, 1957.
Middleton: *Tobacco Coast*, op. cit. (Chapter IV).
Francis Norton Mason: *John Norton & Sons Merchants of London and Virginia, 1750-1795*, Richmond, 1937.
Dumas Malone: *Jefferson and His Time*, Vol. I, "Jefferson the Virginian," Boston, 1948.
I. Noël Hume: *Excavations at Rosewell in Gloucester County, 1957-1959*, Paper 18, Bulletin 225, U.S. National Museum, 1962.
Thomas Tileston Waterman: *The Mansions of Virginia*, Chapel Hill, 1946.
A. Lawrence Kocher and Howard Dearstyne: *Shadows in Silver*, New York, 1954.
Edward H. Thompson: *People of the Serpent*, Boston, 1933.
Louis B. Wright (editor): *Letters of Robert Carter, 1720-1727*, San Marino, Calif., 1940.
James Wharton: *King Carter, the Man*, Kilmarnock, Va., 1950.
I. Noël Hume: "Wine Relics from the Colonies," *The Wine and Spirit Trade Record*, August 16, 1958.
Sheelah Ruggles-Brise: *Sealed Bottles*, London, 1949.
Whiffen: *Public Buildings of Williamsburg*, op. cit. (Chapter IV).
Robert Beverley: *History and Present State of Virginia*, 1725, ed. Louis B. Wright, Chapel Hill, 1947.
Mary Stephenson: *Cocke—Jones Lots, Block 31*, Colonial Williamsburg Ms. research report, 1961.
Jesse Dimmick: "Green Spring," *William & Mary Quarterly*, 2nd Series, Vol. IX, No. 2, Williamsburg, April 1929.
Jane Carson: *Green Spring Plantation in the 17th Century, House Report*, Ms. report prepared for Virginia 350th Anniversary Commission, 1954.
Louis R. Caywood: *Green Spring Plantation*, Yorktown, 1955.
Thomas Tileston Waterman and John A. Barrows: *Domestic Colonial Architecture of Tidewater Virginia*, New York, 1932.

I. Noël Hume: *Excavations at Tutter's Neck, James City County in Virginia, 1960-1961*, Smithsonian Ms., 1961.

L. H. Jones: *Captain Roger Jones of London & Virginia*, Albany, 1891.

Louis des Cognets, Jr.: *English Duplicates of Lost Virginia Records*, Princeton, 1958.

CHAPTER VII

Goodwin: *Williamsburg in Virginia*, op. cit. (Chapter IV).

Edward M. Riley: "The Ordinaries of Colonial Yorktown," *William & Mary Quarterly*, 2nd Series, Vol. XXIII, No. 1, Williamsburg, January 1943.

Virginia Sutton Harrington: *Final Archeological Reports on Developed Units in the Town of Yorktown*, National Park Service Ms. report, 1939.

John W. Griffin: *Archeological Investigations at and Near the Archer Cottage Yorktown*, National Park Service Ms. report, 1958.

Charles E. Hatch, Jr.: *Yorktown and the Siege of 1781*, U.S. National Park Service Historical Handbook Series No. 14, Washington, 1954.

John C. Goodbody: *Basic Interpretation Paper—Raleigh Tavern*, Colonial Williamsburg Ms., 1955.

Mary E. McWilliams: *Raleigh Tavern, Block 17, Colonial Lot 54*, Colonial Williamsburg Ms. research report, 1941.

Colonial Williamsburg, Official Guidebook, Williamsburg, 1955 (no author).

Jones: *The Present State of Virginia*, op. cit. (Chapter III).

Noël Hume: *The Buried Treasure of Williamsburg*, op. cit. (Chapter IV).

James M. Knight: *Archaeological Report, Block 29, Area G*, Colonial Williamsburg Ms., 1947.

Harold R. Shurtleff: *Data on the Public Goal*, Colonial Williamsburg Ms., research compilation, 1934.

William Hone: *The Every-Day Book and Table Book*, Vol. III, London, 1831.

Cotter: *Excavations at Jamestown*, op. cit. (Chapter III).

Cotter and Hudson: *New Discoveries at Jamestown*, op. cit. (Chapter III).

Alfred Marks: *Tyburn Tree its History and Annals*, London (no date).

George W. Dalzell: *Benefit of Clergy in America & Related Matters*, Winston-Salem, 1955.

Lloyd Haynes Williams: *Pirates of Colonial Virginia*, Richmond, 1937.

337

Principal Sources

Henry P. Johnson: *The Yorktown Campaign and the Surrender of Cornwallis 1781*, New York, 1881, reprinted 1958.

St. George Tucker: "Journal of the Siege of Yorktown, 1781," ed. Edward M. Riley, *William and Mary Quarterly*, 3rd Series, Vol. V, No. 3, Williamsburg, July 1948.

Thor Borresen: *Final Report on Redoubt No. 9, Second Parallel*, National Park Service Ms. report, 1938.

Edward B. Jelks: *Archeological Study of British and Confederate Earthworks on South East Side of Yorktown*, National Park Service Ms. report, 1955.

Ffoulkes: *Arms & Armament*, op. cit. (Chapter III).

Albert Manucy: *Artillery Through the Ages*, National Park Service Interpretive Series No. 3, Washington, 1955.

Homer L. Ferguson: *Salvaging Revolutionary Relics from the York River*, Mariners' Museum Publication No. 7, Newport News, 1939.

Fred Frechette: "Cornwallis Fleet 'Found' in York River," *Richmond Times-Dispatch*, August 2, 1954.

Joseph W. Geddes: *The Probable Form and Appearance of the Original Church* (Hickory Neck Episcopal Church), Ms. of speech delivered there October 28, 1934.

Historic St. Luke's Restoration: Smithfield, Va., published by the restoration committee, 1953.

Helen Campbell: "Few Questions Answered by Excavations at Bruton Church," *Virginia Gazette Supplement*, June 28, 1957.

Maria Bauer: *Francis Bacon's Great Virginia Vault*, 1939.

Maria Bauer: *Foundations Unearthed*, Glendale, Calif., 1940.

Whiffen: *The Public Buildings of Williamsburg*, op. cit. (Chapter IV).

Helen Bullock: *Bruton Parish*, Colonial Williamsburg Ms. research report, 1936.

CHAPTER VIII

J. C. Harrington: *Glassmaking at Jamestown*, Richmond, 1952.

J. Stuart Daniels: *The Woodchester Glass House*, Gloucester, 1950.

W. A. Thorpe: *English Glass*, London, 1949.

I. Noël Hume: "A Century of London Glass Bottles, 1580-1680," *The Connoisseur Year Book*, London, 1956.

Wright: *The Cultural Life of the American Colonies*, op. cit. (Chapter VI).

William Ward Condit: "Virginia's Early Iron Age," *The Iron Worker*, Vol. XXIII, No. 3, Lynchburg, Va., 1959.

J. Paul Hudson: "Augustine Washington," *The Iron Worker*, Vol. XXV, No. 3, Lynchburg, Va., 1961.

Henry C. Mercer: *The Bible in Iron*, The Bucks County Historical Society, Doylestown, Penn., 1941 edition, revised by Horace M. Mann.

Cotter: *Excavations at Jamestown*, op. cit. (Chapter III).

John Smith: *Travels and Works of Captain John Smith*, ed. A. G. Bradley, Edinburgh, 1910.

Carson: *Green Spring*, op. cit. (Chapter VI).

Caywood: *Green Spring*, op. cit. (Chapter VI).

Tyler: *Narratives of Early Virginia, 1606-1625*, op. cit. (Chapter III).

Susan M. Kingsbury (editor): *Records of the Virginia Company of London*, Vol. III (1607-1622), Library of Congress, 1933.

Louis R. Caywood: "Green Spring Plantation," *Virginia Magazine of History*, Vol. LXV, 1957.

C. Malcolm Watkins: *The "Poor Potter" of Yorktown*, Smithsonian Ms., 1961.

Mary A. Stephenson: *The Coke-Garrett House*, Colonial Williamsburg Ms. research report, 1953.

Williams: *Pirates of Colonial Virginia*, op. cit. (Chapter VII).

A.B.C. Whipple: *Pirate*, New York, 1961.

CHAPTER IX

Watkins: *The "Poor Potter" of Yorktown*, op. cit. (Chapter VIII).

Smith: *Travels and Works*, op. cit. (Chapter VIII).

J. Paul Hudson: *A Pictorial Booklet on Early Jamestown Commodities and Industries*, Williamsburg, 1957.

Mills Brown: *Cabinetmaking in the Eighteenth Century*, Colonial Williamsburg Ms. research report, 1959.

Ethel Hall Bjerkoe: *The Cabinetmakers of America*, Garden City, N.Y., 1957.

Mary Stephenson: *Colonial Lot 354*, Colonial Williamsburg Ms. research report, 1952.

I. Noël Hume: *Report on Archaeological Excavations on the Peter Scott Site*, Colonial Williamsburg Ms. report, 1958.

Principal Sources

Eric P. Newman: *Coinage for Colonial America*, American Numismatic Society, New York, 1956.

Mary Stephenson: *Colonial Lots 263, 264, and 265*, Colonial Williamsburg Ms. research report, 1955.

I. Noël Hume: *The Anthony Hay Site: Report on Archaeological Excavations of 1959-1960*, Vols. I & III, Colonial Williamsburg, Ms. report, 1961.

Humelsine: *Colonial Williamsburg: The President's Report 1960*, op. cit. (Chapter IV).

Karl Geiringer: *Musical Instruments*, London, 1949.

I. Noël Hume: *The Printing Office: Archaeological Report*, Colonial Williamsburg Ms. draft, 1958.

Noël Hume: *Excavations at Rosewell*, op. cit. (Chapter VI).

CHAPTER X

J. C. Harrington: "Dating Stem Fragments of Seventeenth and Eighteenth Century Clay Tobacco Pipes," *Quarterly Bulletin of the Archaeological Society of Virginia*, Richmond, September 1954.

J. C. Harrington: "Tobacco Pipes from Jamestown," ibid., June 1951.

Adrian Oswald: "The Archaeology and Economic History of English Clay Tobacco Pipes," *Journal of the Archaeological Association*, Third Series, Vol. XXIII, London, 1960.

Adrian Oswald: "English Clay Tobacco Pipes," *The Archaeological News Letter*, Vol. 3, No. 10, London, April 1951.

J. Paul Hudson: "Seventeenth Century Glass Wine Bottles and Seals Excavated at Jamestown," *Journal of Glass Studies*, Vol. III, Corning, N.Y., 1961.

I. Noël Hume: "The Glass Wine Bottle in Colonial Virginia," ibid.

I. Noël Hume: "A Seventeenth Century Virginian's Seal," *Antiques*, Vol. LXXII, No. 3, New York, August 1957.

George B. Griffenhagen and James Harvey Young: "Old English Patent Medicines in America," *U.S. National Museum Bulletin 218*, Contributions from the Museum of History and Technology, Paper 10, Washington, 1959.

Stephenson: *Cocke-Jones Lots*, op. cit. (Chapter VI).

C. Malcolm Watkins: *North Devon Pottery and its Export to America in the 17th Century*, Paper 13, U.S. National Museum Bulletin 225, Washington, 1960.

I. Noël Hume: "German Stoneware Bellarmines—an introduction," *Antiques*, Vol. LXXIV, No. 5, New York, November 1958.

M. R. Holmes: "The So-called 'Bellarmine' Mask on Imported Rhenish Stoneware," *Antiquaries Journal*, Vol. XXXI, London, 1951.

Alfred Coxe Prime: *The Arts & Crafts in Philadelphia, Maryland and South Carolina, 1721-1785*, Topsfield, Mass., 1929.

Catalogue of the Frank P. and Harriet C. Burnap Collection of English Pottery, Nelson-Atkins Gallery of Art, Kansas City, 1953.

Mason: *John Norton & Sons*, op. cit. (Chapter VI).

J. F. Blacker: *The A.B.C of English Salt-Glaze Stoneware*, London, 1922.

F. H Garner: *English Delftware*, London, 1948.

W. B. Honey: *English Pottery and Porcelain*, London, 1952.

Hugh Tait: "Southwark (Alias Lambeth) Delftware and the Potter, Christian Wilhelm," *The Connoisseur*, Vol. CXLVI, No. 585, London, September 1960.

Carl Bridenbaugh (editor): *Gentleman's Progress, The Itinerarium of Dr. Alexander Hamilton, 1744*, Chapel Hill, 1948.

W. J. Pountney: *Old Bristol Potteries*, Bristol, 1920.

Bernard Rackham: *Early Staffordshire Pottery*, London, 1951.

Donald C. Towner: *English Cream-Coloured Earthenware*, London (no date).

I. Noël Hume: "Rouen faïence in eighteenth-century America," *Antiques*, Vol. LXXVIII, No. 6, New York, November 1960.

Carlisle H. Humelsine: "The Revelations of Archaeology," *Colonial Williamsburg Report by the President for the Year 1958*, Williamsburg, 1959.

John Goldsmith Phillips: *China-Trade Porcelain*, Cambridge, Mass., 1956.

Index

Index

344

Index

ment of, 130; table of (1709), 155; bottle (glass), 64, 65, 95, 109, 110, 125, 130-3, 148, 151, 182, 205, 218, 238, 239, 244, 266, 268-71

winemaking, 205

Wingina (Indian chief), 16

Wormeley, Capt. Ralph, 270

Wray, James, 136

wrecks, 174, 180, 182, 295, 322

Wren, Sir Christopher, 77

Wundes, Johannes, 53

Wythe, George, 272

Yancey, John, 328

York River, 4, 27, 56, 74, 117, 180-5, 231, 277, 295, 302, 307, 308

Yorktown, 6, 72, 102, 103, 110, 153-5, 175; Battle of (1781), 175, 176, 180, 187; battlefield, redoubt 8, 178; battlefield, redoubt 9, 175, 176; battlefield, redoubt 10, 175, 176; Civil War defenses, 175; Digges House, 221; pottery kiln at, 221-5; roads of, 221; ships sunk off, 180-5, 327; Visitor Center, 307; *see also* Swan Tavern

Zouche, Sir Edward, 198

352